Markets and marketing in developing economies

Markets and marketing in developing economies

Edited by

REED MOYER
Professor of Marketing

and

STANLEY C. HOLLANDER
Professor of Marketing
Both of Michigan State University

Prepared under the Sponsorship of the
AMERICAN MARKETING ASSOCIATION

1968
RICHARD D. IRWIN, INC., HOMEWOOD, ILLINOIS
IRWIN-DORSEY, LIMITED, NOBLETON, Ontario

Printed in the United States of America
Library of Congress Catalog Card No. 68–30852

To Sue and Selma

Preface

This collection of articles grew out of a request of the Marketing Education Committee of the American Marketing Association to advance the
field of marketing in the area indicated by this book's title. We were free
to select the method of achieving the goal. The editors elected to collect
and publish the papers found in this volume. Their publication serves two
purposes: to disseminate in one volume the results of research in the area
by a number of scholars from several disciplines, and, hopefully, to stimulate the conduct of additional research on the subject.

To help foster the second purpose the editors have prepared a selected
annotated bibliography, located at the end of this volume. It is not meant
to be comprehensive. Thus, we have tried to prevent its becoming another
bibliography on international marketing, several of which are already
available. Instead it covers the items which will be relevant to the scholar
interested in pursuing research in the field of marketing's role in economic
development.

Even though the classification is necessarily somewhat arbitrary, the
articles included in this volume do tend to fall into two groups. One major
set emphasizes the ways in which the developing country environments
influence marketing, while the other is concerned with marketing influences upon the economic environment of the developing nations.

Preston's article, which introduces the first section, examines the relationship between marketing employment and economic level. Of course
correlation does not indicate causation, but few readers are likely to disagree with the author's treatment of trade employment as the dependent
variable in the relationship. As is appropriate for a discussion of marketing
in countries where government is likely to play a particularly active role,
the next four articles examine some of the ways in which public policy is
likely to affect developing-country distribution. Berg traces the history and
marketing implications of the socialist philosophies that now dominate
government and public thought in the new African nations. Bauer touches
upon a number of developmental topics, but pays especial attention to
types of trade regulation that have become important on the African
scene. Henley looks to a very different aspect of public policy, the marketing results of protectionism versus free trade in Central- and Latin-
American common market areas. Abbott directs our attention to the
neglected opportunities for more positive governmental participation in
marketing development through increased inclusion of marketing considerations in the national planning process. Finally, the first portion of

the book concludes with Currie's statement of the ways in which marketing programs must be adapted to environmental constraints.

The second half of the volume presents statements of the ways in which marketing can influence the economic climate for better or for worse. The first subset of two articles tends to emphasize the worse rather than the better. Adams studies an often overlooked developmental situation, the American Indian reservation, and notes the ways in which the white trader influences progress. Glade and Udell discuss the deleterious effects that flow from the absence of the "marketing concept" among Peruvian businessmen. The last three articles outline some of the entrepreneurial characteristics and resources of traders. Mintz searches for truly entrepreneurial value schemes and finds them, literally, in the marketplace, among the petty traders. Alexander reports on the place of trade as a spawning ground for industrialists, while Miracle presents programmatic advice for utilizing both traders' and farmers' potential resource accumulation capacities.

We are indebted to the authors whose articles make up the bulk of the volume. In all but a few cases the papers were invited by the editors. We asked those who were doing important research in this field to share the fruits of their work with readers of this volume. In several instances the articles published here are modestly revised versions of papers published earlier but deserving of wider circulation. They are reprinted here to bring them to the attention of a larger audience with research interests in this growing field.

We have included contributions from scholars in several disciplines. Research into marketing's role in the development process lends itself admirably to a multidisciplinary approach. There are contributions here from economists, economic historians, marketing specialists, and anthropologists.

The articles also cover a wide geographical range, including aspects of marketing in all underdeveloped regions of the world except those in the cold climate areas. Papers deal with marketing in a number of different countries in Africa, Asia, Latin America, the Middle East, and even a primitive backwater in southwestern United States.

These articles are not definitive, nor is the range of the articles all-encompassing. Again, a comment made by one of the volume's editors is appropriate here: "Much remains to be done on a number of fronts. This work represents a first step down a long road whose end is dimly perceived." The editors encourage interested readers to "join the walk."[1]

July, 1968   REED MOYER
                                          STANLEY C. HOLLANDER

---

[1] Reed Moyer, *Marketing in Economic Development* (East Lansing: Institute for International Business Management Studies, Michigan State University, 1965), p. 6.

Contributors

JOHN C. ABBOTT, who holds an M.A. from Cambridge University and Ph.D. from the University of California (Berkeley) is the deputy director, Economic Analysis Division, of the Food and Agricultural Organization in Rome, with special responsibility for field programs in economics and marketing. He initiated the FAO series of Marketing Guides relating to conditions in the developing countries and has authored a number of journal articles, several dealing with marketing aspects of economic development.

WILLIAM Y. ADAMS is associate professor of anthropology at the University of Kentucky. His A.B. degree is from the University of California (Berkeley) and his Ph.D. from the University of Arizona. He gathered much of the material for his dissertation and for his contribution to this volume while employed as an Indian trader at Shonto Trading Post on the Navajo Reservation. For seven years he played a key role in the archeological expeditions growing out of the construction of the Aswan High Dam. He has published widely in the fields of ethnology and archaeology.

ALEC P. ALEXANDER is associate professor and chairman of the Department of economics at the University of California, Santa Barbara. Both his A.B. and Ph.D. degrees are from the University of California (Berkeley). In addition to his present teaching affiliation, Professor Alexander has taught at his alma mater and at Northwestern University. From September, 1954 to June, 1956 he conducted research in Turkey as a Ford Foundation Fellow. In 1963 he was senior research analyst for the Greek Center of Economic Research in Athens, Greece. He has published several articles on industrial entrepreneurship in Greece and Turkey.

PETER THOMAS BAUER is professor of economics at the London School of Economics where he specializes in the field of economic development. Trained at Scholae Piae in Budapest and Cambridge University, Professor Bauer has also held teaching positions at Cambridge and Yale Universities. Among his many publications in the area of economic development are *West African Trade, The Economics of Underdeveloped Countries* (with B. S. Yamey), and *Economic Analysis and Policy in Underdeveloped Countries.*

ELLIOT J. BERG is professor of economics and associate director at the Center for Research on Economic Development at the University of

Michigan. He previously taught at Harvard University, and from 1964–66 was project director, Harvard Advisory Group, Liberia. Professor Berg has been a consultant to A.I.D. and the Ford Foundation and in 1967 served as economic adviser to the Kenya Government Public Sector Salaries Commission. He has written extensively on labor problems in western Africa.

LAUCHLIN CURRIE, who is presently a visiting professor at Simon Fraser University, has had a long and distinguished career in education and public service. He has taught at Harvard University, Fletcher Graduate School, Michigan State University, and at several institutions in Colombia where he has resided since shortly after World War II. From 1939–1945 Professor Currie served as administrative assistant to President Roosevelt. He has also served on a number of governmental missions both for the United States Government and for the government of Colombia. Among his recent publications are: *Accelerating Development* and *Obstacles to Development.*

WILLIAM P. GLADE, JR., professor of business and economics at the University of Wisconsin, received his Bachelor's and Master's degrees as well as his Ph.D. at the University of Texas. His research interests in economic development have taken him to a number of Latin American countries over the past decade and a half. His publications include: *The Latin American Economies: A Study of Their Institutional Evolution* and articles on various aspects of economic development.

DONALD S. HENLEY is assistant professor of marketing at Michigan State University. His D.B.A. is from Harvard University. While at Harvard he was a research associate working primarily in Central America where he did extensive research into management and marketing practices of Central American manufacturing firms. More recently Professor Henley has been involved in research work at Michigan State University's Latin American Market Planning Center, studying the urban food marketing process and the counter flow of manufactured goods to rural food shed areas in LaPaz, Bolivia.

STANLEY C. HOLLANDER, professor of marketing at Michigan State University, holds a Ph.D. degree from the University of Pennsylvania. He edited a recent special international issue of the *Journal of Retailing,* and is the author of numerous articles and monographs on retailing and marketing history, management and theory. He has been a consultant to the United Nations Industrial Development Organization, as well as to other public and private organizations.

SIDNEY W. MINTZ is professor of anthropology at Yale University. He has a B.A. Degree from Brooklyn College and a Ph.D. from Colombia

University. His field research abroad has carried him to Puerto Rico, Jamaica, Haiti, and Iran. In 1967 Professor Mintz was vice president and president-elect of the American Ethnological Society. Among his publications are *Worker in the Cane: A Puerto Rican Life-History* and articles on anthropology including several on peasant markets in Jamaica, which have received wide currency among marketers.

MARVIN P. MIRACLE is associate professor of agricultural economics and chairman of the Comparative Tropical Economics Program, University of Wisconsin. He previously taught at San Francisco State College and for a year was research associate at the Food Research Institute at Stanford University. His degrees are from Oklahoma State University and Stanford University. Professor Miracle conducted extensive research in many areas of western and eastern Africa, India, and Latin America, and has published many articles on agricultural economics problems in Africa. His recent publications include: *Maize in Tropical Africa* and *Agriculture in the Congo Base: Tradition and Change in African Rural Economics.*

REED MOYER is professor of marketing at the Graduate School of Business Administration, Michigan State University. Professor Moyer has a Bachelor's degree from Harvard University, a Master's degree from the University of Wisconsin, and a Ph.D. from the University of California (Berkeley). Before entering teaching he was a business executive in the coal mining industry. Among his publications are: *Competition in the Midwestern Coal Industry, Marketing in Economic Development,* and a number of articles in professional journals on international marketing, marketing research, and energy economics.

LEE E. PRESTON, associate dean of the School of Business Administration, University of California (Berkeley), has degrees from Vanderbilt University and Harvard University. He has taught at the University of California (Berkeley) since 1958 with the exception of 1961–62 when he served as staff economist for the Council of Economic Advisers. He has also held posts at the Center for Economic Research, Athens, Greece, as a visiting professor at the American University at Cairo, Egypt, and as a visiting professor at Lingnan Institute of Business Administration, Chinese University of Hong Kong. Among his many articles, monographs, and books are: *Studies in a Simulated Market,* with Norman R. Collins, *Concentration and Price-Cost Markets in Manufacturing Industries,* with Norman R. Collins and *Consumer Goods Marketing in a Developing Economy: The Case of Greece.*

JON G. UDELL is assistant dean and director of the Bureau of Business Research and Service in the Graduate School of Business at the University of Wisconsin. He has also taught at Cornell University. His Bachelor's, M.B.A. and Ph.D. Degrees are from the University of Wisconsin. Professor

Udell has authored numerous articles on economic development, marketing management, business economics, and consumer behavior which have appeared in the professional journals. He also has to his credit several research monographs including *A Model of Non-Price Competitive Strategy*.

Table of contents

Introduction

A few years ago one of this volume's coeditors wrote that "marketing has been almost totally neglected in the literature on economic development. Instead, most theoretical and empirical studies in this area stress the importance to development of such things as capital formation, land reform, educational reform, and improved productive techniques."[1] A number of factors probably contributed to this neglect, including the intangibility of marketing, the association of marketing with high-level, not low-level economies, the inattention to marketing problems in economists' competitive models, and allied with this point, the feeling that marketing is a passive, accommodating activity which will be performed somehow once production is increased.

Recently this condition has changed somewhat. Marketing is still ignored, both in the literature and in developmental plans, but not as consistently as formerly. The Agency for International Development has funded sizable research projects in marketing in several Latin-American countries. They are aimed solely at linking marketing with the developmental process. AID is also creating national market planning centers to implement the research. In agricultural marketing the U.N.'s Food and Agriculture Organization has been active in training and other activities designed to improve marketing practices.

This increased interest in marketing's role in development has carried over into academic research and writing. This volume represents the fruits of some of this research.

The emphasis in these papers and in much of the other research on the distributive sector in developing economies centers on the food industry. These research efforts may focus at any of several points in the distributive chain. Some study aspects of the supply-gathering function; others look at trade in local village markets; still others analyze food store marketing in the larger cities. Whatever form they take, this emphasis on some aspect of food marketing is understandable. In many less developed countries, 40–65 percent of the consumer's budget may be spent on food. The leverage here is great. Modest improvements in efficiency in food distribution can spell relatively large gains in real income, food

---

[1] Reed Moyer, *Marketing in Economic Development* (Institute for International Business Management Studies, Michigan State University, 1965), p. 1.

1

price reductions freeing part of the consumer's income for expenditure for other commodities.

Improved marketing may perform other functions that speed development. The preceding paragraph demonstrates the gains accruing to the consumer from improved marketing. The farmer may benefit as well. An effective marketing system permits an increase in farm output moving into commercial markets. Much of the farm production in backward countries is produced in the subsistence sector. This is true not only in primitive societies but in the hinterlands in more developed economies. Development schemes seek to monetize the subsistence sector by inducing surpluses which may be sold in commercial markets. Effective marketing intermediaries aid this process in several ways. Because of their familiarity with market conditions, they may make known marketing opportunities of which producers may be unaware. Additionally, they may make credit available, store commodities, provide transportation facilities, and perform a host of other activities which facilitate production.

But their developmental role goes beyond the performance of these functions. Distribution systems link markets with markets and producers with markets. And in so doing they equalize and distribute goods from surplus to deficit areas under conditions of shifting demand and supply. Consumers and producers are separated geographically. Moreover, the production cycle differs from the consumption cycle. Food products are consumed at fairly regular intervals; they are harvested intermittently. These conditions require the intermediation of distributors to maintain an effective flow of goods both geographically and through time. If this distributive job falters, the development process is bound to suffer as well.

There is another possible function of marketing whose validity is disputed by some writers in the field of developmental economics. This is the activity that marketers perform calling to the attention of those in the hinterland an array of consumer goods whose utility has been verified by traditional consumers but whose consumption has been ignored by those in or on the margin of the subsistence sector.

The Glade-Udell article in this volume presents a variant of this theme. The traditional view holds that backward countries have dual economies, a modern (monetized) and a subsistence. The Glade-Udell study of Peru uncovered the existence of a modest amount of latent purchasing power in the sierra (subsistence) sector as evidenced by deposits in rural credit coops. The thrust of their paper is that it is up to marketing specialists to intermediate between the potential consumers and the producers to insure that goods satisfying the needs of the sierra folk are produced. The phenomenon of latent purchasing power in rural areas, ready to be tapped by enterprising firms, has been observed in other underdeveloped regions.[2]

Dissenters would argue that the consumer has abundant opportunities to spend what little income he possesses on goods of his own choice, without the urging of marketers.

An interesting historical note is the similarity between the basic functions performed by traders in primitive society today and their counterparts during the Commercial Revolution and before. The linking of markets, accumulating supplies, breaking bulk, building capital, and matching supplies with demand were performed by the merchant capitalists several centuries ago. Historians recognize the key role these capitalists played in the precondition period of the Commercial Revolution leading up to the Industrial Revolution and during the Industrial Revolution itself. Then, traders contributed substantially to development by creating a pool of entrepreneurs. To progress, economies must move, relatively, out of agriculture and into industry. But a key to this shift is the adequate supply of risk-taking, trained entrepreneurs necessary to direct the nascent industrial enterprises. The merchant class was a prime source of industrial entrepreneurs for various reasons.

The same condition applies today, as Professor Alexander points out in his article. Ironically many of these entrepreneurs come from the merchant class not because trading is valued but because it is held in contempt. Marketing in developing economics has two strikes against it: It is either ignored, attention shifting to production, finance, and other activities presumed to contribute more toward development, or it is attacked as a parasitic function, not only contributing nothing to the economic system but draining it of vitality as well. Because he stands between consumers and producers and apparently creates nothing of tangible value, the trader is treated with disdain. This attitude toward him probably accounts partly for the relatively large numbers of foreign traders in most underdeveloped regions of the world. Discriminated against, foreigners often move into trading as the only available means of supporting themselves. Many move out of trading and into other lines of economic activity and into more social respectability when their trading profits give them the opportunity to move. Many of these expatriate traders advance economic growth in their adopted countries by bringing skills and training that the countries' natives sadly lack.

Alexander indicates that traders are more likely than others to become industrial entrepreneurs for several reasons: (1) they already have entrepreneurial experience and have acquired skills in negotiating, buying,

---

[2] Observed by Donald A. Henley in his AID-supported work in Bolivia, and in I. D. Barnet, "Stimulating Development through Consumption-Oriented Policies," *International Development Review*, September, 1964, pp. 21–23.

selling, etc., which are readily transferable from merchant to industrial entrepreneurship; (2) they are closer to the market; hence, they are aware of profit-making opportunities in industry; (3) they are used to uncertainty and feel capable of coping with it; and, (4) their trading experience provides the capital (through profit accumulation) necessary to invest in industrial undertakings.

We have shown a similarity between one aspect of development today (the creation of an entrepreneurial pool from the merchant class) and development during the Industrial Revolution. It is useful to draw historical analogies in accounting for current phenomenon, but care must be taken not to rely too heavily upon them. Conditions are never quite the same. Professor Mintz's observation bears repeating. He asks whether economic development will be easier or harder to accomplish today in backward countries than it was a century or two ago. It will be easier because of the ready transfer of productive techniques and facilities from the developed to the underdeveloped regions, but harder because, in one sense, history will not repeat itself. When the Western countries developed, they had external territory (colonies or virgin land, for example, the American West) to move into and, to some extent, to exploit. This exploitation provided profit opportunities for traders and industrialists which no longer exist.

Our generalizations and observations need qualification for another reason. We have discussed the developmental role of marketing as though the function is performed by a homogeneous set of entrepreneurs. Obviously, this is incorrect. As the articles in this volume show, marketing in some form may be performed by itinerant peddlers and "mammies" at one end of the spectrum and representatives of international firms at the other. The contributions they make to economic development may differ as night differs from day. Analysis calls for separating the effect on development of the various types of intermediaries.

There is a danger when prescribing remedies suggested by research findings to disregard the secondary effects of the suggestions. This danger exists in the prescription of marketing remedies as well as in other areas where economic processes are concerned. Where this problem exists, we need, in the economist's parlance, general, not partial equilibrium analysis. Consider the following example. We have suggested some of the important functions which marketing performs to facilitate development. If some of these functions are not available or are inadequately performed, output may suffer. Thus, the unavailability of satisfactory storage facilities or insufficient price information may reduce the farmer's income below what he could receive if those deficiencies were removed. But what is the total effect of the improvement in these marketing services? The farmer might benefit by increasing the prices received for his goods and therefore increasing his income. The higher income then may be used to purchase personal consumption goods and farm supplies and to finance added farm output. These steps may lead to additional growth in the economy and, through a multiplier effect, to even more growth.

But what is the other side of the coin? If the improved marketing leads to higher prices paid to the farmer, they may spell higher prices paid by the consumer, whose real income as a result is reduced. This reduced income lessens demand for other commodities with attendant adverse effects on the internal growth process.

There are other similar situations. For example, several of the papers in this volume as well as articles elsewhere point to the existence of monopolies and resultant monopoly profits in some trade segments in developing economies. These monopolies are usually viewed with op-probrium. Their monopoly power permits them to elevate prices above the competitive level with obvious adverse effects on the consumers' real income and with second-order repercussions on the development process. Here again though, the loss to one segment of society is offset by a gain to another. We might ask: To what use does the trader put his monopoly profits? They might serve as a much needed pool of investment capital, a *sine qua non* of development. Or, of less value to the economy, they may finance the purchase of luxury goods. We should note in passing that in a number of underdeveloped countries, especially in Africa, the government has established state trading companies as monopolies, part of whose purpose is to tap monopoly profits to help finance the developmental effort.

Or consider the following. Marketing reform may call for the introduction of more capital-intensive goods to improve efficiency and reduce spoilage. These improvements may be better storage facilities, improved food-handling equipment, or more efficient transport units, among others. But in capital-poor countries, the use of more capital-intensive facilities in one sector probably means less capital-intensive processes in another. P. T. Bauer's appeal not to confuse technical with economic efficiency applies with force in this example and others like it. Where capital is scarce, marketing reformers might well emphasize the use of better techniques, new organizational forms, and improved quality of management instead of innovations requiring capital outlays.

In all of these cases, one must balance the benefits gained against the losses from the introduction of the innovation. The net effect may not be as obvious as the proponents of glib solutions would have us believe.

In a concluding chapter, we summarize findings of the articles which follow, and draw conclusions from them, where appropriate. It might be well at this point, nonetheless, to indicate a couple of strains which run through several of the articles so that the reader may be on the lookout for them. He will doubtless find other common threads.

These papers confirm theoretical reactions to malfunctioning marketing arrangements. These include:

Stimulus	*Response*
1. Retail price control	1. An inadequate production response with consequent shortages.
2. Restrictions on entry into trade through licensing and other means.	2. Elevation of prices and profits and reduction in the volume of trade with a resultant dampening effect on production. Fewer outlets reduce the integration of the subsistence rural sector into the monetized urban and village economy.
3. State trading monopolies	3. Shortages as well as the creation of substitute marketing channels through black markets and smuggling.

The articles in this volume emphasize the contributions to development which marketing may make. It is also apparent that marketing may deter economic growth as well. Professor Adams' account of the Shonto trader is a case in point. This store proprietor's strong monopoly position and his continued efforts to maintain it doubtless slowed growth of the Navajo tribe he served. It is possible that the monopoly trading companies in West Africa have had a similar effect on the area they serve. These firms' interests may be served by maintaining a high level of import and export business at the expense of the development of import-substitution industries within the country.

We emphasize the *possibility* of this deterrent effect. Their strong market position permits activities and decisions which benefit them and slow down intended industrial growth, but it is not altogether clear that they have so misused their market power. Indeed, some neutral observers contend that these firms have advanced the internal development process. Their dominant position leads to the need for scholarly studies of their impact on the countries in which they operate.

Other deterrents to development stem from artificial restraints on competition imposed directly or indirectly by trading interests. These may take the form of licensing laws, marketplace restrictions, coercive attempts to thwart competitors' actions, and other legal and nonlegal measures.

Influence of the
ENVIRONMENT on
marketing

The Clark-Fisher thesis holds that tertiary employment increases relative to total employment during the course of economic development. The thesis has both supporters and critics, and empirical investigation has not yet produced definitive results. Professor Preston contributes to the debate a cross-section analysis of commercial employment in countries at different stages of development. His findings tend to support the thesis in a modified form; they also suggest a basis for estimating the "normal" size of the commercial sector in relation to the state of development.

LEE E. PRESTON*

The commercial sector and economic development

A considerable debate took place a decade ago concerning the changing relative importance of different types of economic activity—and particularly of commercial and service activities—during the course of economic development. The discussion was cast in terms of the three broad economic activity categories identified by Colin Clark:[1] (1) primary production—agricultural and extractive activities; (2) secondary production—manufacturing and other activities changing the form of materials; and (3) tertiary production—all other activities, including commerce and services. Clark suggested that the process of development was marked by an increase in the relative importance of secondary, and then tertiary, activities as sources of income and employment. The growth of the tertiary sector was also stressed by A. G. B. Fisher,[2] and the proposition that tertiary activities tend to loom larger in the total economy, and particularly to account for larger shares of total employment, as countries increase in wealth came to be termed the Clark-Fisher thesis.

The relative growth of the distributive trades in the course of development is a crucial element in this proposition. Trade accounts for nonnegligible amounts of employment in nearly all economies, and typically for one fourth to one third of all tertiary employment. In addition, for all

* University of California, Berkeley.

[1] Colin Clark, *The Conditions of Economic Progress* (London: Macmillan & Co., Ltd., 1951).

[2] A. G. B. Fisher, *Economic Progress and Social Security* (London: Macmillan & Co., Ltd., 1945); and "Production, Primary, Secondary and Tertiary," *Economic Record*, Vol. XV (1939), pp. 24–38.

their diversity, marketing activities may be somewhat more similar among economies than personal services or some other tertiary activities. If so, any general tendencies at work might be more clearly reflected in the scale of marketing activities than in tertiary activities as a whole. Finally, the challenge to the Clark-Fisher thesis set forth by Bauer and Yamey,[3] Holton,[4] Minkes,[5] and others focused specifically on the character and scale of marketing activity in poor countries.

The series of comments exchanged by Fisher and the critics ended in a semantic argument with no firm conclusion.[6] In the subsequent decade, considerable development has occurred in countries around the world, and larger and more reliable collections of comparative data have become available. It thus appears that the Clark-Fisher thesis—and more specifically the size of the commercial sector in developing economies— merits a reconsideration in the light of more recent events and current knowledge. Such a reconsideration is particularly important in view of the increased emphasis being placed upon marketing and other nonproduction activities in development studies and plans.

THE THESIS AND THE CRITICS

The thesis that tertiary employment, and particularly marketing employment, should grow relative to total employment in the course of development was initially put forward as both a theoretical and an empirical proposition. It was argued that the development process was marked by a transition from subsistence to market economies, and therefore by a relative increase in the scale of distributive activity. Further, as people become wealthier, their consumption was said to shift relatively away from goods, particularly foods, and toward services. In addition, labor productivity was thought to have increased more rapidly in goods production than in trade and services. With all of these factors at work, as average income levels increase, a greater share of the labor force should tend to become occupied in tertiary activities, and particularly in

---

[3] P. T. Bauer and B. S. Yamey, "Economic Progress and Occupational Distribution," *Economic Journal*, Vol. LXI (1951), pp. 741–55.

[4] R. H. Holton, "Marketing Structure and Economic Development," *Quarterly Journal of Economics*, Vol. LXVII (1953), pp. 344–61.

[5] A. L. Minkes, "Statistical Evidence and the Concept of Tertiary Industry," *Economic Development and Cultural Change* (1955), pp. 366–73.

[6] A. G. B. Fisher, "A Note on Tertiary Production," *Economic Journal*, Vol. LXII (December, 1952), pp. 820–34; A. G. B. Fisher, "Marketing Structure and Economic Development," *Quarterly Journal of Economics*, Vol. LXVIII (February, 1954), pp. 151–54; A. G. B. Fisher, "Tertiary Production: A Postscript," *Economic Journal*, Vol. LXIV (September, 1954), pp. 619–21; S. G. Triantis, "Economic Progress, Occupational Redistribution and International Terms of Trade," *Economic Journal*, Vol. LVIII (September, 1953), pp. 627–37; and Peter T. Bauer and Basil S. Yamey, "Further Notes on Economic Progress and Occupational Distribution," *Economic Journal*, Vol. LXIV (March, 1954), pp. 98–106.

trade. Scattered data from various rich and poor countries were frequently cited as evidence of this tendency.

The critics challenged both the argument and the data. It was noted that changes in marketing and service activities due to development may be qualitative as well as quantitative, and the need for some types of activity is eliminated by the development process just as the need for others arises. Income increases may permit diverse changes in food quality, and in the quality and quantity of manufactured goods and housing, as well as increased consumption of services. The assumed differences in rates of productivity change, based on evidence from rich countries, may not appear in poor ones; and, in any event, if productivity differences among sectors are reflected in relative price changes, any tendency for service consumption to increase may be partially offset by price increases. Finally, it was argued that available data for poor countries failed to reflect economic reality and, therefore, that the empirical support for the thesis was spurious.

The theoretical points made by both proponents and critics of the thesis have merit, but the significant question is the net effect of this complex of forces on the structure of economic activity. This question is most readily resolved by an empirical test, and therefore the appropriateness of available data for purposes of this test becomes a crucial issue. In the earlier discussion, the critics charged that available data seriously understated the amount of tertiary activity in poor countries—and therefore led to overestimates of the tendency of such activity to increase with increases in income—for two reasons:

1. Labor in poor countries is typically unspecialized. The same individual may act as primary producer, handicraft or factory worker, and also perform marketing or service activities. Indeed, the small-scale producer typically assumes some responsibility for the marketing of his own produce, at least at an intermediate market level and perhaps to final users. When these production-and-marketing workers are enumerated as "agricultural workers," "handicraft workers," etc., a substantial commitment of labor time to tertiary activity escapes observation and the resulting data are, therefore, inaccurate.

2. Economic units in marketing or service activities in poor countries frequently coincide with the family unit, and family members other than the household head may participate in the economic activity on a part-time or "as needed" basis. In addition, women, children, and men not qualified for other work frequently engage in ambulatory vending or service activities. Both of these sources of additional tertiary labor effort typically escape coverage in official data.

These two points taken together were considered to invalidate the available occupational data as evidence of the relative importance of marketing or service activities in underdeveloped economies. The statistical association between the scale of tertiary activity and indicators of development was, therefore, said to be illusory. The true association was between development, occupational specialization, and the reduction of underemployment.

Although there is considerable substantive accuracy in these observations, even with respect to the comparative occupational data now available, they probably should be taken as qualifications to the results of empirical analysis, not reasons to reject empirical studies altogether. With respect to the ancillary marketing activities of primary or secondary producers, the important point is that these activities *are* ancillary. The farmer who takes his produce to town for sale is not primarily engaged in food marketing. The participation of family members in the producing unit is by no means restricted to tertiary activities and is probably even more characteristic of agriculture. The visible presence of street vendors, shoeshiners, and beggars in the tourist-populated capitals of poor countries can easily create an inaccurate impression of the importance of these activities in their economies as a whole. (Compare data on automobile ownership in poor countries with the traffic jams in their capital cities!)

With respect to all of these apparent expenditures of labor time on marketing and service activity, the distinctions between work and leisure, *under*employment and *un*employment—distinctions which are obvious in rich countries—are very difficult to draw. Although the exclusion of part-time and casual trade and service workers is a source of inaccuracy in much of the available data, the enumeration of all these people as full-time workers would also be inaccurate. Whether the shopkeeper's wife spends her morning in the store gossiping with the customers, or at home gossiping with the neighbors, she remains a lady of leisure. The shopkeeper, on the other hand, whether busy or not, should be and will be enumerated as a sales worker by any conscientious census taker.

COMPARATIVE OCCUPATIONAL AND INCOME DATA

The preceding comments are intended to suggest that officially collected and reported occupational data, although subject to important qualifications, may be taken as indicative of the actual distribution of the labor force between principal types of economic activity in different countries. The major collection of data is that published in the International Labor Organization *Yearbook*. These data show the distribution of the economically active population by countries and by eight major occupational categories, three of which are relevant for our purposes:

  6. Commerce.
  7. Transport, storage and communication.
  8. Services.

The commerce category consists of wholesale and retail trade, finance, insurance and real estate. Trade employment accounts, in fact, for the great bulk of the total in nearly all countries. The three listed categories taken together may be said to comprise the tertiary sector of economic activity. It would be desirable for present purposes to group the data more directly about marketing activities alone, excluding purely financial operations and including those elements of agriculture, manufacturing, transport, and storage associated directly with marketing. However, such regrouping is impossible with the available data, and it is clear that the commerce category contains the bulk of marketing personnel and relatively little else. The share of commercial occupations, and of all tertiary occupations, in the economically active population as computed from this source will, therefore, be the focus of analysis.

The summary indicator of the level of development selected for this study is the Gross Domestic Product (GDP) per capita, expressed in U.S. dollars, available from the *United Nations Yearbook of National Accounts*. Like the occupation data, these also are subject to important questions with respect to both relevance and accuracy. Although the GDP figures are probably more appropriate as indicators of relative states of development than as measures of real income (the context in which they are most frequently criticized), their accuracy is undoubtedly correlated with the level of development itself. Fortunately, our immediate analytical purpose can be served if the data are viewed as correct only within rough orders of magnitude.

The income and occupation data used in this analysis are tabulated in the Appendix, along with the computed ratios of commercial and all tertiary occupations to the total active population. Both sets of data refer to various years around 1960. It is not necessary for our purposes that observations for all countries be taken at a single date, or even that the two variables for each country be observed in the same year, since neither should be expected to change very greatly from one year to the next. Lack of perfect consistency in the timing of observations may have some effect on our results, but these problems are probably no greater than those of qualitative comparability and reporting accuracy inherent in data of this type.

Parallel observations are available for 79 countries. Unfortunately, none of the communist countries is included.[7]

STATISTICAL ANALYSIS

We initially test the hypothesis that the share of all commercial occupations, and of all tertiary occupations, in the economically active

[7] A similar analysis of these data focusing on the ratio of manufacturing to nonmanufacturing employment outside of agriculture for a sample of 25 countries was presented by W. Galenson, "Economic Development and the Sectoral Expansion of

population (hereafter referred to as the C/LF and T/LF ratios) is positively associated with the GDP per capita. It is desirable to examine both the commerce sector and the larger tertiary grouping in order to check for differences in the closeness of the relationship. An initial summary tabulation (Table 1) suggests some degree of association between the variables. The four GDP classes in this table reflect more or less natural breaks in the data; the absence of a large population of "middle income" countries (GDP $500–$799) is notable.

Inspection of the data reveals five poor countries in which the computed C/LF ratio is so high as to suggest either errors or important

Table 1

GDP PER CAPITA AND C/LF AND T/LF RATIOS, 79 COUNTRIES

GDP Per Capita ($U.S.)	Number of Countries	Average C/LF Ratio	Average T/LF Ratio
0–199	29	8.93	22.56
200–499	28	9.80	29.71
500–799	6	13.22	42.23
800–over	16	15.50	43.49
All Countries	79	10.90	30.80
(Avg. GDP = $450.3)			

Source: Appendix.

noncomparabilities in reporting procedures. These data were therefore excluded from the statistical analysis, but are reintroduced in the following section.

Both linear and exponential regression equations were computed, as follows:

$$Y = aX^b \ (0 < b < 1), \text{ estimated as } \log Y = \log a + b \log X$$
$$Y = a + bX$$

Where:

$Y_1 = $ C/LF ratio; $Y_2 = $ T/LF ratio; and $X = $ GDP per capita.

Additional equations were also computed using the rate of growth of GDP, total and per capita, and the share of agricultural occupations in the labor force as explanatory variables. However, the failure of these computations to yield substantially stronger or different results, and the inter-correlations among the variables, suggest that only the two-variable regressions merit attention.

The exponential equation is theoretically the more appropriate. We would certainly expect an intersection at or near the origin, and some retardation in the relative growth of nonproduction activities should be anticipated at some GDP levels. However, over the range of the 74 observations, the straight line provides an equally good fit for both dependent variables. The regression results are as follows (standard errors in parenthesis):

Linear functions:
$$Y_1 = 6.1 + .008\,X \qquad\qquad R^2 = .54$$
$$(.0008)$$

$$Y_2 = 18.6 + .021\,X \qquad\qquad R^2 = .58$$
$$(002)$$

Exponential functions:
$$\log Y_1 = -.17045 + .44\ \log\ X \qquad R^2 = .50$$
$$(.05)$$

$$\log Y_2 = .22867 + .74\ \log\ X \qquad R^2 = .58$$
$$(.05)$$

(Antilogs of the constants are .676 and 1.693, respectively.)

The two regression equations for Y_1, the C/LF ratio, are plotted in Figure 1, where their close correspondence over most of the range of the data is apparent.

These results mean that for the entire collection of 74 observations, differences in GDP per capita explain about half of the differences in the

Figure 1

REGRESSION RESULTS, 74 COUNTRIES

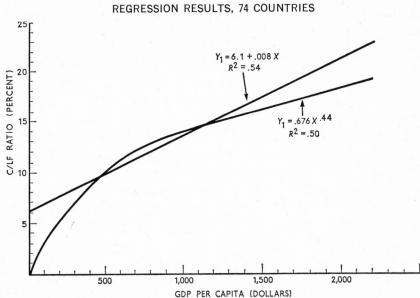

relative importance of commercial occupations, and of all tertiary occupations, in the active population. Reading from the linear functions, our expectation, subject to a considerable margin of uncertainty, is that differences of $100 in GDP per capita among countries will be accompanied by differences in the same direction of 0.8 percentage points in the relative share of commercial occupations, and differences of 2.1 points in the share of all tertiary occupations, in the labor force. Reading from the exponential functions, we expect an increase in the C/LF ratio of 4.4 percent (*not* percentage points), and in the T/LF ratio of 7.4 percent, to accompany increases of 10 percent in per capita GDP.

AN ALTERNATIVE INTERPRETATION

These results produced by the mindless computer suggest the presence of a fundamental relationship, but one which is either relatively weak or badly obscured by noncomparabilities among the observations. We have, therefore, plotted all of the data and experimented with a number of subsidiary groupings and alternative formulations. We focus here only on the C/LF ratios.

The results of this analysis are shown in Figure 2, and may be summarized in the following comments:

1. Three of the observations—Hong Kong, West Berlin, and Luxem-

Figure 2

ALTERNATIVE VIEW OF THE DATA

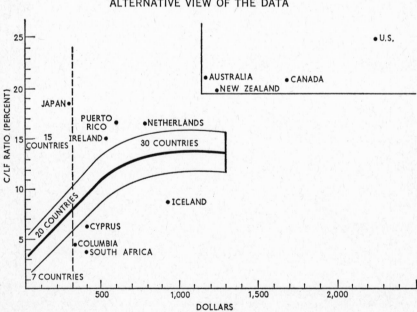

bourg—are more accurately described as cities than countries. They have the high C/LF ratios in relation to income that one would expect of urban trade centers. They have been excluded, therefore, from further consideration.

2. Observations for the four "new world" countries of Australia, New Zealand, Canada, and the United States stand quite apart from the main body of the data, and suggest either a substantial shift in the level or a different form of any functional relationship present.

3. Much the greatest variation of C/LF ratios is found among the lowest income countries—those with less than $300 GDP per capita. Thus, any accurate description must recognize the wide dispersion of these values. Some of the low ratios may be due to underreporting of the types mentioned previously; some of the ratios are, on the other hand, suspiciously high. On balance, it appears that the larger group of poor countries unquestionably have lower shares of their labor forces in commerce than do the intermediate and rich countries. For example, even if allowance is made for underreporting, and if the five countries excluded from the statistical analysis are now included, only 11 of the 42 low-income countries have C/LF ratios as great as 10. By contrast, only 10 of the 36 countries with GDP above $300 have C/LF ratios below 10, and all but one of these low-ratio countries are in the $300–$500 GDP range.

4. Leaving aside the three cities, the "new world" countries, and high-ratio poor countries, a continuous functional relationship may serve as a fairly accurate describer of the remaining collection of observations. One such relationship is illustrated by the heavy curve in Figure 2. Within the arbitrary bounds of plus and minus two percentage points of this curve, 43 of the 79 observations fall. The suggested curve is not readily described by any simple algebraic approximation, and it is perhaps more accurate to describe it in terms of three phases:

a) An almost linear trend of 1.75 points in the C/LF ratio for each $100 change in GDP, for GDP up to $500 per capita;
b) A much slower rate of increase—about .75 points for each $100—in the $500–$1,000 GDP range;
c) A leveling off at a C/LF ratio of 14–15 for countries approaching $1,000 GDP per capita and above.

By far the most numerous variations from this suggested pattern are, of course, among the poor countries. Fifteen of them fall above the plus-2-point limits of the curve, and seven fall below. Even if the latter are all discounted as due to underreporting, something like one third of the poor countries have relatively high C/LF ratios by this standard. The seven substantial deviations within the middle range of the data are individually indicated in the figure.

The result of this rather *ad hoc* analysis is that there appear to be three quite different groups of countries with respect to the relationship between the scale of commercial employment and the level of income:

The four rich "new world" countries, with their very high C/LF ratios;

About one third of the poor countries, with the high C/LF ratios anticipated by Bauer and Yamey and other critics of the Clark-Fisher thesis;

The main body of the data, consisting of more than half of the observations, in which the suggested positive function gradually retarding to an upper limit of 14–15 percent provides a reasonably accurate general description.

IMPLICATIONS

The several theoretical propositions underlying the Clark-Fisher thesis may be called upon to explain the increase of the share of commercial employment in the labor force as suggested by the foregoing analysis. Two additional factors probably contribute to the upward trend as well. One is that changes in the composition of *goods* consumption made possible by increasing incomes tend to generate increases in the relative scale of marketing activity. For example, as GDP levels rise within the $200–$700 per capita range, the shift in consumption is not so much toward services as toward durables, style merchandise, and branded and packaged foods.

These changes in *goods* consumption lead to increased marketing activity both because the goods themselves are new to the economies in question, and therefore require introduction and explanation, and because, even when familiar, these kinds of goods require continuing marketing effort in the form of demonstration, service, advertising, and personal selling in a way that traditional staples do not. The second additional factor is that increases in income permit not only increases in consumption but also increases in the variety of goods from which consumption choices are made and in the convenience with which merchandise is made available to all kinds of final users. These increases in both variety and convenience involve additional marketing effort, both capital and labor.

The retardation in the expansion of the commercial sector at the levels shown here should probably be interpreted as an *ad hoc* phenomenon associated with the particular production-consumption mix possible in economies in the $800–$1,200 per capita GDP class around 1960. Thus, we should view the 14–15 percent ceiling as a "current" rather than a "natural" limitation. The higher ratios of the four "new world" countries probably reflect a number of features in which they are unique—relative underpopulation, and large geographical distances between numerous market centers, for example—as well as their high levels of income. Also, there may be larger differences in productivity between the production and marketing sectors of these economies, because of rapid rates of technological change prior to 1960. If so, a balanced output of goods and marketing services would require relatively more labor in marketing, and less in production, in these countries than in others. However, as other developed countries become more like the United States and Canada both in the qualitative composition of consumption and in levels of productivity and income, it is probably more reasonable to anticipate an upward shift in the entire functional relationship than a maintenance of the present ceiling on marketing employment in the occupation structure.

The principal implication—or perhaps it is only a contention—of this analysis is that we may meaningfully speak of the "normal" size of the commercial sector in economies at different stages of development, at least for countries that make fairly extensive use of markets as the mechanism of distribution. The expected level of commercial employment, given the level of income or other development criterion, can be estimated only with broad limits, and we would expect it to change over the long term in response to qualitative changes in the production-consumption mix. However, even with these limitations, if the notion of a normal or expected relationship is accepted, it then becomes possible both to forecast changes associated with continued development and to identify economies in which the scale of marketing activity clearly deviates from "normal."

Projecting an expansion of commercial activity along the normal path for countries in the process of development has direct implications for manpower and educational requirements, urban land use, and financial practices. Further, as commercial activities increase in relative scale, the efficiency with which they are conducted and their contribution to the development process loom larger in the total complex of economic activity. Both the functional importance of marketing and its anticipated relative increase in scale should draw the attention of public and private planners to the trade sector and its special problems in countries beyond the "takeoff" stage of development.

Economies in which the size of the commercial sector is clearly different from that implied by their position in the international income distribution present individual analytical problems. In some instances, data collection and reporting differences no doubt indicate discrepancies where none exist. Other deviations may be due to important individual structural characteristics, including the degree of urbanization and the closeness of contact with more highly developed countries. Japan, for example, is an industrialized and urbanized country with a highly developed marketing system, in spite of its relatively low levels of per capita income. The same factors probably explain the large upward deviations for Puerto Rico and the Netherlands.

For the relatively poor countries, a large apparent excess of commercial employment may well indicate a major task for development policy and a major source of labor for industrial or agricultural expansion. The ability of an excessive number of persons to subsist in commercial occupations necessarily implies that the cost of marketing is higher than necessary, and thus that final prices are increased and the expansion of demand retarded. The elimination of redundant commercial employment may well be a requisite of vigorous development based on market principles in such economies. Private firms seeking to introduce new lines of merchandise into such markets may find it necessary to establish their own marketing agencies (thereby increasing the redundance of resources in the short run) in order to eliminate the depressing effect of the traditional trade structure on the growth of demand.

Some interest also attaches to economies that appear to be putting relatively little labor effort into commerce according to this standard. Low commitments of labor resources to trade might be due to extreme inequality of income, so that the per capita figure misrepresents typical income levels, or to the specific composition of production and consumption and to dependence on marketing facilities in other countries. South Africa is probably an example of the first, and Iceland of the second. Where such individual explanations do not suffice, a low commitment of resources to commerce may indicate that the growth of domestic demand is being held back by inadequate marketing effort and that welfare benefits in the form of convenience and merchandise variety are being foregone. Both private investment and public encouragement of the expansion of trading facilities and activity may well be called for.

A final point of some importance is that taking account of differences in the scale of commercial activity due to income differences serves to define the scope for organizational change within the trade sector. One might initially observe that the substantial association between commercial employment and income, regardless of differences in organizational characteristics, suggests that these latter are unimportant. It is possible, however, to point to some evidences of organizational impact even in these gross data. For example, the highly concentrated and integrated marketing system of Finland uses only 11.6 percent of the labor force, whereas the fragmented trade sector of Italy—with a per capita GDP one third less than Finland—uses 13.2 percent. More important, perhaps, is the implication that for the great bulk of countries in which the size of the commercial sector is approximately "normal" relative to their income levels, improved marketing efficiency and an increased contribution of commerce to the development process probably involve the redistribution of effort within the trade sector rather than an overall change in its size. Thus, the focus of policy can shift to a more careful analysis of needs and opportunities by kind of business, function, and location, problems that can be approached only on a country-by-country basis.

The virtue of the comparative analysis presented here is that it places the unique marketing structure of each country in some perspective in terms of its level of development and its position relative to other countries. Further, we have tried to identify both the core of validity and the important qualifications to the proposition that that trade sector will experience relative growth in the course of development. Marketing activity provides the mechanism by which producers are made aware of new production and demand opportunities and the vehicle by which the fruits of development are brought to final consumers. Thus, for countries beyond the "takeoff" stage, expansion of commercial employment should be viewed as a normal part of the development process.

APPENDIX

GDP PER CAPITA AND OCCUPATION DATA, 79 COUNTRIES, 1960's

Country	Continent	GDP Per Capita (1)	Commerce (2)	Commerce Transportation, and Services (3)	Total Active Population (4)	$Y_1 = \dfrac{Col\,2}{Col\,4}$ % (5)	$Y_2 = \dfrac{Col\,3}{Col\,4}$ % (6)
			Active Population			Ratio	
Mozambique	Africa	45	23,093	154,685	1,672,129	1.40	9.27
Nepal	Asia	50	57,849	173,438	4,153,455	1.40	4.16
Tanganika*	Africa	52	15,381	27,799	39,179	39.25	71.00
Pakistan	Asia	63	1,474,516	4,450,450	30,205,981	4.88	14.73
India	Asia	67	7,653,571	28,100,105	188,675,000	4.06	14.90
Indonesia	Asia	69	2,193,978	5,980,736	32,708,614	6.71	18.29
Thailand	Asia	78	779,904	1,601,114	13,836,974	5.64	11.57
Haiti	N. Am.	80	61,608	148,435	1,747,187	3.52	8.47
Congo	Africa	87	91,640	218,166	6,198,933	1.48	3.60
Bolivia	S. Am.	104	57,046	147,838	1,058,725	5.40	13.98
Korea	Asia	105	785,000	2,011,000	8,653,000	9.07	23.24
Paraguay	S. Am.	111	41,708	159,988	616,640	6.78	25.93
Taiwan	Asia	115	200,645	731,051	2,993,029	6.70	24.42
United Arab Republic	Africa	116	629,966	2,234,304	7,769,067	8.11	28.75
Ceylon	Asia	122	246,234	832,599	2,993,349	8.22	27.83
Rhodesia*	Africa	134	24,730	59,950	96,110	25.73	62.37
Northern Rhodesia*	Africa	134	6,060	18,780	32,270	18.06	58.20
Syria	Asia	138	141,126	375,260	1,244,760	11.33	30.01
Tunisia	Asia	147	62,710	174,130	1,327,520	4.72	13.12
Peru	S. Am.	148	112,126	252,226	2,475,339	4.52	10.18
Surinam	S. Am.	148	11,300	15,150	96,500	11.70	15.46
Iran	Asia	159	355,005	1,218,491	6,066,638	5.85	20.01
Morocco	Africa	159	473,000	551,000	3,291,000	14.37	16.74
Guatemala	N. Am.	164	52,561	163,618	967,814	5.43	16.94
Ecuador	S. Am.	179	91,734	330,800	1,483,734	6.18	22.32
Ryukyu*	Asia	180	76,000	156,349	405,000	18.76	38.60
Philippines	Asia	191	911,000	2,320,000	10,266,000	8.88	22.60
Honduras	N. Am.	192	26,500	33,130	580,440	4.58	5.69
El Salvador	N. Am.	198	50,400	176,130	806,590	6.24	21.80
Turkey	Europe	201	403,764	1,327,441	12,993,245	3.11	10.21
Fiji Islands	Oceana	212	6,213	21,633	93,257	6.66	23.65
Iraq	Asia	215	91,738	436,395	1,795,277	5.11	24.35
Federation of Malaya	Asia	216	195,192	589,692	2,164,861	9.01	27.22
Portugal	Europe	218	272,754	897,285	3,423,551	7.96	26.21
Algeria	Africa	220	174,349	398,017	3,508,934	4.96	11.35
Mauritius	Africa	221	18,802	65,655	187,401	10.03	35.29
Gabon*	Africa	240	8,160	18,010	22,000	37.10	81.86
Nicaragua	N. Am.	249	15,273	56,367	329,976	4.62	16.97
Brazil	S. Am.	250	1,073,997	4,469,577	17,117,362	6.27	26.11
British Guiana	S. Am.	250	18,303	55,117	161,407	11.33	34.16
Hong Kong	Asia	258	131,279	483,342	1,211,999	10.83	39.85
Japan	Asia	284	9,010,000	18,930.000	47,650,000	18.90	39.73

* Countries omitted from statistical analysis.

Country	Continent	GDP Per Capita (1)	Active Population		Total Active Population (4)	Ratio	
			Commerce (2)	Commerce Transportation, and Services (3)		$Y_1 = \dfrac{\text{Col } 2}{\text{Col } 4}$ % (5)	$Y_2 = \dfrac{\text{Col } 3}{\text{Col } 4}$ % (6)
Mexico	N. Am.	288	1,074,593	2,957,332	11,332,016	9.48	26.10
Colombia	S. Am.	301	203,774	931,950	3,755,609	5.42	24.81
Greece	Europe	310	266,070	859,408	3,638,601	7.31	23.61
Spain	Europe	322	911,800	3,066,900	11,634,200	7.84	26.36
Martinique	N. Am.	330	8,062	23,320	91,333	8.82	25.27
Panama	N. Am.	348	30,721	108,386	336,969	9.12	32.04
Costa Rica	N. Am.	358	21,412	71,043	271,984	7.87	26.10
Jamaica	N. Am.	361	60,281	212,498	606,823	9.93	34.92
Cuba	N. Am.	370	232,323	732,230	1,972,266	11.83	37.12
South Africa	Africa	386	224,005	1,292,070	4,551,301	4.92	28.38
Cyprus	Europe	403	16,230	60,445	235,358	6.90	26.53
Chile	S. Am.	409	225,300	345,500	2,356,000	9.56	14.60
Argentina	S. Am.	474	904,989	2,900,565	7,599,071	11.90	38.17
Ireland	Europe	474	163,584	429,943	1,108,108	14.76	38.81
Italy	Europe	490	2,661,000	6,424,000	20,134,000	13.21	31.90
Trinidad	S. Am.	532	30,200	106,700	267,100	11.31	40.10
Israel	Asia	579	104,700	406,700	843,100	12.41	48.16
Puerto Rico	N. Am.	581	127,000	368,600	754,700	16.82	48.60
Austria	Europe	656	369,389	1,182,496	3,369,815	10.96	37.07
Finland	Europe	750	236,381	666,688	2,033,268	11.62	32.80
Netherlands	Europe	767	675,899	1,945,355	4,168,626	16.21	46.66
West Berlin	Europe	893	174,000	530,000	1,056,000	16.48	50.19
German Federal Republic	Europe	931	3,730,000	10,597,000	26,993,000	13.81	39.25
Iceland	Europe	937	5,806	19,837	63,595	9.12	31.50
Venezuela	S. Am.	975	304,375	982,650	2,406,725	12.64	40.84
Denmark	Europe	975	313,351	927,127	2,093,631	14.97	44.29
Belgium	Europe	1029	538,300	1,649,900	3,694,400	14.57	44.66
Norway	Europe	1035	186,814	613,625	1,406,458	13.28	43.67
United Kingdom	Europe	1078	3,160,351	10,260,212	22,610,046	13.97	45.37
France	Europe	1113	2,596,700	7,611,700	19,705,600	13.18	38.63
Australia	Oceana	1211	827,911	2,019,249	4,225,096	19.60	47.78
New Zealand	Oceana	1281	163,037	434,442	895,363	18.21	48.49
Sweden	Europe	1313	438,526	1,323,699	3,244,026	13.51	40.80
Switzerland	Europe	1316	346,215	960,844	2,512,411	13.78	38.26
Luxembourg	Europe	1333	25,347	45,797	135,139	18.75	34.01
Canada	N. Am.	1767	1,323,000	3,598,000	6,727,000	19.66	53.49
U.S.A.	N. Am.	2324	16,827,000	40,743,000	74,618,000	22.53	54.55

Sources: (1) United Nations, *Yearbook of National Accounts Statistics, 1963,* Table 3A. (2) International Labor Office, *Yearbook of Labor Statistics, 1964,* Table 4.

Many of the governments of developing countries, especially in Africa, are strongly influenced by socialist doctrine. Part of the dogma is to attack the merchant as being parasitic, hence subject to takeover by the state. But, Professor Berg argues, the lack of trained personnel, the difficulty of centralized decision making and other adverse political and cultural factors make successful state control of distribution difficult to achieve. Furthermore, government control in this sector leads to a mis-allocation of resources. He documents his case with discussion of marketing policy in Guinea and Tanzania.

ELLIOT J. BERG*

Socialist ideology and marketing policy in Africa†

INTRODUCTION

On the ideological level, "socialism" has won the day in Africa. Politically aware intellectuals or political leaders who do not believe that socialism is the true and clear path to rapid economic development are in the minority. It is often thought, that because "African Socialism" means so many different things to those who speak in its name, it has no common ideological content. That is not true. Despite the diversity of socialist doctrines, most Africans who call themselves "socialists" do hold in common certain underlying economic attitudes or preconceptions.

All of them, first of all, view "capitalism" as an unsuitable system for Africa. It is the economy of the colonizers; it is old-fashioned. It is inadequate to meet the pressing development needs of poor countries. Individual enterprise can't be counted on to mobilize resources on the required scale, and the market mechanism is a wasteful, highly imperfect regulator of economic activity. Local entrepreneurs are few, local sources of capital rare. At best, capitalist development would mean development by foreigners and permanent economic dependence on the outside world.

Even if all of this were not true, "capitalism" would still be unaccepta-

---

* University of Michigan.

† This paper is a revised and expanded version of an article which appeared in the *Quarterly Journal of Economics,* November, 1964.

ble on ethical and social grounds. It rests on the exploitation of man by man. It is inhuman. It alienates each man from his brothers, preventing a full flowering of the human personality.

These ideas and attitudes are not much different from those occupying the mainstream of European socialist thought. Their specifically African quality is found in the persistent theme that socialism is fundamentally in harmony with the communal traditions of African society, and in the stress given to several of the universal criticisms of capitalist economic organization: the identification of capitalism with colonialism and the unproductive, parasitic role of the merchant.

While socialists in Africa (and in most of the underdeveloped world) share this world view, concrete economic policies vary widely in states that proclaim themselves socialist. But through all socialist doctrine and practice there runs a general policy orientation which gives definable economic substance to socialist ideology. Several aspects are of most relevance here.

It is first of all clear that in all socialist approaches, the State is to be the driving force in development. It is not only to undertake new initiatives, but to intensify existing controls over private economic activity.

In most of Africa, government has always been the major element in the economy even though the public sector commands a smaller proportion of total output than in advanced Western countries. The presence of the state is exercised through its economic controls and regulations, and by its predominance in the money sector. And the minimum tasks required in the continent's present stage of development (law and order, physical infrastructure, education, transportation) imply a very large government role even under the most "liberal" economic policies conceivable. But in the "socialist model" the state has a much greater place—in the creation and operation of industrial and agricultural enterprises, in control of marketing, in price regulation and in general management of the economy.

Related to the predominance of the state is an emphasis on direct economic controls, underlying which is a lack of faith in individual profit-seeking and the market mechanism as efficient instruments of resource allocation and mobilization. This is most strikingly evident in socialist policy tendencies with respect to the distribution sector of the economy. Government monopoly of all or part of foreign and domestic trade is regarded as desirable and necessary. To some extent this is economic nationalism; it springs from a desire to reduce the influence of big foreign firms and alien small traders. For it is one of the most important facts of economic life in the underdeveloped world in general and Africa in particular that commerce, both internal and external, is largely in the hands of foreigners—Europeans, Levantines, Asians, non-local Africans in Africa. But behind it there is usually the conviction that private commerce is inefficient—that prices are too high, profits too great and the number of traders too large, and that the merchant class is profoundly parasitic, a group of useless exploiters. For all these reasons it is essential to "democratize the channels of commerce," as President Touré has put it—i.e., to nationalize trade.

This penchant for full or partial state take-over of the trading sector is stimulated by the belief that since trading is a simple matter its nationalization can provide an easy and rich source of development finance. In both Guinea and Mali the planned profits of the nationalized trading sector, for example, were to provide much of the local expenditure for the first post-independence development plans—in Mali about one-third and in Guinea about 60% of total domestic investment.

ORIGINS OF SOCIALIST ATTITUDES

It is worth considering briefly the roots of these attitudes and ideas on economic policy. In part they rest on imported ideology. Much of the distaste and distrust with which African elites view "capitalism" reflects the Marxist world view—however modified or heretical in form—which colors the thinking of so many national leaders in Africa. Capitalism is to them simply the projection of colonialism and imperialism, much as Lenin said it was.

Another factor important in explaining the "anticapitalist" spirit abroad in Africa is the image of capitalism and the general economic attitudes inherited from the colonial period. Thus colonialism and capitalism are so closely identified in African thinking not only because of Marxist-Leninist doctrine but because most Africans have seen it to be so. Behind them is a half-century of history cluttered with memories of price-fixing arrangements, government-bestowed monopoly privileges, restrictive wage and labor market policies, forced labor—all dependent on an alliance between colonial governments and private (almost exclusively foreign) enterprises, and most of them involving a sacrifice of African interests. It is hardly surprising that "decolonization" and a reduction of the roles of private enterprise should seem related.

Moreover, the colonial experience in most of the continent was scarcely designed to encourage an appreciation of the economic potentials of individual initiatives in a relatively free market. Economic policy in colonial Africa was most often paternalist, *dirigiste*, anti–free enterprise to the core. More often than not, African peasants were told what to produce, who to sell it to, where, when, at what price. In a number of countries, even the African instinct of survival was discounted; Africans were forced to grow some crops in excess of normal needs, as a guarantee against famine. Wage earners in much of the continent were not until recently thought by colonial officials or employees to be capable of spending their incomes "sensibly," nor were African farmers and traders presumed to be sufficiently alive to price and profit to assure urban food supplies at reasonable prices. Markets had to be "organized," commodity and labor supplies "regularized." Extensive price controls, monopolistic allocation of sales and purchases, regulation of entry into trade, commerce and industry—most of the armory of a benevolent *dirigism* found its way to Africa.

In the early years of the colonial presence this was no doubt inevitable and necessary. Preconditions for the effective functioning of markets had to be established. But it tended to persist in much of the continent when its utility was doubtful. That it did so reflected the economic tastes of colonial administrators in charge of economic policy, most of whom had little understanding of and sympathy for the struggles of the market place. They took a dim view of the competitive market, its "disorderliness" and seeming wastefulness; they rarely saw the point of having two sellers (or buyers) where one might do. And they had a particularly low estimate of the merchant, who—as they saw it—grew fat buying cheap and selling dear, exploiting the ignorance and improvidence of the ordinary African. The educational and disciplinary aspects of market decisions were never appreciated. And that the market might in some measure contain corrective tendencies, or reflect underlying forces of supply and demand, these and similarly homespun notions of the economist, were badly received in Africa. When retail prices rose, the instinctive reaction was to damn the traders and look for conspiracy.

These are the habits of thought passed on to independent Africa by its colonial rulers: misunderstanding and mistrust of the market mechanism; an ingrained belief in the ability of government to manipulate economic variables, no matter how contrary the underlying market conditions; an inability to perceive the potential uses of the price system in allocating resources through decentralized decision-making. It is no surprise that so much African thinking on economic development policy runs in terms of state enterprise, direct state controls over production, marketing, and prices, suppression of middlemen, and state-directed activity in general. Aside from the impulses in this direction arising from ideology and from internal political considerations, it represents continuity with the past.

THE GUINEA EXPERIENCE

Consideration of socialist development policies in Africa invites a glance at the experience of the Republic of Guinea.[1] Alone of all the

---

[1] This account relies heavily on personal observations and unpublished mimeographed documents gathered in Guinea. For further discussion see: J. Charrière, "La Guinée: Une experience du Planification," in *Cahiers Internationaux*, 1960; "Ou en est

French territories in Africa, this small country of some three million proud and spirited people took its independence when offered it in 1958. Its dynamic political leadership was convinced of the efficacy of the socialist "model" as outlined above and was dedicated to economic transformation along socialist lines.

Its tasks were enormous. Despite their capture of political control, few Guineans had experience in dealing with economic problems, either on the level of the state or the firm; at independence, only a handful held high level technical or administrative posts in government, and almost none knew managerial responsibility in the small private sector. . . . Yet three months after independence almost all French civil servants were gone. Gone too was French economic aid, which had provided most of the development finance during the postwar period, and the protected market in France for coffee and bananas—which accounted for 80 percent of Guinea's export earnings in 1957.

The new government attacked its problems with vigor and confidence. One of its first acts, taken three months after independence, was to set up a state trading monopoly limited at first to trade in exports and key imports. This limited role of the state trading organization was soon found to be unsatisfactory: the domestic wholesale and retail trade remained in private hands, so the state had simply imposed itself on the existing "colonial" structure, adding, as it were, another layer of middlemen. The scope of state trading was thus extended; it was given a complete monopoly over foreign trade and domestic wholesaling.[2] The process was completed in 1960 by the extension of state shops to the retail level.

The state trading venture has proved to be an unmitigated disaster, afflicting the whole economy. An inexperienced Guinean management soon found itself in charge of what was in effect the largest trading firm in Africa. Despite some gallant efforts, the distribution system rapidly fell a victim to a massive administrative muddle. Goods were ordered for which there was no demand, or in quantities far beyond normal needs. Desired staples were frequently in short supply because of inadequate inventory policies and irregular deliveries. The old "colonial" evil of the "tied" or "conditional" sale become common enough in state shops to call for the public denunciation by President Touré. Poor inventory control in warehouses resulted in the rotting of perishable items.

It was not long before Guinean urban consumers came to know

la Guinée?" in *Problèmes d'Outre-Mer*, Vol. I (June, 1963), pp. 75–76; and J. Miandre, "L'experience guinéene," in *Esprit*, October, 1963, pp. 514–32.

[2] It was reasoned that the state could "nationalize" importers' profit margins, earn 15 percent on the sale of imports, and thereby raise 6 billion Guinean francs (about $24 million) in three years, or 60 percent of the domestic investment component in the Plan.

shortages, poor quality goods, long queues and black markets. Consumers of imports in the interior were even more badly served. And the export sector suffered from sparse and unreliable deliveries of pesticides, fertilizers and other imported inputs.

The absence of consumer imports, or their low quality, combined with low prices fixed for meat and fish, affected the production and marketed supply of local foodstuff and export crops. The flow of meat, fish and rice to urban centers shrank as producers either withheld their output from the market, or diverted their supplies to neighboring countries, mainly Sierra Leone and the Ivory Coast. Smuggling became the order of the day, absorbing not only the existing private traders who were hobbled and harrassed by official regulations, but new entrants besides. Coffee found its way to Liberia and the Ivory Coast; Guinea's 1962 export of coffee was half the level of previous years. Diamonds also left the country illegally. Some imports increased fantastically, for reasons that are not clear; imports of cotton prints, for example, rose from 158 million francs in 1959 to 2.3 billion in 1961 and 1.8 billion in 1962. Most of these textiles were almost surely smuggled out of the country to finance either smuggled imports from neighboring countries or capital flight. The propensity to smuggle was aggravated by the drastic depreciation of the Guinean franc in the (free and illegal) money markets on Guinea's borders.

Troubles were compounded by price policies decreed with cheerful disregard for market forces and in particular without recognition of Guinea's geographical situation. Shortly after independence, for example, President Touré decided, as a symbol of the intentions of the new regime, to sell rice (a gift from the Chinese) at a price well below that prevailing in neighboring countries. In a matter of weeks the rice disappeared from the country, sold across the border at the higher prices prevailing there. Similarly, the government decided that certain basic goods, such as cement, would be sold in the interior either at the same prices as in the port city of Conakry, or at a subsidized price. The aim was to favor consumers in the interior, on whom transport costs weighed heavily. But the subsidized items also found their way across the borders, since the delivered price in the Guinean interior was substantially lower than across the border.

These difficulties in state trading organization and policy are a major factor in the poor performance of the Guinea economy since 1958. The state farms, which were to be the cornerstone of agricultural development, never got off the ground, despite the import of hundreds of agricultural machines; most of these machines were soon abandoned for lack of maintenance and spare parts. Marketed agricultural output has probably fallen since 1958. Of the numerous industrial projects listed in the first Three Year Plan (1960–1963), only a few had been completed by

1967, and most of these were of dubious viability, because of scale, location, or input supply problems. The 1960–1963 plan and the (unpublished) seven year plan that followed it, had no apparent relationship to policy. By 1963, Guinea faced a severe balance of payments crisis, and was unable to meet its debt service payments on loans from the Soviet Union and Eastern European countries. Despite an inflow of foreign aid of perhaps $50 million a year, which made Guinea one of the world's most "aided" countries ($15 to $20 per capita per year), the economy has been prostrate since the early 1960's.

Part of this unhappy record was no doubt attributable to the precipitous withdrawal of the French. Part of it, too, is due to the methods and content of early Soviet economic aid. But the major responsibility rests with Guinean economic policy, particularly in the trading sphere.

Despite the obviously faltering performance of the economy, reform has been proved difficult. In March 1961, the system of internal distribution was on the verge of complete collapse. Imports were piling up in Conakry while the interior was without staples. The government was forced to comandeer all available trucks in Conakry to move goods to the interior. Shortly thereafter adaptations were made; the state trading organization was decentralized and a greater role for private traders was announced. But aside from some administrative reshuffling, little basic change occurred. Fundamental reappraisals were hindered by the need to maintain ideological purity, and unwillingness to look cooly at all alternatives. Official economic discussion in fact became increasingly divorced from reality. Despite persistent economic crises (in 1963 there were food riots in a number of urban centers), and the periodic announcement of basic reforms involving changes in price policies and return of more of the distribution sector to private hands, there has been little real change in policy.

TANZANIAN MARKETING POLICIES

With the decline of Guinea's economy and the end of the N'Krumah regime in Ghana in 1966, the mantle of socialist leadership in Tropical Africa has fallen to Tanzania.[3] It has more people (10 million), a larger monetized sector, and—because the transition to independence was smoother—a more orderly administration. The flavor of its socialism is also somewhat different—or at least it was until 1967. It has been a generally more open and democratic society, more flexible and experimental in its approaches both to politics and to economics.

In February 1967, Tanzania took a turn to the left in its domestic

---

[3] The United Republic of Tanzania consists of the mainland (Tanganyika) and Zanzibar. The discussion refers only to Tanganyika.

policy. In a declaration made at the town of Arusha, President Nyerere proclaimed that Tanzania had decided to launch herself more firmly on the socialist path to development.[4] The major means of production are to be put in the hands of the farmers and workers of Tanzania; there is to be a "total absence of any kind of exploitation"; "self-reliance" and austerity must guide the development effort. Accompanying the declaration of principle was the announcement that 24 companies were henceforth nationalized, including the banks, the main flour mills, and several trading companies.

Even with the changes of early 1967, Tanzanian policy toward the distribution sector has been much more cautious than Guinea's. The general goal has been the same—to reduce and eventually eliminate private control over distribution. But action toward this goal has not been hasty, and the means used have been different than in Guinea.

Four main instruments of policy have been emphasized. First, agricultural cooperatives have been organized to serve as primary marketing units in rural areas. Cooperatives in Tanzania date from well before independence; between 1952 and 1961 their number grew from 172 to 857, most of them among coffee, cotton and tobacco growers.[5] Upon independence in 1961, "It was decided that the cooperative form was well-suited to the African setting and to the achievement of independence in the economic sense: control of the economy by the indigenous people rather than by expatriates and others non-African in origin."[6] A crash program of expansion therefore was initiated.

Secondly, the marketing boards existing before independence have been increased in number; there were 12 boards in 1966. Their functions vary. Only two of them maintain price stabilization funds. One (cotton) controls all the aspects of handling the crop, including transportation and ginning. At the other extreme is the Seed Board, which only serves as a licensing agency.

In the area of wholesale trade and the handling of imports and exports, the imposition of direct public sector control has proceeded particularly slowly. In 1962 the Cooperative Supply Association of Tanganyika (COSATA) was organized, to serve as wholesale supplier to the cooperative movement. In 1963 Government bought a major interest in a European importing and exporting firm International Trading and Credit Co. of Tanganyika, Ltd. (INTRATA). INTRATA has been given exclu-

---

[4] A useful summary of the Arusha Declaration and the events following it is M. Lowenkopf, "The Meaning of Arusha," in *Africa Report* (Washington, D.C.) March, 1967, pp. 8–13, also pp. 22–23.

[5] The United Republic of Tanzania, *Report of the Presidential Special Committee of Enquiry into Cooperative Movement and Marketing Boards* ('Dar-es-Salaam, 1966), p. 5.

[6] *Ibid.*

sive importing rights for certain goods, markets some exports and is exclusive marketing agent for several staples (sugar and cassava). In February 1967 INTRATA and COSATA were merged, along with the several newly nationalized large trading companies, to form the State Trading Corporation. The wholesale trade remains nonetheless predominantly private; the State Trading Corporation handles only 20% of Tanzania's imports, though about half of the imports of non-technical consumer goods is now in its hands. Private importers and wholesalers retain control over technical goods—transport and medical equipment and supplies and household appliances.[7]

In retail trade, finally, a policy decision was made in 1963 to install a large number of consumer cooperative shops around the country. The decision was explicitly based on the need to Africanize trade.[8] While numerous shops were established, retail trade still remains very largely dominated by small private traders, mainly Asian.

From these policies in the trading sector there have resulted no catastrophic consequences on the Guinea scale. But there have been problems sufficiently serious and disillusioning to call for an extensive study in 1966 by a Special Presidential Committee of Enquiry. The Committee report provides numerous insights into the problems of state control over marketing in an African setting.

The agricultural cooperatives, first of all, have performed very poorly. The Committee found widespread dissatisfaction among farmers. Many of them complained that the cooperative societies, which were to protect them from middlemen exploitation, ". . . instead place us under another worse type of middleman under the cloak of cooperative societies and marketing boards."[9] They complained "of the continuous economic plunder which we endure from the corrupted employees and committeemen of the cooperative societies and unions"; of inefficiency and the existence of too many marketing boards; of "unnecessary delays (which) run for

---

[7] United Republic of Tanzania, *Background to the Budget; and Economic Survey, 1967–68* (Dar-es-Salaam, 1967), p. 37–38.

[8] ". . . with the formation of COSATA in 1963 the political decision was made to establish many consumer shops. It must be emphasized that the motivation for this decision was not that the profit margins were excessive: on the contrary the available evidence is that competition had kept them very low indeed. The political decision was a consequence of the fact that the bulk of the retail trade in Tanganyika was in the hands of Asian merchants who had not identified themselves with the aspirations of Tanganyika nationalism and whose commercial dominance appeared to be an obstacle to the full development of the Africans, who made up some 98% of the population. The hostility was compounded by the fact that many of the Asian commercial enterprises were linked by family and caste ties and by the failure of most Asian merchants to bring Africans into their firms in any meaningful way." (*Report of the Presidential Special Committee of Enquiry into Cooperative Movement and Marketing Boards*, 1966, pp. 46–47.)

[9] *Report of the Presidential Special Committee of Enquiry into Cooperative Movement and Marketing Boards*, 1966, pp. 3–4.

days and cause us to incur unnecessary expenses for food and sometimes storage charges." The farmers further complained of "improper and unfair grading of produce," of the methods used to fix prices, and of "continual political threats which are imposed on us when we want to air our views."[10]

In its analysis of the problem, the Committee of Enquiry listed the following difficulties: (1) Since the co-ops were imposed from above, members usually don't know what they are for, don't regard them as belonging to farmers, and don't really exercise democratic control over them. (2) Appropriate manpower is scarce, in two senses: There aren't enough trained employees available, nor enough honest ones. (3) Skilled staff and advisory services are lacking. (4) The co-op movement is too susceptible to political interference, manifested by "exaggerated demands for the premature registration of societies . . . deployment by commissioners of the scarce personnel and scarcer vehicles of the Cooperative Development Division. . . . (and) the frequent political pressure to open consumer cooperatives without adequate public demand or appreciation. . . ."[11] (5) Private traders, in collaboration with some officials who have allowed themselves to be used, have been hostile to the co-ops.

The venture into wholesaling has been, if anything, less successful than the policy on cooperatives. The Committee of Enquiry puts it politely when it notes that COSATA "failed to prosper"; the reasons were "undercapitalization, poor management, overly-rapid establishment of retail branches, and insufficiency of trained personnel."[12] Government efforts "to rescue COSATA by giving it exclusive rights to import and deal in certain goods only resulted in raising the prices for those articles and in cushioning COSATA against the consequences of its inefficiency by concealing the extent of it, and thus postponing the day when the realities of COSATA's situation had to be faced. That day arrived in early 1966, when the decision was taken to withdraw some of COSATA's operations and to turn its management over to INTRATA."[13]

The Government's policy on control of retail trade through consumer cooperatives has been an even more decisive failure. The Committee commented as follows:[14]

Without exception, all of these shops were run at a loss. . . . Under capitalized and without genuine strong demand on the part of the prospective customers,

---

[10] *Ibid.*

[11] *Report of the Presidential Committee of Enquiry into Cooperative Movement and Marketing Boards,* 1966, p. 11.

[12] *Ibid.,* p. 45.

[13] *Loc. cit.*

[14] *Report of the Presidential Special Committee of Enquiry into Cooperative . . . ,* 1966, p. 47.

the COSATA shops had the added burden that the COSATA management (including its expatriate advisors) were oriented mostly towards overseas wholesale trade, that there was no reservoir of Africans experienced in retail trade except as individual vendors, that there was no programme for training, and that managerial attention was constantly diverted from making the existing shops profitable to the need for opening up new shops as a result of the overwhelming political pressures. As a result of these losses, which contributed to COSATA's own financial problems, COSATA credit and financing have been withdrawn from the consumer shops.

Aside from trained manpower scarcity and diversion of managerial energy, the retail stores were crippled by the application of romantic notions of management; they were run by committees, not by managers. Many basic decisions, moreover, were taken on political grounds.[15]

One of the major difficulties of the retail cooperatives is that they are not operated by managers, much less by well-trained managers. They are operated by committees which employ the staff and fix their terms of service, buy the commodities, fix the resale price and perform all the other functions which a manager should perform. It would be bad enough if the committees consisted in people who had experience in the running of stores, but they have had none. This difficulty is compounded by the fact that when the committes are in dispute with outside expert advisors they may receive political support over the ineffective objection of the Cooperative Development Division; such a political decision is the course of least resistance today, but it results in financial losses which must be borne by the public.

Not enough information is available to estimate the cost burden imposed on the Tanzanian economy by its post-independence marketing policies. That there have been substantial economic costs is beyond question. By official admission reductions in farmer incomes in several areas amounted to approximately 2% of total farmer proceeds, from cooperative society stock and cash losses alone. Up to now the extent of damage has not been comparable to that which occurred in Guinea—in part at least because the network of private trade in Tanzania remains more or less in place. However, the coexistence of public and private marketing sectors in Tanzanian conditions, cannot be regarded as stable. The layers of middlemen, for example, are more numerous than before, since the State Trading Company has a monopoly over the import and wholesaling of basic consumer goods, but must rely on the Asian traders for most retailing. Similarly, the exclusion of private traders from dealing in basic commodities in the rural areas will probably mean their gradual elimination from the rural trade. Nor are the political goals of greater African control really assured under the present system.

[15] *Ibid.*, p. 47–48.

These facts, combined with the intensification of socialist ideology since the Arusha Declaration, suggest that the state sector will take an increasing share of the marketing function. In this respect it is revealing that even before the Arusha Declaration, the Government felt compelled to reject some of the more hard-headed recommendations of the 1966 Committee of Enquiry—for example, its recommendation to pull back on cooperative activity at the retail level.[16] Developments in 1967 give further reason to expect a waning private sector role in marketing. The "anti-exploitation" aspect of the Arusha Declaration has been taken up with zeal and has given rise to numerous excesses; African traders in vegetables, who buy from farmers in areas around Dar-es-Salaam, for example, have been called "exploiters," and water sellers in the capital fell under similar approbrium and were due to be deported to rural areas until a noisy outcry from civil servants forced reconsideration of the order. The point is that it is becoming increasingly unacceptable ideologically for an African to engage in trade on any scale. Since it is not acceptable either that Asian domination of trade persist, the only way open is future expansion of the state (directly, or through centrally-organized cooperatives) into the whole field of marketing.

THE UNSUITABILITY OF THE SOCIALIST MODEL

It is not the business of outsiders—at least outsider economists—to quarrel about the suitability of the goals set out by socialists in Africa. It is legitimate, however, to consider the probable effectiveness of socialist policies in advancing the goals of economic growth and change which socialists want. For a number of reasons, suggested in the Guinea and Tanzania narratives, the socialist path to development, and particularly socialist policy in the distribution field, is ill-suited to present African circumstances.

Organizational weaknesses

The first and most obvious reason is Africa's scarcity of people equipped by training, experience or education to manage the economy. To an extent unmatched in most of the underdeveloped world, positions of skill and responsibility were until recently in the hands of non-Africans. This was true almost everywhere in the public sector until a decade ago, and remains true throughout the private non-agricultural sector,

---

[16] *Report of the Presidential Special Committee of Enquiry* . . . , 1966, p. 48 and *Proposals of the Tanzania Government on the Recommendations of the Special Presidential Committee of Enquiry into Cooperative Movement and Marketing Boards, Government Paper #3, 1966*, p. 12.

with the possible exceptions of Ghana and Nigeria. One main reason for this was the limited availability, until recent years, of upper level education; as late as 1958 there were only about 8,000 Africans graduated from all the academic secondary schools below the Sahara, and about 10,000 others were studying in universities—more than half of these in Ghana and Nigeria.

In these figures lie the most severe indictment of colonial rule. African governments are trying to make up for it with an enormous educational effort. But trained people necessary to man the bureaucracies of the new states will not be available for at least a decade in most of the continent. The vital middle levels, now exceedingly shallow, are likely to remain so for even longer, as universities continue to absorb most secondary school graduates. Under these circumstances, to put heavy and exacting new burdens on the state is to invite trouble—waste and inefficiency at the least, economic dislocation on the Guinean scale at the worst.

A state trading system inevitably involves greater centralization of decision making and larger-scale, more complex organization. It therefore demands more technical and managerial skills—at least of the kind requiring formal training. This is seen most clearly on the retail level, where decisions on what to buy, where to locate shops or stalls, selling prices, whether to give credit, etc., can be made, and usually are made, by hundreds or thousands of traders, most of them without formal training or education. And most of this is done without a single accountant or high level administrator.

Introduction of a state trading system therefore involves serious misallocation of human resources. It requires more human skill per unit of sales. It involves waste of the considerable skill, experience, talent and human energy found in the existing community of private traders; it substitutes acquired skill, in this sense, for the raw capacity and energy mobilized by the search for profit. It deprives other public sector activities of needed trained manpower. While trained teachers are wanting, and general administration is shoddy, it is dubious wisdom to have trained and able people fixing and enforcing prices, authorizing import licenses, running cooperatives or retail stores.

Transfer of trading functions to the public sector also involves an inefficient or wasteful use of capital resources. The factor mix in trade tends to become more capital-intensive under state trading arrangements, especially on the retail level and in rural trade. To the extent that entry into petty trade is restricted, and attempts are made to "rationalize" the trading structure, bigger inventories, more and better warehousing facilities and more elaborate accounting procedures are required. More capital will thus be required in the distribution sector. Moreover, a greater proportion of the available capital will be absorbed in this sector, as investment capital provided by private traders (foreign and indigenous) is withdrawn from domestic use. Public sector resources available for other purposes are reduced.[17]

The extension of direct state control over trade thus involves a misallocation of human and capital resources, and so would be questionable from an economic point of view even if state trading were as efficient and effective as private trading. This however is a most unlikely possibility.

All enterprises in Africa, as in most less developed areas, operate under extremely difficult conditions. The climate is hard. Distances are great. Communications are uncertain. Skilled workers, supervisors and managerial abilities are hard to find. Suppliers of machinery, spare parts, raw materials and other imports are far away. Ancillary services are few. All of this makes the successful operation of even the simplest enterprises a demanding task.

The distribution sector shares these problems. It also has to meet special demands. In addition to the usual functions of internal trade— getting goods of the right kind, quality and quantity, at the right place and time—it involves credit, transport and other decisions: decisions on which crops to purchase, to whom credit should be granted, transport charges to be made. It demands especially critical activity in the areas of inventory controls and protection against theft and deterioration. The export-orientation of African economies (between 24 and 60% of marketed output in African countries is exported) creates further demands: trading in export markets is highly specialized and delicate, demanding quick decisions, high standards of quality control, close attention to timing of deliveries. It does not lend itself well to the rougher arrangements possible if production is only for enclosed local markets.

All of these functions can be performed by state trading organizations, some more easily than others. Marketing boards and bureaus have taken over part of the export trade in most of the continent without excessive difficulty. They have, however, often retained private traders as primary buying agents. Also, there are many commodities which do not lend themselves easily to state trading. The Ghana Timber Marketing Board, for example, has had periodic difficulties with the consistency of quality grading.[18] And in Tanzania the agricultural cooperatives have run into trouble with pyrethrum, which deteriorates rapidly if not processed at the right time.

At the same time that the economic environment makes the difficulties of successful operation of trading and other enterprises unusually de-

---

[17] In most African countries a major constraint on foreign aid is the lack of local cost financing. Assuming the existence of reasonably well-designed projects, every dollar of local capital made available can bring in four or five dollars of foreign aid. The cost of state trading ventures, then, in terms of sacrificed capital investment, may be much larger than the original public investment involved.

[18] See *West Africa*, March 17, 1962, p. 296.

manding, these difficulties limit the span of managerial control. Lack of middle level personnel, of accounting infrastructure, of ancillary services to perform specialized functions, of good communications—all of these not only mean more uncertain decision making, but much greater problems of managerial control. In these conditions decentralized decisions are bound to be more efficient, and control over operations more effective, than centralized decisions and controls.

Political influences

The influence of politics on economic decision making is another factor important in weighing the prospects of successful development along socialist lines. Public enterprises (including cooperatives imposed from above) are subject to intense political pressures of various sorts, all of which reduce their efficiency. Political interference is inevitable in the most basic decisions—on personnel, price and location policies for example. It is of course true that political considerations are never absent from important economic decisions in any society. But in African conditions these are likely to assume overwhelming dominance, even on relatively insignificant matters. One reason is that African societies are all highly "politicized"; the primacy of politics was a fact during the struggle for independence, and remains an important element in the thought and actions of most African leaders today. The notion that economic and political decisions *should be* separated does not find easy acceptance.

Even more relevant is the fact that the kinds of decisions a state enterprise must make—in marketing or other sectors—touch so many economic nerves with so much weight, they are bound to push economic efficiency considerations into the background. Where there is much unemployment, for example, the issue of who gets a job is no small matter; the difference between having a job and not having one is often the difference between success and failure, between returning to the village and staying in town, between relative comfort and despair. At the same time, family loyalties are powerful, and anyone responsible for hiring who does not favor family members (largely defined) finds himself subject to enormous pressures to do so and possible family rejection if he does not. Under these circumstances hiring and firing decisions cannot possibly be made on relatively objective efficiency or suitability criteria.

It is the same with other basic economic decisions—whether an agricultural co-op (or state trading unit) should open a buying post in a given rural area, for example, or whether it should deal in a particular minor crop. The marginal cost of either opening new buying posts or buying minor crops are usually greater than the marginal returns. But the potential gains to the farmers immediately affected are substantial; it may mean the difference between having to carry crops ten miles to market or not having to carry them at all, or perhaps the difference between some money income and none. Whether more or less buying posts are established, and what crops are bought, are therefore likely to be politically determined. And the relative political pressures in presence are not such as to lead to economically rational decisions. Those who stand to benefit from a particular decision are affected heavily, while the general interest is thinly spread. Moreover, the instruments of central administrative control and screening tend to be poorly developed, and it is in any event difficult for central screening bodies, responsible for national economic policies, to continually resist strong political pressures generated from below. Bad decisions—that is, economically inefficient decisions—are therefore highly probable.

Internal corruption

There is a final factor, at once so banal and so basic that it is hard to know just how much to make of it. This is the matter of controlling misappropriation of funds—corruption as that term is generally used, and pilferage both by employees and others. On the face of it, it is hard to see how state marketing systems, especially on the retail level, can keep losses from theft to manageable proportions. The problem does not arise from defects of character. It exists in advanced industrial countries, and is indeed a major problem for retail establishments everywhere. But it is a problem that is particularly troublesome in Africa, as in all countries in earlier stages of development.

One reason is that the relationship between income earned "legitimately" (i.e., through salaries) and income that can be earned through petty thievery is such as to stimulate thievery. In an industrial country a sales clerk in a small retail shop cannot raise his income very appreciably by fraud without undertaking a fairly complex exercise in larceny. But in an African country relatively big increases in income are easier since salaries are so low relative to cash flow. The instruments of internal control, moreover, which have been in part developed to restrain the baser propensities of employees in advanced countries, do not exist in poor countries. The whole array of bookkeeping and accounting tools, as well as the various devices designed to reduce risks of losses through theft (machine registered receipts, separation of sales and cashiering functions, bonding, private police, etc.) are either not feasible or too expensive for most enterprises in less developed countries. Police agencies, thirdly, are limited in extent and effectiveness; combined with the rudimentary state of accounting and inventory control procedures, this makes detection unlikely. Finally there is the underlying fact, that in Africa, as in all areas in early stages of development, distinctions between the organizational and the private purse are hazily drawn. The

habit of handling other people's money, and appreciation of the restraints it imposes, are not deeply embedded in these societies.

Innovative character of private trade

All of the above are reasons for believing that state trading organizations will perform the normal trading functions with much less efficiency
and at a much higher cost than private traders. There is another consideration, of a slightly different character. This has to do with the creative
role of trade, the development of new markets and new production in the
agricultural sector. This relationship of a dynamic distribution sector to
agricultural development deserves special attention.

More than any other region, Africa is a continent of subsistence farmers. The majority of Africans are only slightly committed to the money
economy; they spend most of their lives in the village, where their main
productive activity is the growing of food for their own consumption.
Under these circumstances the key to agricultural modernization and
growth is fuller peasant commitment to the money economy. Villagers
must be induced to use their land, their energies and their time differently from in the past by growing more for the market. This transfer of
resources within the village from subsistence production and traditional
activities and cash crop production is in Africa's present stage, the
essence of development. It does not by itself guarantee self-sustaining
growth, but it is a revolutionary step in the growth process.

There are plenty of examples of how an aroused peasantry shifting its
energies to cash crops can work great economic transformations. In the
space of two decades after the turn of the century, in a country almost
without infrastructure and with very little assistance from government,
Ghana's peasants made their country the world's greatest cocoa producer. In the Ivory Coast the creation of a road network, a period of
good prices and an active distribution sector led African farmers to a
five-fold expansion of coffee production and doubling of cocoa output in
the 15 years after World War II. The more recent surge in African export
crop production in Kenya offers another example.

If we ask why more such transformations have not occurred, or why
some seem to be arrested, half-finished, a number of obstacles become
apparent: unsuitable soil, climate, including rainfalls; expensive or inadequate transport facilities: lack of knowledge; absence of tools required
for small technological changes (plows, for example); problems of devising suitable credit arrangements under systems of "communal" land
tenure; and others. Two factors, however, seem of particular significance
and generality. The first is neglect of the peasant, the fact that in only a
few countries have African villagers in the past received extension services, roads, marketing facilities, good prices and other assistance which

government might give them. Secondly, rural Africans in most of the continent still have relatively few demands for new goods, and the money income needed to buy them. Want levels remain low. It is not, of course, that they would not like more money income; it is that they are not willing to make the changes in ways of life that are required to get more income.

This last point deserves special emphasis, for not only is it open to misinterpretation, but it is uncongenial to much thinking on development, among socialists as well as others. In order for marketed output to claim a larger share of village resources the peasant must be induced to switch from tried and proven activities to new and unknown ones. The peasant and his family must work harder and give up "leisure" or customary pleasures or activity in the village. In addition to new outlays of effort, all of this involves uncomfortable departures from customs and may involve new risks, a greater dependence on the market, and even outlays of money. It is hard to see why he should make these changes unless he is first convinced that new goods and services are in fact important elements of a better life. His preference for more income as against his present way of life must be increased.

In these conditions, socialist attitudes and approaches lose most of their relevance. The socialist appeal for land distribution, common in other parts of the underdeveloped world as a means of mobilizing the peasantry, are devoid of meaning in sub-Sahara Africa where land is still relatively abundant, and landlordism a rare problem. Approaches designed to squeeze the peasant into greater production for the market are unpromising. State levies on the agricultural sector whether by price policies or direct deliveries, can be effective only where agriculture has become monetized and specialized. Peasants still mainly or largely in the subsistence sector cannot be bullied into the market; full retreat back to subsistence is too easy. . . . Since life in most African villages is not so oppressive as it is in many other parts of the underdeveloped world, and since many African villagers would find it possible to reduce their demands for goods from outside the village, the result of attempts to squeeze the peasant sector, and subsequent peasant dissatisfaction, can easily be "sabotage" in the Veblenian sense—"a conscious withdrawal of efficiency."

The African peasant, then, cannot easily be pushed into the market. He must be pulled into it, encouraged, and enticed by positive inducements, among which the most effective is no doubt that most banal of incentives, the possibility of higher real income. Large-scale transformation of the subsistence sector is unlikely to be achieved unless villagers see some close relation between their greater effort and a better life, and unless they come to believe that consumption of more goods is essential to this better life.

To the extent that this is true, it not only raises serious doubts about the meaningfulness of most socialist prescriptions for agricultural development, but also means that socialists in Africa must face certain unpalatable contradictions between their policy ideas and the exigencies of rapid growth—for example, that rapid growth demands some individualization of land tenure, the emergence of a rural bourgeoisie composed of the more energetic or more fortunate peasants, and the accentuation of rural income inequalities. And with respect to marketing policy, it implies that abolition of private trading can only be obtained at the price of slower economic growth. For aside from their lower efficiency, state trading companies are poorly designed to engage in the kind of want-creating activity that private merchants in Africa, indigenous and expatriate, have always undertaken. The agent of the state trading firm is unlikely to roam remote villages with goods of tempting quality and style and, if necessary with credit as well, in order to whet peasant appetites for money income and cajole them into new lines of production. He is not, in short, likely to be a creator of markets. In the area where the distribution system has its most vital role to play—maintenance and expansion of the flow of marketed output from the villages by stimulating the demand for consumer goods—a nationalized trading system is most deficient.

Geographical problems

Another major pitfall for socialist solutions in Africa has its basis in geography. Africa has the highest ratio of frontiers to total areas of any continent. Goods and people have always flowed over these frontiers in the past, usually with few restrictions. Effective controls were scarcely possible, traders roamed at will between countries, and when prices in one country moved out of line with those in neighboring countries, smuggling on a large scale tended to develop.

The most striking examples are to be found in postwar West Africa, where bits and chunks of British colonies, with few import restrictions and relatively low price levels, jutted into the protected, high-price French African land mass. Trade between areas under British and French control existed before the colonial frontiers were established, and resourceful groups of African traders served these areas without regard to frontiers.

The mechanism and extent of smuggling is known only in broad outline, but there is enough evidence to indicate that it is a large-scale phenomenon, involving thousands of people, millions of dollars, and an institutional framework that includes specialized transport, established marketing channels, and free (illegal) foreign exchange markets in border towns and cities, almost all in African hands. Export commodities (cattle, smoked fish, cocoa, coffee, peanuts, diamonds, etc.) are involved, and consumer goods.

In West Africa, until the late 1950's at least, the foundation of the contraband trade was export of cattle and smoked fish from savannah regions in French West Africa (Niger, Mali, Upper Volta, northern Togo and Dahomey) to the British territories. These exports generated sterling, which was used to finance illegal import into the franc areas of textiles, bicycles, spirits, lamps, costume jewelry, cola nuts, matches and a wide range of other goods. A Franc-Sterling Study Mission estimated that total exports from British to French West Africa amounted to 12.2 billion metropolitan francs in 1956, of which 8.5 billion was contraband; British West African imports from French West Africa were estimated at 7.5 billion metropolitan francs, of which 4.5 billion was contraband.[19]

Not only consumer goods but export crops too passed over borders, whenever differentials in the prices offered to growers in the French and British areas made it profitable. Thus in some years in the 1950's as much as 60,000 tons of peanuts crossed from Nigeria to French Niger to take account of the subsidized produced prices prevailing in Niger. In 1954–55, it was estimated that 8,000 tons of Ivory Coast cocoa fled to Ghana, where the Ghana Marketing Board maintained its producer price at a high level compared with world (and Ivory Coast) prices. In 1960 the flow of cocoa from Ghana to the Ivory Coast may have been as high as 25,000 tons. And in 1962 an estimated 8,000 tons of export commodities were smuggled from Eastern Nigeria to benefit from higher prices in the Cameroons.[20]

Smuggling has up to now been less prevalent in other parts of the continent, mainly because price structures in Southern and Central Africa were less dissimilar, and exchange controls less widespread, and trade in East Africa has been relatively free. But recent Congo experience shows how quickly new channels of trade across neighboring frontiers can develop; with domestic inflation, an unrealistic rate of exchange and exchange controls (as well as new and chaotic political arrangements), a significant amount of Congolese production, both of manufactures and raw materials, leaves the country illegally. Its proceeds finance purchases of needed imports and hard currency balances abroad.

Suppression of smuggling is exceedingly difficult when conditions for its flowering are present. Frontiers are long. Often the ethnic groups are the same on both sides, which makes general restriction of movement of people hard to enforce. The smugglers are at least as inventive as the government officials trying to control them, and it is usually possible for

---

[19] Chambre de Commerce de la Côte d'Ivoire, "La Contrabande par Terre en Afrique Occidentale Francaise," (mimeo, n.d.).

[20] *West Africa*, June 29, 1963, p. 733.

the smuggler to find some customs officials who are willing to look the other way for a slight consideration. A government determined to crack down on smuggling can, of course, slow the contraband trade. But the expense and trouble of effective control is very considerable.

A control that was effective, moreover, might have serious political consequences. Almost everybody seems to benefit from smuggling. Producers of smuggled beef, fish and export crops get higher prices for their products. Consumers get cheaper, better, more varied goods. The level of employment and the wage bill is probably increased, since the ratio of workers and wage payments to sales volume is no doubt greater in the labor-intensive contraband trade than in legal commerce. Where African traders are the main agents of the contraband trade there is also a redistribution of profit income from established (mainly expatriate) trading firms to African traders.

It is, of course, the government that is hurt: its customs revenues decline, its price policies are undermined, income is redistributed from public to private sectors, and respect for the law is diminished. But any government that successfully supressed smuggling might find itself reaping a political whirlwind, for the list of injured private interests would be imposing.

The smuggler casts a long shadow in Africa. He imposes restraints, actual or potential, on independent economic policies. All of the instruments of direct economic control, as well as price policies generally, will —unless they are in harmony with those prevailing in surrounding countries—threaten to activate or enlarge the current of contraband trade. This will occur, for example, if relatively low prices are paid for locally marketed export crops; or if austerity policies are introduced, restricting the import of luxury goods and raising their price; or if rate policies on railroads result in internal price distortions; or if exchange controls and restrictions on capital outflows become burdensome. The smuggler also threatens protected local industry with illicit competition.[21]

The difficulty of framing independent economic policies under these circumstances is obvious. This is, of course, true not only for socialist policies, but for all public policies. As conceived in Africa, however, socialist policies involve a greater degree of direct economic control and manipulation of market variables, so the potential restraints implicit in the smuggling phenomenon have more bearing on them. Unless common policies are laid down by geographically-related groups in African states,

---

[21] In the early 1960's, for example, Gambian imports of matches amounted to 55 boxes per year per capita; most of it was smuggled to Senegal, where the local product was higher priced and of poorer quality. The Federal Minister of Finance of Nigeria publicly estimated at 15% of the proportion of Nigerian cigarette consumption produced by smugglers in 1961, and emphasized the threat to the Nigerian tobacco industry.

each of them is at the mercy of policies followed by their neighbors. In this sense, African states have a more limited command over their economies than is probably the case anywhere in the world. Socialism in one country is not possible in Africa.

CONCLUSION

Ideology—ideas about how the world works—is important in understanding economic policy. One set of ideas has been considered in this paper—those generally described as "socialist"—and their suitability for Africa has been appraised. Much of the analysis undoubtedly is applicable to underdeveloped areas elsewhere. A large body of mankind in particular shares the African socialist view that the trader or merchant is a bad guy, trade the next thing to daylight robbery, and state control in trading a necessary and desirable element in any progressive economic policy aimed at growth.

This is not a new or unique viewpoint. It seems to be the case in fact that almost nobody anywhere has ever had much good to say about merchants. Literature is graced with few merchant heroes; medieval merchants were all right, even glamorous, when they engaged in long distance, foreign trade and provided they became merchant princes, bought land, and got themselves and their children into something more respectable. But *internal* trade has always been at least faintly disreputable, and petty trade usually odious. Not even in the writings of the economists is there much appreciation of the merchants' positive role. None perhaps are so harsh as Marx, but the trader moves through the history of economic thought as a shadowy and suspicious character.

These attitudes and ideas have had little discernible effect on public policies in Western countries. In Africa and other less developed areas, however, they have had immediate impact. With its emphasis on the exploitative nature of trade, the intellectual and ideological heritage has encouraged state takeover of the distribution sector. Other factors work in the same direction—notably the colonial heritage, the predominance of foreigners in the community of traders, and the fact that so few of the elites in the new states have themselves had any experience as traders.

It is one of the unfortunate facts of history that the underdeveloped countries have come on the world scene at a time when prevailing ideas on economic policy are peculiarly unsuitable to their real needs and possibilities. This is particularly dramatic in the case of "socialist" ideas in Africa. It has been argued in this paper that the African state cannot and should not bear the burdens that African Socialists would put upon it. Lack of trained people, limited capacity to control the economy, the special character of agriculture, the unusually demanding conditions of the economic environment which make centralized decision-making difficult, the political and cultural factors which hinder economically rational public sector decision-making and management—all of these considerations make successful state-directed development efforts improbable. In the distribution sector the socialist preconceptions are particularly inapplicable. The extension of state trading involves a misallocation of human and capital resources. State trading organizations lack the initiative, flexibility and dynamism necessary to fulfill the market-creating role essential for agricultural transformation. State trading is almost certain to be inefficient: the difficulties of the African environment makes centralized decision-making especially hazardous, and allows a much smaller span of managerial control; it is extremely difficult to resist political pressures on decision-making; control over mishandling of funds presents special problems. With these kinds of obstacles, state trading ventures are destined to be expensive burdens at best, economic catastrophes at worst.

The most interesting and important question may be not whether state trading is doomed to inefficiency but whether there are any feasible alternatives. Where there is a class of African traders ready and willing to perform marketing functions, one obvious alternative exists: to transfer as many trading activities as possible to these individuals. In this case, ideology is the major obstacle, for it is only the fear of creating a rich class of merchant-exploiters which prevents the transfer of trading functions to the private sector.

Where there are no indigenous traders to speak of, as in the case of Tanzania and a number of other countries in Africa (and elsewhere), the problem is a good deal more difficult. Here it is Utopian to believe that economic analysis can—or indeed should—prevail over national sentiment. It is simply asking too much of any society that it accept a situation whereby non-indigenous, racially different people maintain an overwhelmingly predominant position in a vital economic sector. This means that strenuous efforts have to be made to create or nurture an African trading class—through credit policies, government purchasing policies, advisory services, and the like.

The costs and risks of such policies are substantial. They reduce the average income of ordinary Africans and create windfall gains for a chosen few. It is not to be expected that implementation of such policies would be administratively sanitized, with the state dispensing favors in neutral fashion, encouraging those who have demonstrated ability and competence in the struggle of the market place. In fact, who gets what contracts and other advantages will depend on personalities, on political and ethnic considerations. But similar problems exist in even greater dimensions in state trading systems, and because entry into small-scale trade is easy, market restraints over abuses are at least conceivable.

This may not be a satisfactory solution to the economic purist on the outside, nor would indigenous socialists find it attractive, since it involves the deliberate buildup of a local bourgeoisie. But in such matters, where powerful ideological currents of socialism and nationalism come together, it is hard to find more feasible alternatives.

The need to husband scarce capital in developing countries makes the apparently excessive use of labor in the trade sector more rational economic behavior than appears at first glance. Steps should be taken therefore to reduce entry barriers to trade in order to expand trade volume and prevent monopoly profits. If governments desire to increase the participation of Africans in trade at the expense of expatriates, Professor Bauer suggests the use of outsiders rather than the restriction of entry. Tracing the detrimental economic impact of restrictionism, Bauer makes a compelling case for freedom from government interference in the distributive sector.

P. T. BAUER*

Some aspects and problems of trade in Africa†

INTRODUCTION

This paper examines, from the African standpoint, the principal aspects of trade in Africa, and suggests improvements to enable it to serve better the African interest. In particular it considers the defects of commerce in Africa, the possibilities of efficient modernization, and the merits of encouraging labor-intensive service industries.

Highly selective treatment is inevitable in the examination of these topics.[1] I shall review some aspects and implications of trade which I hope are of some general interest, which are prominent in public discussion and which have given rise to government action. I shall proceed largely, but not only, by setting out issues rather than by suggesting policies. The distinction between description and analysis on one hand, and suggestions for policy on the other, will be made clearly throughout.

* London School of Economics and Political Science.

† This article originally appeared in substantially the same form as presented here in *Economic Development in Africa* (Oxford: Basil Blackwell, 1965). Permission of the publisher to use the article is gratefully acknowledged.

[1] I may mention here one general limitation. I shall deal only with trade outside the so-called subsistence sector. There is exchange and trade in locally produced goods and services within the subsistence economy, usually confined to the village, tribe and some other narrowly restricted community.

I begin with two points which are partly introductory but which also bear on the substantive discussion.

First, I shall deal with specific issues which bear on trade as an instrument for an effective deployment of resources and for the promotion of their growth. A discussion in terms of specific topics may understate the wide and pervasive influence and potentialities of trade in the underdeveloped world. Trade contributes to material progress in various ways, including among others by the husbanding of scarce resources, notably capital; by the extension of markets, with the resulting promotion of specialization and of production for sale, and thus the creation of an agricultural surplus (chiefly by providing a market for agricultural produce and at the same time bringing new crops, methods and inducement goods to the notice of farmers and within their reach); by stimulating the accumulation of capital; by bringing to prominence and influence trader-entrepreneurs accustomed to an exchange economy; and by acquainting people with the processes of the exchange economy and promoting the habits and attitudes appropriate to it. Moreover, by linking local communities to the outside world and acquainting people with the habits of a money economy, trade promotes (for good or evil) the disintegration of the traditional local attitudes, customs and institutions.

These considerations are particularly relevant to the situation in Africa where subsistence production is still so extensive. Production for wider exchange and sales is indispensable for the achievement of even a reasonable standard of living. The inducement and even the possibility of production for wider markets depend greatly on the terms on which producers can buy or sell, which in turn are much affected by the effectiveness of the trading system which is therefore of great significance for the progress of the peoples of Africa, as of most underdeveloped countries.

My second point concerns the ambiguity and complexity of the concept of the African interest. The concept of a group interest is rarely simple. Even disregarding the important and complex philosophical problems of the interest of a community, and of the time-horizon envisaged (involving the interests of different generations), there still remains the highly relevant problem of the discrepancy between the interests of different groups or sections of the population. Whenever economic specialization has made some progress, members of each specialized group can improve their relative position (and up to a point also their real income) by restricting their numbers, and thus increasing the scarcity value of their services. Any benefits gained are at the expense of the rest of the community; and the economic cost of such measures from a less effective allocation of resources usually appreciably exceeds the benefits to the sectional interests.

AFRICANIZATION AND RESTRICTIONS ON FOREIGN TRADERS

In almost every African country foreigners are prominent or even predominant in trade outside the subsistence sector.[2] In all major countries the import and export trade is largely handled by foreigners, who often also play a large role in subsequent stages of the distribution of imports and in the earlier stages of the assembly of exports. This situation is often regarded as anomalous; and the predominance of foreigners in external trade is often termed as a monopoly situation.

The use of the term monopoly here is unfortunate. It reflects and encourages confusion between two logically and practically quite distinct situations, the first in which an activity is largely in the hands of a geographically or ethnically distinct group, and the second is one in which those in a particular activity can exercise a degree of monopoly by deliberate restriction of supply or entry, which enables them to secure prices, trading margins, or returns on capital, higher than would prevail under more competitive conditions. The two types of situation are quite distinct, and one can, often does, exist without the other. The frequent identification of these two types of situation is particularly unfortunate in African conditions because there the predominant position of foreigners sometimes is accompanied by a measure of monopoly, but often it is not, and this difference is obscured by the indiscriminate use of the term to cover both. And as I shall suggest shortly, the confusion is apt to issue in policies designed to limit the predominance of expatriates, which in fact strengthen whatever element of monopoly they may possess.

The prominence of foreigners in African commerce reflects the advantages of the possession of capital and of access to it, as well as of skills and attitudes such as technical and administrative skills, thrift, ability to perceive and take advantage of economic opportunity, and various other aptitudes and attitudes, derived in part from the background of societies long accustomed to the ways of a money economy. Foreigners, including foreign traders, have been prime agents of economic change in Africa, and have been largely responsible for linking these economies to the outside world, and for the provision of human and material resources which have made these links possible.

The prominence of non-Africans in trade does not in itself imply the presence of monopoly in the usual meaning of the word. There is, nevertheless, a substantial degree of concentration in external trade in several African territories, notably West Africa. The principal reason for

---

[2] I use the term foreigner or expatriate as synonymous with non-African. Many of the European, Indian and Levantine traders have lived for decades or even generations in Africa, and it is therefore inaccurate to refer to them as foreigners or expatriates. But these terms are less cumbersome than non-African, and I shall use them to refer to people of non-African origin.

this is to be found in the large capital requirements in some branches of tropical trade, which in turn derives from the long distances and poorly developed communications, and also from the necessity of financing local intermediaries and often even local producers, because of the low level of liquid capital in the indigenous economies. The wide and rapid swings of prosperity and depression also tend to benefit those with large capital by enabling them to weather the slump, and even to buy up firms in difficulties. In one or two instances historical accident, such as the administration of certain territories by chartered trading companies, has promoted concentration. A high degree of concentration is in itself likely to result in a situation in which trading margins are wider than if the number of competitors were larger. This likelihood is enhanced if there are market-sharing agreements among the firms, agreements which are facilitated when there are few firms. A substantial measure of concentration and periodic market-sharing agreements have been prominent in the external trade of British West Africa, an area in the economic life and development of which external trade has been of the greatest importance.

Both the width of the trading margins and the stability of market-sharing agreements are much affected by actual and potential competition, notably by the presence of outsiders (that is, both firms other than those which account for the high degree of concentration, and firms not participating in or observing the market-sharing agreements), by the number of participants in the market-sharing agreements, and by the possibility of the entry of effective new competitors. In practically all branches of trade outside small-scale retailing, the most effective competitors of foreign trading firms are other foreigners and foreign trading firms. Such actual or potential competition may come from three sources: foreign firms with experience of some other branches or stages of trade in the local country; foreign firms with trading experience elsewhere, notably some other poor country; and foreign firms engaged in economic activity other than trade in the same country. Empirically, the first two categories have been much the more important. The technical and administrative skills and experience, the knowledge of market conditions, and at times the local connections of such enterprises, are of obvious value in challenging the position of established firms.

It would seem that neither the high degree of concentration, nor the market-sharing agreements have generally secured substantial monopoly profits, or exceptionally wide gross margins to the firms for any prolonged period, except when government controls have restricted entry or stifled competition.[3] Without such controls the advantage of the posses-

---

[3] There are a few exceptions where special circumstances, notably control of important transport or port facilities, have placed certain firms in a particularly strong position. This was of some significance in the past, for instance in the trade in oil palm products in Eastern Nigeria. It is of no general interest or importance at present.

sion of large capital is generally not sufficient to sustain monopolistic margins or profits for long.

However, the combination of the prominence of foreigners in trade, and of a high degree of concentration in external trade, present difficult political and administrative problems, even without monopolistic practices, organized barriers to entry, or abnormally wide profit margins. Indeed the absence of these aspects and practices enhances the dilemmas of policy which are often ignored in a politically highly charged atmosphere. In many African countries (and indeed throughout the underdeveloped world) there are controls to ensure larger local participation in trade by prohibition or severe restrictions of the immigration of foreign traders and trading employees, restrictive licensing of trading enterprises, and rationing or licensing of supplies. They are almost invariably said to be introduced to increase the volume of trade in African hands. This formulation ignores the essential problems and their attendant dilemmas.

Such restrictions diminish the aggregate volume of trade and of economic activity in the territories concerned, and they thus affect adversely the economic interest of African producers, consumers and workers. They do this because the activities of more efficient firms and individuals are reduced to provide opportunities for less efficient firms and individuals. Moreover, it is virtually certain that the volume of trade handled by African traders is reduced by these restrictions. It is of course true that African traders whose activities depend on these restrictions would be displaced or find their scope curtailed. But the expansion of the total trade which would come about in the absence of these restrictions would benefit the African traders in those stages of trade, or in those distributive activities which would still remain in African hands. On all but extreme assumptions, the total volume of trade handled by African traders would increase even though some would be displaced in certain branches of trade. This conclusion is reinforced if the effects of the activities of foreigners on the growth of the economy as a whole are considered.

In practice, however, those who benefit from the restrictions and would lose by their removal are aware of these losses (or even overestimate them), whereas those who would benefit from their removal do not realize this. The losses from the removal of restrictions are direct, localized and are readily perceived, whereas the benefits would be widely diffused, would be indirect (in the sense of reaching the beneficiaries at one or more removes only), and would permeate the economy only gradually. The losses suffered by African trading interests would also suggest that the subservience of Africans to foreign merchants had increased. This type of asymmetry in the perception of benefits and losses from the imposition or removal of restrictions is usual.

Let me now consider some further economic effects and implications of these restrictions. In the trading activities in which they are imposed, competition is reduced and the trading margins of both Africans and foreigners are widened. Where the controls are effected by restrictive licensing and allocation of supplies, they result in windfall profits to the favored traders, secured at the expense of their customers, and at the expense of those excluded from the protected activity. The wider distributive margins affect adversely the customers of the traders, including farmers who have to pay more for their supplies, and to receive less for their products, and they therefore generally tend to reduce the growth of production for the market. Moreover, such regulations necessarily exclude numbers of people from trading, many of whom for various reasons may be substantially disadvantaged by this enforced restriction on their occupational mobility. And whatever the basis of allocation of licenses and supplies, it necessarily implies an element of privilege and favoritism. This sets up obvious political, social and administrative strains, particularly in multi-racial societies.

Such regulations and controls are also apt to convey misleading ideas about commercial activity and of its difficulties and rewards. They ensure easy profits. As a result both the favored traders and other members of the community tend to underestimate the difficulties and risks of commerce, and indeed to regard it as involving no more than the mere collection of riskless and effortless profits, which indeed it largely is in these conditions. So far from promoting commercial and economic education, and serving to train members of the local population for a more effective participation in economic life, such controls have the effect of misleading people about the tasks of commercial life, which leaves them less rather than better prepared to face subsequent vicissitudes.[4]

There are thus substantial disadvantages in attempts to promote the interests of African traders by restriction on competition in trade, especially by restrictive licensing and by the control and allocation of supplies. These disadvantages are particularly important when a large part of the economy is still in the subsistence stage, because, as already noted, the ability and readiness of subsistence producers to produce for the market is much affected by the volume, variety and terms of the available trading services.

It does not, however, follow from the foregoing that deliberate government action may not be required in this sphere. For instance, without it the local population may feel that it is separated from the outside world by an impenetrable layer of alien traders. This in itself may induce a sense of dependence, which is sharpened when these traders are

---

[4] These arguments apply whether the favored traders are private firms or co-operative societies. The position of co-operative societies is considered in section 5, below.

members of economically and socially more advanced communities. And when the degree of concentration is high, both the feeling and the reality of dependence on particular firms are naturally further increased. This can lead to a politically explosive situation, particularly when some or many of the expatriate traders have over a period of years achieved considerable prosperity, even though their profits may not represent either abnormal returns on capital, or monopolistic margins.

There are no simple solutions to the problems and dilemmas of such a situation. The drastic suggestion sometimes heard for the elimination of expatriates from all or most branches of trade would severely retard economic progress in areas where continued growth cannot be taken for granted.

The most appropriate course must depend on local circumstances, particularly on social, political, economic and administrative conditions and possibilities. It would be affected by the extent, depth and intensity of the feelings of masses of producers and consumers, which often may differ considerably from those ascribed to them by vocal groups of local traders. Although generalized policy recommendations are of very limited use, I nonetheless offer some suggestions which I hope will serve as starting points for the reader's reflection.

For social, political and economic reasons it may be thought desirable to subsidize Africans in various branches of trade. The costs of such a policy should be brought out into the open and borne by the community as a whole in accordance with some recognized canons of equity, which are presumably reflected in the tax structure as far as it is politically and administratively possible. This suggests that wherever possible assistance should take the form of a government subsidy. This ensures that the cost is appreciated, and is borne by the community at large, and not by an arbitrarily selected group, namely by the customers of traders, and by those who are excluded from trade by the restrictive measures designed to protect African traders. Such a subsidy is also less likely to impede economic development than a rise in the cost of trading services.[5]

A subsidy could be given to African traders, co-operative societies or government-owned corporations or government departments engaged in trade. It could also be given to expatriate firms to encourage the employment of Africans in responsible posts. For instance, a subsidy could be related to the proportion which payments to Africans bear to total salary payments in certain senior grades. This would in effect be a subsidy designed to promote the training of Africans in trade. Service with unsubsidized trading firms (i.e., firms unassisted except for this particular subsidy) is suitable training for independent commercial activity, and

---

[5] Whether a subsidy is less of an impediment depends largely on the system of the subsidy and the structure of taxation.

possibly for subsequent industrial activity as well. It is likely to be more fruitful training than independent commercial activity in an officially-created non-competitive environment, that is in conditions in which profits are virtually assured. An increase in the number of Africans in senior positions with foreign firms would also help to serve to dispel some of the popular misconceptions about the activities of these firms and about their profits.

Thus direct government subsidy for securing African participation in trade offers a wider range of possibilities than protection of African traders by the restriction on their competitors, a policy which is inflexible and circumscribed, besides having the other special disadvantages already described.

I may refer to another specific suggestion. Given the admission of a certain number of expatriates to an African country, it would promote economic development if they were allowed to move freely between different occupations and activities without being prohibited from entering any particular activity or range of activity, especially trade.[6] If they are allowed to move between different commercial activities, they are likely to deploy their capital and skills in directions yielding the highest return, and they will thereby usually contribute most to economic development. They will normally engage in those activities in which the Africans are least likely to compete effectively in the near future, since it would be uneconomic for foreigners to enter these. This suggestion runs counter both to current practice, and to widely-held notions. It may indeed prove politically impracticable if opposition to foreigners is especially vocal and effective in particular activities.[7]

ALLEGATIONS OF REDUNDANCY IN AFRICAN MARKETING CHANNELS

In many poor countries in Africa (and elsewhere) a large number of intermediaries is a conspicuous feature of the local scene. This multiplicity of intermediaries is often held responsible for the high costs of distribution and is widely regarded as a major defect of African commerce. This complaint is not so highly charged politically as those about the prominence of expatriates, but it is a frequent and influential theme of the official literature, and it has had important effects on the course of

---

[6] On political and social grounds this may not apply to mining, or to the acquisition of real property. This, however, has no bearing on the argument of the text.

[7] The case for this suggestion may be strengthened if such immigrants are given permission to reside for a given number of years, but without expectation of political rights, or assurance of an extension of this period.

events.[8] It was largely responsible for the introduction of restrictive licensing of ginneries and traders in the cotton industry of Uganda, a series of measures which has not only raised the cost of these activities, and reduced the marketing facilities serving Africans but has also secured large monopoly profits to favored licensees. This type of complaint was also partly responsible for the establishment of export monopolies over all major West African agricultural produce, which has had very far-reaching results.

The argument is that unnecessary intermediaries place themselves within the distributive chain thereby raising its costs. As a corollary the compulsory elimination of these redundant intermediaries is proposed. However, neither these suggestions, nor the consequent policy proposals stand up to examination.

The complaint invites the question why the allegedly redundant intermediaries are not by-passed by those with whom they deal. An intermediary will normally be used only if the price he charges for his service (that is, his margin) is less than the value his customers place on his service. He will be by-passed without official intervention if he provides no services (that is if he is redundant), or if his services exceed the costs incurred by his customers if they performed these services for themselves. This will happen unless neither of the parties served by them realizes that it would be cheaper to by-pass them, or unless institutional arrangements prevent the adoption of more economic direct methods of dealing. Let me consider these possibilities.

The allegedly redundant intermediary necessarily must stand between another middleman and the producer, or between a middleman and the final consumer, or between two middlemen. Thus at least one of the parties served by the supposedly redundant intermediary is himself an intermediary. Even if it were true that the average farmer does not know his marketing alternatives, or could not perform simple commercial calculations, a redundant intermediary would still be eliminated if his middleman customer could effect a saving by dealing direct. It is most unlikely that those who live by trading, and whose profits and livelihood thus depend on their margins, would ignore economic opportunities in their own field of business, or fail to take advantage of them. Moreover, there is ample evidence of the awareness of African farmers of their marketing alternatives, and of their eagerness to sell at the best price; and this is not surprising in view of their low cash incomes and of the

---

[8] For instance the following characteristic passages in the official *Report of the Nigeria Livestock Mission* (London: H.M. Stationery Office, 1951) well illustrate these complaints . . . "the handling of almost the entire trade by a host of redundant dealers and middlemen, the frequent handlings of stock" are among the factors that "represent for Nigeria economic wastage on a prodigious scale and in large measure accounts for the unjustifiably wide gap between the prices received by the producer and those paid by the consumer," p. 95.

often low opportunity costs in the disposal of their time.[9] Thus, an intermediary whose margin exceeds the value of his services to the parties served by him will be by-passed.[10]

Thus the compulsory elimination of classes of intermediaries (say, itinerant buyers or commission agents) implies that their services must be performed at greater cost (in terms of real resources) by one or other of the parties between whom they stand. This implies an uneconomic measure of vertical integration, together with a reduction in the marketing alternatives open to the parties. These adverse effects are serious in underdeveloped countries which are least able to afford the resulting waste.

Institutional arrangements sometimes deny customers the right to use certain methods of marketing. For instance, restrictive practices may prevent customers from by-passing middlemen even if they preferred to do without their services. This is against their interests. Such practices are much more significant in developed than in underdeveloped countries, though they are not unknown in the latter. For instance, in some West African ports market women are said to have prevented fishermen and their wives from retailing their catches. But clearly the interests of the fishermen will not be served by a compulsory restriction in the numbers of intermediaries whose monopolistic position would thereby be strengthened.

African producers are often said to be prevented from selling their crops on the best terms because they are indebted to particular intermediaries and have to sell to them. But a compulsory reduction in the number of trader lenders aggravates the situation of the producers instead of improving it. Such a measure reduces the volume of credit available to producers, and thereby weakens their position. The combined terms of the loan and the price would be worse; and it is this combination which concerns them. The weakness of the seller derives from his need for a loan; reduction in the number of potential lenders aggravates this weakness. This is a specific example of the general point that the position of the customers of traders is usually not improved by a compulsory reduction in the number of traders, since this merely reduces the alternatives open to customers.

It is also often suggested that there are too many intermediaries or processors at any particular stage in the distributive chain, and that this results in unnecessary multiplication of facilities which raises overheads which in turn forces the intermediaries to pay producers unnecessarily

---

[9] But even if they did not know the alternatives open to them, or more generally their own commercial interests, their position is unlikely to be improved by a compulsory reduction of the services available to them.

[10] This is so unless the customers are not free agents for institutional or other reasons, a matter which I shall consider later in this section.

low prices. However, such a situation could be expected to induce the intermediaries to bid up producers' prices to get larger supplies, which would then lead to the elimination of the redundant intermediaries. There is indeed ample specific evidence in Africa that the so-called excessive competition tends to raise producer prices rather than depress them. If there really were significant economies in the operation of fewer and larger trading and processing establishments, the interest of intermediaries and processors and the responsiveness of producers to the higher prices offered by them, could be expected to establish such a market structure with a relatively small number of local units, without compulsion. A situation would result in which the possibilities of the economies of scale are balanced with producers' valuations of the convenience of marketing (especially the proximity of traders or processors), and of the availability of a range of independent alternatives. This again is amply confirmed by empirical evidence in many African territories. For instance, it is borne out by the contrast in a number of countries between the few large timber processing enterprises compared to the multiplicity of cotton ginneries. This reflects the economies of scale in the former activity and their absence in the latter, which prevents larger ginneries from offering significantly more favorable terms to the producers than do the smaller dispersed units.

The multiplicity of intermediaries in a large measure reflects certain essential aspects of the economies of many African territories. The principal factor behind this multiplicity of intermediaries is that production for sale is undertaken by large numbers of farmers who individually produce on a small scale. As they have little storage capacity and small cash resources they have to sell in small lots at frequent intervals. Moreover, many or most farmers operate far from the points of assembly, the principal markets or the ports of shipment. There is a heavy cost of assembling and conveying to the distant market large numbers of small parcels of produce.

Even the simple economics of this matter are so imperfectly understood that a numerical example may be useful. If each of five farmers situated twenty miles from the nearest village or town himself marketed his own very small weekly output, this would require five round trips of forty miles each. If, however, one middleman (who may in fact be one of the farmers acting for the others) intervenes and carries the produce to the market, the number of journeys is reduced by four-fifths, saving scarce and valuable capital (in the form of animal or truck transport), as well as labor. This last economy may also be important, since, even if there is a general surplus of labor, the harvesting of produce has to be accomplished within a given short period so that at times the farmer cannot afford to leave his holding. The same principle applies at the next stage; if each small middleman carried his purchases direct to the large markets the number of journeys would be greater than if another intermediary stepped in and carried the purchases of several traders; and so on all along the line.

The task of bulking cannot be avoided. So long as there is competitive entry into trade the producer is not affected whether the performer of the service of bulking and transport is remunerated by salary or by the profits of trade. If the farmers formed themselves into a co-operative society, these services would be undertaken by the servants of the co-operative society, whose time and effort would still have to be paid for.

Thus the distributive task in these economies absorbs a large volume of resources. The type of resource used depends on the relative supplies and prices of different resources, especially of capital and labor, on technical conditions, and also on institutional factors. Compared to conditions elsewhere, capital in African economies is generally scarce relative to unskilled labor. The lack of telephones and the low level and poor quality of the roads increase the capital required for a given flow of production and consumption. Most intermediaries are themselves poor so that they operate on a small scale; and small-scale distribution requires comparatively little capital and training. For these reasons, distribution tends to be labor-intensive.

There are some institutional factors originating outside commodity distribution which enhance the labor-intensive nature of trading activity in Africa. These are the restrictions on the access to land, and, more important, the establishment of minimum wages for hired labor in organized industry and commerce. These regulated wages do not apply to small-scale trade, nor of course to self-employment which is prominent in small-scale trade, an overflow activity into which are forced those who cannot secure wage employment.

In short, although the marketing arrangements in commodity distribution, especially small-scale trade, in Africa, are technically primitive compared to those in economically more advanced societies, they are not wasteful in African conditions. Arrangements which are economically efficient in one society will not be efficient in another where the availability of resources is different. Thus attempts to force marketing arrangements more closely into line with those prevailing elsewhere lead to waste. This applies notably to measures designed to bring about a larger measure of vertical integration by enforcing direct dealing between consumers and producers through the compulsory eliminating of intermediaries. Such measures increase unnecessarily the capital and administrative skills required in distribution (that is, they enforce increased employment of a scarce resource which can be used elsewhere), while setting free manpower with little or no alternative opportunities. They thus raise the real cost of marketing. They also deny marketing facilities to many producers, which may prevent them from entering the exchange economy or remaining within it.

PREVALENCE OF RESTRICTIVE TENDENCIES

Complaints about the prominence of expatriates, and those about the alleged wastefulness of the multiplicity of middlemen, usually stem from different sources and move on a different plane. But they often issue in similar policies, which reinforce an important and undesirable feature of African trade, which has received little publicity. This is the prevalence of restrictive tendencies.

There is in many African economies a pronounced tendency towards restrictionism, which draws strength from two distinct sources: the pressure of sectional economic interests and tribalism or xenophobia. As already noted, the tendency towards restrictionism is a feature of economies in which there is some measure of specialization. In such societies people often try to increase the scarcity value of their services by restricting entry into their own or related activities, because by such means they can improve their relative position and up to a point their real income.

. . . .

Although for obvious political and administrative reasons such measures are particularly effective and popular when directed against foreigners or members of ethnically or linguistically distinct groups, they are often directed also against other members of the local population (other than the beneficiaries).

For instance, it is well known that in West Africa there has for many years been a vocal and politically influential opposition to the activities of expatriate traders. Less familiar is the frequently equally vehement opposition to the entry or activities of Africans from other tribes, regions or districts. Such opposition is often directed against people who are ethnically and linguistically indistinguishable from, or even identical with, those who oppose their entry and activities, so that the essentially economic basis of the opposition is clear.

In recent years and decades there has been much officially supported restrictionism in many important branches of African commerce (including transport) effected by such measures as the restrictive licensing, the establishment of zonal monopolies, the confinement of trade to certain markets, and various other devices.

Restrictionism in trade raises the cost of the indispensible service of commodity assembly and distribution and reduces the alternatives of the population. By narrowing markets it retards the expansion of production for the market as well as the growth of specialization, and thus the development of the economy; for these reasons it not only retards the growth of agricultural production for sale but also increases the frequency and severity of local shortages, especially of food. It increases the unemployment stemming from the lack of co-operant resources (including the uneven local incidence of the scarcity of these resources) by preventing the most effective deployment of the available capital and skill. It also retards the spread of ideas and of new techniques and thus confines economic horizons. It enhances people's sense of dependence on the privileged traders which exacerbates political tension especially, but not only, when these are foreigners. It often strengthens the position of local monopolies. It leads to the growth of pressure groups and to political and economic strife. Further, in many African territories the local population itself is heterogeneous, so that restrictionism is particularly likely to result in extensive fragmentation of the economy.

Such restrictive measures, which are now so effective, have been introduced in many underdeveloped countries at a comparatively early stage of their development. Many of the African economies have hardly emerged from tribal restrictionism before being overtaken by more narrowly economic restrictionism. Thus they have not experienced the comparatively long spell of unrestricted activity of the earlier history of the developed countries. Moreover, in European countries certain forms of restrictionism, notably the local monopolistic restrictions, disintegrated in the course of the accelerated economic advance of the eighteenth and nineteenth centuries. The early emergence of economic restrictionism (superimposed on or even juxtaposed with tribal restrictionism) affects adversely their economic position and prospects. Very poor economies, in which advance from a subsistence to an exchange economy is necessary for material progress, are particularly harmed by such restrictionism.

A specific example serves to illustrate some implications of the foregoing discussion. It has been known for many years that there is a large internal trade in local produce in Nigeria, much of it over long distances. There are wide seasonal fluctuations in the prices of these products and also large inter-district and inter-regional price differences. These fluctuations and differences reflect the narrowness of markets, the poor communications, and the low level of physical and money capital. In such a situation there are considerable possibilities of profits for enterprises with the requisite capital and organization. This was recognized by the United Africa Company in the early 1930s when it entered this trade. Its activities aroused such fierce opposition from local trading interests that the government asked the company to refrain from trading in local produce, and since about 1932 the company has not in fact participated in this trade. This episode incidentally illustrates the divergence between the sectional interests of certain African groups (the traders in local produce) and the interests of the African population as a whole, since the population generally would undoubtedly benefit from the smoother flow of internal trade.

For political reasons the European firms are still barred from participation in internal trade. Indeed they are more effectively barred than in the past, as local trading interests are more vocal and politically influential than in the 1930s. Newspaper and political opinion reflects their interests and views to a far greater extent than it does those of the rural population at large.

A general suggestion arises from the subject of this section.[11]

Governments and administrators could make greater efforts to resist restrictionism. A fairly close study of West African trade and some work on Uganda, suggest that in Africa the political pressures for restrictionism are not overwhelming, especially when they are directed primarily against other Africans. In Uganda the demands for restrictive licensing of ginneries have come entirely from expatriates; and as already noted in West Africa, much of the restrictionism is directed primarily against Africans. Governments and administrators have supported or accepted restrictionism for a variety of reasons, including over-estimate of the strength behind it; failure to recognize the heterogeneity of the African economic interest, especially the discrepancy between sectional interest and that of the rest of the community; the official preference for apparently tidy structures; the failure to see through the hollowness of the arguments for restrictionism; and a failure to appreciate its adverse results. In African conditions official support is very generally necessary for the effectiveness and maintenance of restrictionism. Thus official support should generally be withheld from restrictionism; and it might even be replaced by effective discouragement.

EXAGGERATED HOPES FOR COOPERATIVE TRADING

The co-operative movement is supported by governments in many, possibly most, African countries. The development of co-operative trading societies is widely regarded as the best way to remedy many of the real or alleged defects of African commerce, notably the predominance of expatriates, the high costs of distribution, the liability of producers to exploitation, and so forth.

Government support of co-operative societies takes varying forms, usually representing a mixture in varying combinations of such ingredients as special legislative facilities for the formation and registration of societies; provision of advisory and supervisory services by a government department; official participation in, or control of, decision-making and

---

[11] A more specific suggestion is discussed in section 6 below in the context of the modernization of distribution.

management; financial assistance ranging from the guaranteeing of loans to the payment of subsidies and grants in aid; and restrictions on, or the prohibition of, activities of competing private undertakings; preferential treatment in allocation of licences or supplies; and so forth. Quite often government departments have in fact become partners in co-operative enterprises in which they have become deeply involved. In these circumstances, co-operative societies are really extensions of government departments rather than independent organizations.

The case for government support of the co-operatives is often regarded as axiomatic. Yet the case for it is not obvious. A co-operative society is simply a form of business enterprise whose capital is provided, and whose activities are organized, by its suppliers or customers. A co-operator is both a part owner and a customer of the society.

Generally the economic or commercial services of co-operative societies such as credit, marketing or consumer societies are essentially similar to those supplied by private firms. When a co-operative society does not receive substantial privileges, preferential treatment or financial support from the government, its economic success can be measured by its ability to survive, and to satisfy the commercial needs of its members, who can always turn to private firms if they are not satisfied. If, in such conditions, the society survives or expands, it means that its members prefer it to privately owned firms. Its advantages may stem from various sources, such as efficiency, or perception of commercial opportunities ignored by private firms. Or it may operate in a field where there is little competition among private firms, so that there is room for an independent supplier. Or the society may benefit from the loyalty of its members, or from the knowledge of their credit worthiness, or simply from their preference to deal with their own organization. But whatever the reasons for its success, this provides its economic justification, if it is gained without special privileges and support denied to private competitors.

There are certain other economic activities which cannot be easily undertaken by private organizations but which can possibly be undertaken by co-operatives. These include such important agricultural activities as pest control and soil conservation. These yield indiscriminate benefits, which means that firms undertaking them could not collect charges from the beneficiaries, since the benefits accrue whether or not the beneficiaries pay. Thus they will not be undertaken by private firms. The individual producer may also be reluctant to spend money on these activities as part of his expenditure will accure to the neighbours without cost to them, and his own efforts may be frustrated by their neglect. These difficulties may be overcome by a co-operative embracing all the producers in its area of operation. This could obviously overcome the obstacles which are prohibitive to private enterprise in this field. At the same time it may be preferable to performance of these tasks by a government department, which is unlikely to know conditions in the particular area, or the circumstances of the producers, so well as a local co-operative society. There are great difficulties in the way of establishing such societies in underdeveloped countries, notably Africa. But it is noteworthy that there is a wide area, important for agricultural improvement, in which the co-operative effort would be complementary and not competitive with private effort, and may also be preferable to direct government intervention.

When co-operative societies enjoy sustained and substantial government support, then of course the simple test of survival and progress no longer indicates economic usefulness, because they enjoy advantages which arise from privileges created for them by the government, and not from their commercial efficiency or their ability to satisfy the demands of their members. Thus the basis of rational economic assessment is removed. This is particularly so whenever the support and assistance is general rather than specific, and involves not only, or mainly, financial grants, but such matters as restriction on the activities of competitors, or preferential treatment in the allocation of licences or trading sites. Moreover, there is also the practically very important advantage that once the government has begun to subsidize co-operatives, further help can always be expected in the case of difficulties which the government cannot refuse. The government faces a contingent liability to assist societies which have run into financial difficulties, a liability which may be particularly onerous when these societies have acquired many members with the help of this support.

It is often argued that co-operatives, especially co-operative trading and credit societies, should not be judged on the basis of commercial success, because co-operation is desirable on wider grounds, for instance, by encouraging the virtues of self-reliance and thrift, or acquainting producers with problems of organization and marketing. This may justify government assistance in the form of advisory service or technical assistance. But this can hardly serve as an argument for large-scale government assistance, which becomes practically government participation. Such assistance, and the expectation of its continuation, undermine the self-reliance of the co-operators. Membership is valued not for its own sake but because of the privilege and support enjoyed by the society. Moreover, there is little or no educational advantage in co-operation in such conditions, rather the reverse, since any apparent commercial success is in a large measure the result of the special privileges granted to a society by government rather than of the ability to serve the needs of customers.

Certain special arguments are often urged in Africa in support of the co-operative principle and of government support to co-operatives: that co-operatives to some extent resemble the communal shared economic activity of tribal life and is thus particularly suitable to African conditions; that co-operation helps African farmers to secure loans on tolerable terms, chiefly because the management has personal knowledge of the debtor; and that co-operation redresses the inequality of economic strength between the farmer and the middleman. But in themselves these arguments do not justify government support to co-operatives. If co-operatives are so suitable to African conditions, it would not be necessary to subsidize them. Again, the individual producer is known also to the small trader and money-lender. The high rate of interest on loans to farmers reflects largely the scarcity of money capital, the high cost of administering small loans and the high risks. High rates of interest may also involve an element of monopoly profits, though I believe this to be comparatively unimportant because of the ease of entry into small-scale trade and money-lending. But if competition is weak, this is precisely a condition in which there are opportunities for unsubsidized co-operative enterprise. Essentially the same applies to the alleged inequality in bargaining strength between producers and money-lenders. If this were a substantial factor adversely affecting the terms of trade of producers[12] to be redressed by co-operation, the resulting improvement in these terms would secure the adherence of producers without government support.

It may be argued that such support is still required to overcome initial difficulties even if ultimately the society becomes viable, a suggestion along the familiar infant-industry argument for protection. But this argument is weak, and it would not justify subsidization or support of co-operative societies compared to private undertakings in which the same reasoning could be applied. In any case this has nothing to do with substantial and continued large-scale assistance to the co-operative movement.

Counsel has been darkened in this sphere by misleading comparisons with the success of the British consumer co-operatives over the last hundred years. This analogy is wholly irrelevant for the following reasons, among others. First, the British co-operatives were not subsidized by government. This in itself should suffice to dispose of the comparison. Second, the co-operative movement benefited greatly from the availability of latent managerial and administrative talent among the British working and lower middle classes for which in the nineteenth century and early twentieth century there was very little outlet in commercial or public life, and which was therefore available relatively cheaply to the co-operative movement. In Africa, however, the exact reverse applies.

---

[12] This is unlikely whenever there are a number of competing traders, or whenever entry into small-scale trade is easy (which it generally is, especially because farmers themselves often also act as traders) since actual or potential competition in trade forces the traders to bid for supplies. This compels them to offer prices which secure only competitive returns to the traders, regardless of differences in commercial skill or sophistication between themselves and the producers.

There is a great dearth of administrative and managerial talent locally, and there is ample opportunity in government service or private commerce for this talent, which is therefore not available to the co-operatives. Third, in the nineteenth century, competition in retailing in Britain was often weak, which helped the rapid progress both of the co-operative societies and, towards the end of the century, also of various other new types of retail organizations.

I may now turn to some policy implications of the foregoing. In those activities in which co-operatives compete with private firms, there is no general case for subsidizing co-operative societies rather than private African undertakings. If, however, co-operatives are supported, this is best done by the provision for a limited period of advisory and supervisory services. If it is decided to assist them beyond this limited extent, there is a case for doing so by direct cash subsidies, rather than by restrictions on the activities of the competitors.[13]

If it is thought desirable that the government should participate in a particular trading activity, it would seem preferable that it should do so directly through a government department or a government-owned corporation, rather than indirectly or covertly through government-subsidized co-operative societies, which are co-operatives in name only. It is often thought that government-supported co-operatives represent the best of both worlds in that they serve the public interest without the political and administrative difficulties presented by government operation. The truth seems to be rather the reverse. Such organizations are not subject either to the commercial or competitive test of the market, nor to the public scrutiny to which government agents or corporations are often exposed.

Lastly, it may be better to concentrate or even confine support for co-operatives to activities yielding principally indiscriminate benefits, such as pest control and irrigation (as distinct from ordinary commercial activities), which for reasons indicated earlier in this section cannot be undertaken by private enterprise, but which, at the same time, are not particularly suitable for government departments.

MODERNIZATION AND ENCOURAGEMENT OF THE SERVICE INDUSTRIES

The two final topics which I propose to discuss—modernization, and the encouragement of labor-intensive service industries—may be conveniently discussed together as they are related in the field of policy.

It is not quite clear what is meant by modernization of distribution, which is an ambiguous concept. For instance, it could refer either to an

---

[13] For the same reason as in the analogous instance noted in section 2 above.

increase or to a decrease in the volume of services rendered to the ultimate consumer. Home deliveries to consumers were at times regarded as essential in many branches of retailing in advanced economies, while now they are exceptional in the advanced economies of North America. Again, specialization is generally regarded as a feature of advanced economies, but the department stores and supermarkets of Western countries, as well as of the more sophisticated commercial centres of Africa, are in some ways the opposite of specialization. Capital-intensive or technically-advanced methods are often regarded as characteristic of modern types of economic activity. But the economic desirability of the adoption of such methods is essentially a matter of costs and returns, and it depends on factor supplies, technical conditions, the pattern of consumer wants and institutional arrangements. There is no special merit in adopting capital-intensive or technologically-advanced methods if these absorb a larger quantity of valuable resources in satisfying consumer wants than would simpler methods.[14] The foregoing is simply an example of the familiar confusion of technical and economic efficiency, that is, of the assessment of the results and merits of economic activity regardless of cost.

It is, of course, economically desirable that commerce should be modernized in the sense that it uses resources most productively, and at the same time in a fashion most likely to conduce to their growth. I shall now put forward first some general suggestions, and then one more specific proposal for the promotion of this aim.

First, whenever possible, resources should be used to satisfy consumer requirements at lowest cost, that is, on the basis of economic and not merely technical efficiency. Second, trading enterprises should be allowed to operate unfettered by restrictions which raise their costs and which reduce the alternatives open to their customers. In particular, as far as possible trading enterprises should have unfettered access to new markets and methods, even if this affects existing vested interests. Third, the economic modernization of commerce, in the sense of closer approximation to its conduct in more advanced societies without waste of resources, is likely to be promoted by measures which advance the progress of the exchange economy. These include the suitable modifica-

---

[14] It is sometimes thought that the adoption of capital-intensive methods or of technically-advanced methods in some activities would help to promote technical progress and thereby raise the economy on to a higher plane. This view, which essentially ignores costs, is facile. Among other factors it disregards the fact that as a result of the adoption of these more capital-intensive methods in particular activities, methods elsewhere become less capital-intensive as less capital is available there. Consideration of the allocation of the resources may not suffice to provide criteria for policies designed to accelerate growth. But it does not follow that the adoption of unnecessarily costly methods in certain activities in some mysterious way promotes growth to offset the wasteful allocation of resources which it implies.

tion of the land tenure system, introduction of appropriate taxation, improvement in communications, resistance to restrictionism, and the provision of agricultural extension work.

The trade in agricultural produce for local consumption is an activity which seems to offer considerable scope for economic modernization and which is of great significance for economic progress in Africa. The specific suggestion I would like to make (and to which I referred earlier) concerns this broad area of commerce. It is provoked by the incident mentioned in section 4, the enforced withdrawal of the United Africa Company from internal trade in West Africa in the face of pressure by African trading interests, a pressure which at present would be even more effective and powerful than in the 1930s.

It is fairly obvious and well recognized that the expatriate merchant organizations could contribute substantially to the improvement of the efficiency of internal trade, which in turn would benefit the economy greatly, especially but not only by improving the marketing of crops and thus stimulating the output of local agriculture. African governments might therefore consider the promotion of a company for trading (including warehousing) in local produce, to be owned jointly by a government department or corporation, and by one or more expatriate merchant firms and possibly African commercial interests. Such a company could appoint expatriate merchants as agents either for a fee or for a participation in profits. These firms often have branches in many trading centers, and they would be well qualified to act as buying or selling agents. The experiment might at first be limited in scale and scope to minimize the risk and capital involved and to test its suitability in local conditions. Its extension would depend on results, which would be affected by such matters as the local political situation, the resources of the participating trading firms, and the efficiency of its competitors. It is clear that the experiment would be significant only if competitors were in no way hampered by official restrictions on their activities. Nor must the organization be in receipt of favors, privileges and concessions denied to its competitors. Of course, if successful, the experiment could be extended to other branches of trade and transport, as it already has for manufacturing industry (but not for trading) in some African countries.

The experiment might be politically practicable if the organization were known to be semi-official and to include influential African elements. The improvement in the methods and productivity of local food production is now widely and rightly recognized as a major factor in African progress, and one on which viable industrialization is likely to depend. Progress in this field is much affected by the efficiency of marketing. Moreover, acute local food shortages still occur in many parts of Africa and their removal or reduction could alleviate human misery; and in this sphere again such an organization could make a contribution.

It would also serve to reduce the wide intra-seasonal price fluctuations. It would also provide valuable training to Africans in long-distance commerce. Lastly, it might help in unifying the local economies and counteracting the tendencies towards fragmentation. Altogether, if successful, it might contribute appreciably both to current economic welfare and to the promotion of economic progress. These wider advantages would be additional to any direct profits secured by the organization.

Let me now turn to the question of the encouragement of service industries on the ground of their labor-intensive nature and their significance, therefore, as a source of employment. Service activity, especially distribution, is not necessarily more labor-intensive than other forms of activity. For instance, the large-scale substitution of capital for labor is a characteristic feature of distribution in the more recent development of the advanced economies of North America. But it is true that in emerging economies, distribution, especially small-scale trade, is more labor-intensive than many, or even most, other activities outside the subsistence sector. This is so partly because unskilled labor can be substituted more readily for capital in small-scale distribution than elsewhere, and also because small-scale trading represents one of the overflow activities into which are forced those who cannot secure employment at the institutionally fixed minimum wage.[15] There is a general case for not discouraging trade in emerging societies, since this is a potent instrument in economic advance. Further, there is no reason for disparaging labor-intensive activities in these societies. But at the same time there is no general case either for encouraging or subsidizing an activity simply because it is labor-intensive; there is no merit in encouraging such an activity unless there is a market for the output at a price higher than its real cost in terms of the alternative uses of the resources employed in its production.

---

[15] In large-scale distribution, especially in establishments owned by expatriates, wages are raised above the opportunity costs of labor by this wage regulation. This somewhat hampers the progress, and restricts the activities of these enterprises.

This article highlights the effects on firms in Central America from the creation of the Central American Common Market. For many they have been substantial. Based on extensive field research, this study finds that import substitution and competition have lowered prices, and firms have been compelled to expand and restructure sales organizations. Consumption of many products has increased sharply, apparently from changes in marketing policy.

DONALD S. HENLEY*

Marketing and economic integration in developing countries

INTRODUCTION

The last decade has been singularly marked by a number of attempts—some successful—at economic union in both the developed and underdeveloped areas of the world. Insofar as the latter areas are concerned, the most advanced movements are to be found in Latin America. The Central American Common Market (CACM) is a fully functioning entity with virtually no trade barriers between the member countries, a common external tariff, a regional development bank, and a number of viable regional administrative organizations. The Latin American Free Trade Area (LAFTA) is considerably less advanced than the CACM, but nonetheless encouragingly alive given the many hurdles confronting a full-fledged Latin American common market.

The bulk of the literature dealing with Latin American economic integration concentrates almost exclusively on the impact of union on investment activity and production costs. Essentially, those intimately concerned with a Latin American common market have argued that regional groupings, by the very fact of their existence, will call forth investment in intermediate and capital goods industries. Uneconomically high costs associated with small national markets had heretofore been a deterrent to such investment. Further, specialization and rationalization of existing industry in the various member countries would occur as

---

* Michigan State University.

national economies were grouped, thus leading to increased efficiency and reduced costs.[1]

One cannot denigrate the importance of the effects briefly sketched above. There is good reason to believe, however, that the process through which these desired results occur is not nearly so automatic as seemingly implied in the literature. While the elimination, or at least reduction, of tariff barriers between countries provides a necessary condition for enlarged markets through increased intra-union trade, it does not provide a sufficient condition. There are additional marketing conditions which must be met before the businessman can, or will, respond to the opportunities of a common market. One may also question the nature of the impetus which leads to investment, rationalization, and specialization. Undoubtedly, certain entrepreneurs are drawn by opportunity; equally, others are pushed by competition. The literature largely ignores the latter possibility. Only the barest of implicit recognition is given the beneficial effects arising from the increased competition hopefully engendered by a common market movement. There is good reason to believe that a continuing impulse to growth will result from the clash of companies in the market place and the consequent changes in company practices.

The purpose of this paper is to explore (1) the issues of marketing factors and trade flows and (2) the effects of competitive activity on firm behavior. To a large extent, I will draw on material gathered in 1965 in the Central American Common Market.

SOME THEORETICAL CONSIDERATIONS

It is somewhat surprising that the literature dealing with integration of developing countries places so little emphasis on possible changes in the market place. A priori, it seems reasonable to assume that increased competition would have more than a little beneficial effect on production methods and capital investment, notwithstanding the possibility of some disinvestment. Furthermore, price and product policy adjustments in the face of competition, as well as those arising from new entrants to the markets, may be, as we shall see, important indeed.

James E. Meade is quite explicit with regard to the effect of price changes on consumption patterns, suggesting that the induced welfare effects may be equally as important, or more important than, the production location changes emphasized by Jacob Viner.[2] Scitovsky has force-

---

[1] There have been hopes, for example, that specialization in the auto and steel industries would be possible under the LAFTA agreements. See Raymond F. Mikesell, "The Movement Toward Regional Trading Groups in Latin America," in A. O. Hirschman (ed.), *Latin American Issues: Essays and Comments* (New York: Twentieth Century Fund, 1961), pp. 141, 142. Also, *The Latin American Common Market* (New York: United Nations Economic Commission for Latin America, 1959), p. 20.

[2] James E. Meade. *The Theory of Customs Unions* (Amsterdam: North Holland Publishing Co., 1955), pp. 35–41.

fully argued that the gains to Western Europe from economic integration were probably minimal in terms of the traditional trade-creating, trade-diverting analysis. But, they were likely to be substantial indeed if the effect of increased competition on company practices, especially in the marketing area, were considered. The structure of distribution channels and the enervating effect of traditional outlet practices were also considered by Scitovsky. He saw clear signs of the economic gains to be garnered as these distribution institutions were bypassed or forced to modernize under the pressure of a common market movement.[3] Gehrels and Johnston were equally insistent in arguing that the beneficial effects of increased competition within the EEC would be of far more consequence than any shifts in locus of production within the union.[4]

Although there is a great awareness of the relationship between size of market and production scale economies in the United States economy, there is perhaps less awareness that aggressive merchandising and a low-price, high-volume market orientation are probably at the root of American mass consumption. As one views the price and product policies of many Latin industrialists, there is a strong suspicion that any change in these must be for the better. To the extent that a common market movement forces competition between firms previously protected behind high tariff barriers, one could expect reduced prices, aggressive marketing, and product policy geared to consumer needs. Thus, the market may be widened on the basis of marketing activity.

The arguments presented thus far are, of course, predicated on the assumption that manufactured goods will flow between the member countries of a common market. Business firms must take those steps which make a common market a reality. It is perhaps gratuitous to note that entrepreneurs must be apprised of business opportunities in other union countries and must have access to transport and distribution channels to take advantage of these opportunities.

Raymond Vernon develops in considerable detail the problems of exporting manufactured goods from underdeveloped to developed countries; he notes that marketing factors may be equally as important as the traditional issues of production costs, freight costs, and trade barriers, and often may transcend these in importance.[5] Marketing considerations such as information about potential markets, awareness of consumer requirements, ability to penetrate distribution channels, and adaptation

---

[3] Tibor Scitovsky, *Economic Theory and Western European Integration* (London: Unwin University Books, 1962), pp. 20–32.

[4] Franz Gehrels and Bruce F. Johnston, "The Economic Gains of European Integration," *Journal of Political Economy*, August, 1955.

[5] Raymond Vernon, "Problems and Prospects in the Export of Manufactured Goods from the Less-Developed Countries," in United Nations Conference on Trade and Development Series, December, 1963.

or design of products for foreign markets are all items which bulk large in the flow of manufactured goods between underdeveloped and developed countries. It would be strange indeed if some of these issues were not equally relevant to the movement of manufactured goods *between* underdeveloped countries.

As Sidney Dell notes, when contrasting the rapid increases in intra-union trade in the EEC with relatively slower increases within LAFTA,

. . . in the EEC the channels of trade were all there ready made, transport facilities were available, and the necessary commercial contacts and relations could easily be resumed. In Latin America, on the other hand, it is a question of creating entirely new channels of trade, entirely new commercial contacts, and entirely new sources of supply and market outlets; of attempting, in many cases, to provide transport facilities between points which have never yet had anything of the kind.[6]

MARKETING FACTORS AND TRADE FLOWS

Experience in Central America strongly suggests that the removal of tariffs and related barriers between the CACM countries provided a necessary but not sufficient condition for increased trade. In-depth interviews with over 40 Central American firms indicated that marketing factors were, at certain points in time, the critically important concern in the flow of goods and that marketing barriers often prevented companies from moving into other Central American markets. It should be noted, however, that in the majority of cases these marketing barriers were eventually overcome.

In general, there appear to be three major marketing considerations in the flow of goods: (1) physical distribution, (2) orientation toward regional markets, and (3) securing of adequate distribution outlets.

Physical distribution

At first glance, the problems of physical distribution in a Latin American common market, and probably in most cases of union between underdeveloped countries, appear overwhelming. The historical patterns of trade are such that transport routes generally lead to the major seaports, and thence to the United States, Europe, and the Orient. Rarely are there established and well-traveled sea routes between the Latin American countries. Dell quotes some very revealing figures in this regard. For example, the freight rate for lumber shipped from Mexico to Venezuela was $24 per ton in 1963, compared to $11 from Finland to Venezuela; direct ocean shipment of chemicals from Tampico to Buenos

[6] Sidney Dell, *A Latin American Common Market?* (London: Oxford University Press, 1966), p. 75.

Aires was $54 per ton, whereas transshipment via New Orleans was $46 and transshipment via Southampton was $40; goods shipped from Porto Alegre in Brazil to Montevideo arrive more quickly if shipped via Hamburg.[7]

The factors underlying the transport situation described above are not difficult to unearth. Poorly maintained and equipped port facilities measurably add to the freight costs of goods moving intra-Latin America. Further, the lack of goods movement between the Latin countries necessarily reduces the frequency of service offered and the price at which that service is offered. Not surprisingly, the poor service and high costs act as a deterrent to those desirous of shipping goods. A series of road and rail projects is planned or underway to help alleviate the situation by providing alternative transport routes.[8] One could expect, also, that changes in airfreight would go far toward removing the apparent existing transport bottleneck.

There are indications, however, that the picture is not nearly so bleak as often painted. For example, Hoselitz noted in the early 1950's that road and rail transport problems seriously hampered trade movement between the Central American countries.[9] However, by 1965 there appeared to be no major difficulties in moving goods intra-CACM. A response-to-need occurrence of the type suggested by Hirschman had taken place. As traffic between the CACM countries increased, the regional trucking firms necessary to move products efficiently and reliably developed. Indeed, by 1965 spirited competition on the well-traveled routes was in evidence. Furthermore, over a decade freight rates were halved as volume increased. A circular cause-effect relationship undoubtedly existed, as lower rates meant increased movement of goods, and increased traffic permitted lower charges.

Even within the broad reaches of Latin America there is evidence that trade routes are open. Smugglers, for example, have often managed very well to surmount transport problems. The influx of smuggled food items, ready-made clothing, and plastic manufactures into Bolivia is a clear illustration of the ease with which traffic in manufactured goods can move. While road, rail, and air links will clearly have to be improved, there is reason to believe that the enterprising entrepreneur can solve many transport problems.

In the early stages of integration, it is critical to eliminate all-too-frequent border tie-ups at customs posts. A recent Bolivian-Argentine contretemps has probably been duplicated throughout the length of Latin America. In this particular case, permission to import some 20 freight

---

[7] Dell, *op.cit.*, p. 101.

[8] *Time*, April 21, 1967, pp. 28–29.

[9] Bert F. Hoselitz, "Economic Development in Central America," *Weltwirtschaftliches Archiv*, Band 76 (1956).

cars of Bolivian bananas duty free into Argentina had been granted in Buenos Aires. Unfortunately, news of this relaxation of regulations did not reach the border tariff station most intimately involved. As a result, the bananas sat on a siding and rotted while the matter was adjudicated. Clearly, no businessman dealing in perishables or faced with delivery deadlines will continually submit himself to such harassment and risk. For all practical purposes, a common market will simply be removed from his marketing decisions.

There is some danger that a piecemeal approach to economic integration, i.e., the phased freeing of products such as practiced and envisioned by LAFTA, will not alleviate and may intensify the type of problem described above. It is far easier for a border official to pass all products than to be forced to distinguish between various types of duty-free, preferential-duty, and full-duty items. Indeed, the room for maneuver for the traditional bribe is somewhat staggering to the imagination. On the other hand, complete free-trade conditions between common market countries considerably reduces the scope for such extracurricular activity.

Orientation toward regional markets

Historically, industrialists in developing countries have concentrated their sales efforts almost exclusively on the domestic market. A fundamentally important question is whether this orientation will change, and change substantially, with the development of a common market, thus leading to increased and continuing investment activity. While the Central American and early LAFTA experience suggest a yes answer, the response is somewhat qualified and dependent on the time horizon under consideration.

Highly restrictive tariff barriers between the Latin countries have probably been among the strongest forces shaping a domestic market orientation in Latin America. As a practical matter for the businessman, a critical concern certainly must be the manner in which the historical tariff barriers will be dismantled. In a business community which traditionally has looked to government for protection, one suspects that the elimination of duties and quotas must be an irrevocable certainty, else the highly realistic suspicion exists that too much competition will bring reimposed government restrictions on trade movements.

The problem is clearly seen in the present LAFTA treaty. Items placed on the National Schedule may be removed without great difficulty upon the giving of one year's notice. One questions whether many businessmen would make major investments and organizational changes under these uncertain conditions of continued access to regional markets. Contrast this with the CACM situation in which a major political action is now required to abrogate the existing common market structure. I know of at least one Central American industry in which local firms went out of business and could not, as in the past, appeal to their government for protection from imports proceeding from another Central American country. The company which initiated and survived the competitive struggle had made a substantial capital investment to cut costs and serve a multicountry market precisely because it knew that the old barriers would not be reimposed.

Thus, as one looks at the effect of tariff-reducing policies on firm behavior, there is good reason to believe that the tentative tariff-cutting procedures used so far by LAFTA will simply not bring forth the desired regional orientation of the business community. In my view, the policy followed by the CACM of complete and irrevocable tariff removal for most items, and a definite timed removal on interim protected items, is requisite to bring forth a major reorientation of the business community.

Now, what impels a manager to look outside his national market when tariff barriers are reduced or eliminated? It is assumed in the traditional literature that manufacturers will continually scan the horizon, both domestic and international, for market opportunities. The truth, at least in the developing countries, is that this scanning likely does *not* occur. It is reasonably clear that entrepreneurs in developing countries have been less than marketing oriented in domestic, not to mention international, markets.[10] In many countries, high tariffs imposed to foster new industries have virtually ensured companies a market for whatever they could produce. As a result of the ensuing paucity of competition, few managers have been forced to think imaginatively of their price, product, or merchandise policies.

A realignment of managerial priorities and orientation may, of course, occur naturally as market forces evolve. Increasing incidence of overcapacity in such disparate industries as autos and textiles suggests that the time when a Latin American entrepreneur could confidently depend on his national market for continued and profitable growth may be approaching an end. One of the major pressures for integration in Latin American, in fact, comes from the desire to expand market size for existing industries.

It just may be, also, that a truly definitive movement toward economic integration, such as occurred in Central America in 1960–62, will substantially extend the market horizons of the entrepreneur. The mystique

---

[10] David Carson notes the lack of marketing orientation of European firms. David Carson, *International Marketing; A Comparative Systems Approach* (New York; John Wiley & Sons, Inc., 1967), pp. 195–97. There is little reason to doubt that the same mentality permeates much of the manufacturing sector in the developing countries. In Bolivia, for example, considerably more time is expended on business-government relations than on marketing.

of a common market movement could jolt managers out of their traditional habits. The Central American experience suggests the validity of the argument. Virtually every one of the some 40 firms interviewed by the author in 1965 had invested or were seriously planning a major investment predicated on a five-country market. For the most part, these investments and plans were made following the 1960–62 radical shift in the Central American integration movement. Whether the LAFTA, with its more measured and circumscribed movement toward integration, will significantly alter entrepreneurial expectations and actions is an unanswerable, but important, question.

Another impediment, at least in the short run, to the grasping of common market opportunities may be the lack of reliable production and consumption data in underdeveloped countries. Direct observation of market conditions and opportunities by the entrepreneur is hampered by the difficulties of communication and lack of inexpensive passenger transport between the countries. In situations where there has been little or no historical contact between countries, the uncertainties involved would seem to militate against early substantial investment in capital equipment or marketing to service a common market. Of course, tentative early steps may well be taken in exporting and these may lead to full reorientation of the company's marketing strategy. However, it should be noted that for a variety of products halfhearted efforts may never attain market penetration sufficient to induce the company to reorient itself.

No discussion of the ability and willingness of firms to orient themselves towards a regional market would be complete without an appreciation of the peculiar role played by the international firm. Indeed, the apparent advantage which the foreign international firm has in orienting itself to a common market and exploiting it at the expense of native firms has been noted with some concern.[11] The international firm is, by definition, accustomed to operating multinationally. To the extent that it has operations in more than one country, it has access to information on market conditions and opportunities. By concentrating its production facilities to service a multination market it will most likely reduce costs and therefore has an incentive to consider its operations on a common-market-wide scale.

Constricted distribution channels

In his *Barriers to New Competition*, Bain suggests that marketing barriers to entry by a new firm can be substantial, if not precluding. The type of barrier can be dichotomized as difficulty in (1) obtaining con-

---

[11] See, for example, Dell, *op. cit.*, chap. x, and *The Latin American Common Market*, p. 12.

sumer awareness and providing impetus to shift from an established brand and/or (2) penetrating established distribution channels.[12]

In the former case, the potential new entrant may be required to spend considerably more in advertising and promotion than existing firms merely to acquaint the public with his product, i.e., to surmount the existing identification of a generic product with a specific brand name. Further, to induce change the new entrant is often required to substantially outspend the existing brands. The resultant outlays required to establish a new product may make return on investment marginal at best. Entry is forestalled. In other cases, distribution channels normally associated in the mind of a consumer with a certain product may be preempted by existing firms. For some products, existing distribution outlets may be essential for postsale servicing of a product. In either or both situations, the aspiring firm must either forego entry or develop new channels to the consumer.

With regard to entrance in competition with established brands, I know of no systematic study of brand preference in Latin America. A number of Latin American businessmen have suggested that a major consumer reaction to be overcome is that of negative attitudes toward other Latin-country products. Apparently it has been difficult enough for locally manufactured items to gain acceptance in the early stages of industrialization, without bringing to the consumer further uncertainty in the form of a product from another developing country.[13]

Problems of consumer education may be substantial in areas with low levels of literacy. The popularity of transistor radios could, however, somewhat alleviate this problem. In a study of consumption patterns in two rural Bolivian Altiplano villages, Lindley found fairly high recognition of radio advertising messages, with recognition correlated with level of education and income.[14]

It is difficult, of course, to generalize on the effect of radio on legitimizing brand names. Far more research needs to be done on the effect of mass communication on consumption patterns in developing countries. At best, one can say that the first pioneers in intraregional trade will probably pave the way for later entrants. In Central America, at least, few manufacturers expressed concern over the problem of consumer acceptance per se or excessive advertising costs to penetrate a market.

---

[12] Joe S. Bain, *Barriers to New Competition* (Cambridge, Mass.: Harvard University Press, 1962), chap. iv.

[13] On the other hand, a Guatemalan producer of plastic consumer goods claimed that his products would have had greater acceptance in his home market if they had been stamped "Made in El Salvador."

[14] David K. Lindley, "Communication, Consumption and other Modernization Variables in Two Rural Bolivian Altiplano Villages," (Unpublished master's thesis, Michigan State University, 1968).

Whether they were correct in their assessment of market conditions is, of course, another matter, although it appeared they were correct.

Central American businessmen were far more concerned with another aspect of regional marketing—that of obtaining adequate distribution in other CACM countries. Simply stated, the major problem lay with the inability or unwillingness of traditional importer-distributors to provide necessary merchandising support and follow-through for manufacturers. While these distributors were quite prepared to carry a line and stock it, they were not prepared to "push" the product.

This attitude of traditional distributors was not so debilitating in the national market where manufacturers often utilized missionary salesmen, or could go direct if they so desired. In export markets, however, the use of missionary salesmen or direct sales forces was not a step lightly taken —depending on the volume of sales, of course. Firms whose products required a strong sales effort to achieve entry in the face of established products experienced the greatest difficulty with traditional distributors.

Not all wholesalers were guilty of poor service. And, in some product categories such as cement and cotton textiles, the distribution problem was minor. However, in most consumer goods products difficulties with traditional distributors were sufficient to induce a number of Central American firms to set up wholly owned sales forces and warehouses in other CACM countries. In some cases the investment in equipment, inventories, and accounts receivable was as high as $100,000 per country.

Thus, while marketing barriers to entry were quite high in certain product categories in the early years of the CACM, Central American businessmen proved willing to invest to overcome those barriers. For some companies, the major deterrent to a CACM-wide sales force was a lack of expertise in organizing and managing a multicountry sales force. Almost all companies experienced difficulties in finding and training salesmen who could operate effectively in a generally unsupervised situation.

Foreign-affiliated firms were often in the best position to overcome marketing barriers. In the paint industry, for example, pre-CACM export activity by U.S. firms resulted in the development of a chain of distributors throughout Central America. With the advent of the CACM and local manufacture by affiliates, these distributors were in place and readily available to the new Central American firm. The same advantages were held by the international detergent firms when they started production in Central America. Such companies as Grace with local affiliates in two or more countries were able to utilize these firms to handle multiple lines and thus achieve adequate distribution without the expense and problem of starting a new sales force. This pattern of foreign advantages is likely to repeat itself in the LAFTA.

The Central American experience suggests, then, that there are some substantial marketing barriers to trade. However, these barriers can be surmounted over time, and businessmen appear willing to take the necessary steps to overcome them.

THE IMPACT OF THE MARKET PLACE ON PRODUCTION AND CONSUMPTION

As noted earlier, major stress is placed in the literature on the impact of integration on new investment and production specialization. To a large extent, the beneficial effects of competition in inducing new investment, plant modernization, and product specialization is discounted. In addition, the impact of price, product, and merchandising policy on consumer demand is almost completely neglected. In this section we indicate a number of ways in which the free play of market forces can help bring about precisely those effects which the proponents of integration desire.

Market forces and investment activity

ECLA economists appear to argue that investment activity in a common market results more or less automatically from the attraction of multicountry markets which can be serviced economically from one production location within the market. While this "automatic" response may be true in a number of cases, investment within a common market may also be the result of a company's desires to protect established market positions. A number of students of the foreign investment decision have noted the tendency to invest in response to a competitor's move, the major incentive being to maintain market share.[15] There is no reason to believe that an investment decision placed in a common market setting will be terribly different.

A review of investments made in new Central American companies suggests that market incentives were at least as important as production-cost incentives. In the paint industry, for example, the first U.S.-affiliated firm was drawn by the opportunity to obtain a substantial hold on the whole Central American market, thus gaining a substantial jump on future competitors. This investment move was soon followed by a local distributor of an American firm, who entered into a licensing arrangement for local paint production. The distributor noted that his investment had been triggered by a desire to maintain a profitable product line, which was now threatened by local production protected by a substantial tariff.

---

[15] Yair Aharoni, *The Foreign Investment Decision* (Cambridge, Mass.: Harvard Business School, 1966), pp. 65–68.

While perhaps less clear-cut situations, the entrance of the large international detergent firms into the CACM appeared to be in part a response to the production and sales activity of local firms. A multicountry market was important, but not overridingly so, to gain certain scale economies. Entrance into the CACM by the major Spanish match producer was predicated on this group's perception of production scale economies to be gained. These scale economies were, however, expected to be made possible as a result of instituting merchandising and product-line policies substantially different from those followed by existing firms.

Of course, not all new investment in the CACM has been triggered by competitive forces or responses to the marketing activity of other firms. In any number of cases, firms invested because a larger market made local production economically feasible and the various development law benefits made supplying the market by local production more attractive than exporting. The point is, though, that competitive and marketing factors have played a major role in inducing new investment in the CACM countries.

A trend toward increased productivity and lowered costs is a hoped-for result of a common market movement. The usual argument is that small national markets restrict use of the most efficient equipment, which tends to be highly capital-intensive and geared to large-volume output. With a multinational market, investment in such equipment may be feasible.

Although low levels of productivity in the underdeveloped countries are in large measure a by-product of small markets and insufficient mechanization, one cannot ignore the effect of other, less tangible variables on productivity. Many firms may be operating with obsolete, inefficient equipment because of high protective tariffs and lack of competition. Poor management practices and attitudes are a further deterrent to increased productivity.

Two United Nations studies of Latin American industry—one made in 1950 in the textile industry and the other in 1954 in the metalworking industry—strongly suggest that low productivity levels are due at least as much to poor management as to insufficient mechanization or small plant size.[16] Increased competition, with an attendant profit squeeze, could be expected to force changes in managerial practices and equipment use.[17] These changes may not be easy to make, even under competitive stress; they may not be attempted, however, without an external stimulus.

---

[16] *Iron and Steel Transforming Industries in Selected Latin American Countries* (New York: United Nations, 1955) pp. 76–88, 134–43. *Labor Productivity of the Cotton Textile Industry* (New York: United Nations, 1951), pp. 1–16.

[17] In the textile study cited above, the evidence suggested that a greater modernity of equipment in Peruvian mills, in comparison with mills in the other countries studied, is due in part to the competitive pressure of textile imports.

The motivating force behind many investments by the Central American firms studied appears to substantiate the view that competitive pressures can force modernization and specialization. Perhaps the most obvious situation was that of the Nicaraguan textile firms. Woefully inefficient, these firms invested heavily in new equipment as they took advantage of a five-year transitional period in which they were protected by a declining tariff from other Central American producers. According to projections by an independent textile consultant, these firms reduced their unit costs by some 20 percent as a result of this forced investment.

Under somewhat less pressure, a Salvadorean candy firm invested heavily in laborsaving equipment to meet increasing competition from other CACM firms. The manager of this firm felt that there would be increasingly downward pressure on prices, and hence a need to modernize plant and equipment and lower costs. An edible oil firm invested in a wholly new plant which utilized a lower-cost raw material, as increasing pressure from other Central American producers threatened its position in two major markets. One of the largest Central American match firms put into operation a number of productivity-increasing machines in order to meet the competition of a foreign firm which had newly entered the Central American market.

A move toward product specialization was most noticeable in the textile industry. Scale economies are such in this industry that small firms can survive profitably only if they specialize, at the same time providing a price and service which reduce the attractiveness of these small-volume lines to the larger firms. Under the pressure of the larger firms, and given the enlarged market of the CACM, at least three of the smaller Central American textile firms had narrowed their product line and reduced costs.

Price and product policy

As noted, relatively little emphasis is placed on changes in price levels and product type and quality which result from economic integration. The question of product offering is, however, by no means irrelevant to the problem of inducing a dynamic manufacturing sector within a common market.

Market size in many underdeveloped countries may well be restricted as much by high prices and inadequate adaptation of products to consumer requirements, as by low income levels. Often, local producers of import-substituting products will set their prices just under the protective umbrella afforded by tariffs. The effect of such a price policy is generally to stifle demand. Costs are therefore high because production economies cannot be gained. The typical vicious circle ensues, for with high costs, prices cannot be lowered; with a small volume of production, there is a low level of employment, further restricting demand; etc., etc.

To the extent that products are of the same type and quality of previously imported items, the market may be unduly limited to the upper-middle and upper classes. Lower quality, different pricing and packaging policies, etc., may draw a new group of low- and middle-class consumers into the market, thus stimulating output, investment, and employment.

The issues of price and product type appear, therefore, to be of some concern. First, as import substitution occurs through new entrants into an industry or expanded intra-union trade, what are the effects of product offering? Second, what is the impact of increased intra-union trade on the price and product policy actions of firms in industries in which there is no import substitution?

The Central American data tend to support the view that dynamic price and product policy changes occur as a result of economic integration. The CACM had a major import-substituting effect in three industries studied—detergents, fruit juices, and paints. The data show that substantial changes in price levels and product offering occurred as a result of local production of these items.

In the case of detergents, prices after the start of local manufacture were 67 to 75 percent of the previous import level, with no reduction in product quality. These price reductions, coupled with vigorous merchandising resulted in rapid increases in detergent consumption in Central America, with sales doubling in the four years following the entrance of large international firms. Central American consumption had increased only 50 percent in the previous five years. Local manufacture of fruit juices had an even more dramatic impact on prices than did the start of detergent manufacture, as prices were halved.[18] In addition, can sizes were reduced so that unit price was within the reach of low- and middle-class purchasers. An aggressive policy of merchandising was undertaken. Sales rose dramatically as new purchasers were brought into the market, with Central American consumption doubling within two years of the start of local manufacture and increasing sevenfold within five years.

Local manufacture of paints had a profound effect on both the product variety offered the consumer and the price at which he purchased. Initial manufacturing in the region was undertaken by local firms who produced a medium-quality paint at 50 to 60 percent of the price of the

---

[18] Experience in other food products manufactured in Central America in the last few years suggests that the price movements in juice are not unique. For example, the price of baby food was reduced 25 percent and Gerber's was forced to follow suit on its imported line. The wholesale price of tomato paste dropped 76 percent with the start of local manufacture, and the retail price of catsup was reduced 61 percent.

imported high-quality variety. These companies offered a product which was probably oriented more nearly to the level of Central American development, and as a consequence soon gained substantial market share.

As internationally affiliated firms began production, they did not at first move into medium-priced paints, preferring to remain in the high-priced market which they had previously supplied through imports. The price of these paints was, however, reduced by some 20 percent with the start of local manufacture. Market pressures soon forced a large scale shift into the medium-priced lines. With the advent of local manufacture and adjusted product policies, consumption shifted within a few years from 100 percent high-priced paints to 25 percent high and 75 percent medium-priced. While the demand for paints did not appear to increase because of these price and product policies, it is clear that the consumer was offered a product more nearly suited to his needs, and received more purchasing power to direct toward other manufactured goods.

Increased competition in existing industries developed concurrently with the elimination of trade barriers. Even in industries fairly new to the region—detergents, fruit juices, and paints—competition soon forced changes in marketing policy. In detergents, prices had held fairly steady for two or three years following the start of local manufacture. By late 1965, however, the three large international firms had bought out the local firms and were prepared to do battle with each other for market share. To what extent this competition would result in lower prices, increased advertising, or merchandise giveaways is unknown. Early indications were that prices would fall.

With regard to fruit juices, some price competition had occurred as the two largest Central American firms jousted with each other. A price decline of 15 percent resulted. As of late 1964, prices had stabilized and further declines were not anticipated. Price reductions in the order of 10 percent were recorded in the paint industry as Central American production and intra-union trade increased rapidly. As in fruit juices, prices had stabilized by 1965, and there were indications that competitive tactics had shifted to improved quality, better dealer service, and more attractive packaging and merchandising. Also, as noted earlier, increased competition had forced a shift for some firms from production of high-priced to medium-priced paints.

Substantial changes in competitive action arising from the CACM were noted in three other industries studied—candy, cement, and cotton textiles. Price declines ranging from 10 to 40 percent, depending on product type, were recorded in the candy industry. In addition, certain firms which had comfortably survived pre-CACM quality control problems found that post-CACM competition did not permit this luxury. As a result, changes in production equipment and methods were instituted in order to retain traditional markets. Intra-union trade also gave consumers a greater choice of products and permitted wider distribution for the major Costa Rican producer, which reputedly offered the highest quality products in the region.

Downward price pressures were evident in the cement industry, particularly in the Salvadorean and Nicaraguan markets. Notwithstanding the protective effects of freight costs, prices declined 10 to 15 percent. As freight costs continue to drop and road improvements are made, further price reductions, especially in the Nicaraguan market, are expected.

Price competition in the Central American textile industry started in the lower quality goods as local production increasingly substituted for imported products and brought local firms into competition with each other. Price declines of 10 to 20 percent were noted in the heavier drills and twills. To a large extent companies have attempted to avoid price competition by shifting output into new product lines either not produced or produced in small quantities in the region. Thus, when consumption of grey goods and heavier finished drills and twills was filled by local supply and prices weakened, firms started shifting into lighter goods, printed goods, and special finish items. As a result, competition has been an incentive for new product introduction, as well as a spur to lower prices.

As might be expected, the Central American scene is not one in which every industry is fiercely competitive. There are some industries in which firms have come to market-sharing agreements. It can be fairly stated, though, that these industries were more the exception than the rule in 1965. Indeed, there was some indication that new entrants into previously cartelized industries, with their vision of region-wide markets, would destroy the existing cartels. This was true in the match industry. With the entrance of a Spanish group which refused to abide by previous industry market-sharing agreements, the Central American match industry became competitive to the point of driving two firms out of business.

SUMMARY

The available data from Central America suggest strongly that marketing considerations are critical in the process of economic integration. As noted, marketing barriers to entry were quite high in certain product categories. In many cases, firms were compelled to develop wholly owned sales forces in other regional markets, as traditional distributors were not adequate for the task. A major finding of the Central American case was the willingness and ability of firms eventually to overcome marketing barriers.

Any unbiased reading of the data leads one to the conclusion that marketing factors are critical in investment decisions. This proved to be

true in Central America in the case of new investment and in modernization and specialization of existing operations. Further, import substitution and competition brought both lowered prices and adaptation of
products to meet the needs of lower-income groups. In certain product
categories the increase in consumption attendant with these changes in
marketing policy was truly startling.

From his unique vantage point in the United Nations Food and Agriculture Organization, Mr. Abbott determines the extent to which national economic plans take marketing into account. In most cases marketing gets short shrift. The paper is rich with examples of planning failures resulting from inattention to marketing.

J. C. ABBOTT*

Marketing issues in agricultural development planning

The marketing content of most national development plans is at present very low. Agriculture is the main source of national income in most developing countries. Yet none of the 13 current plans examined in the course of this study assigned a major role to the marketing of agricultural products in their development strategies. In only three did the financial allocation to marketing exceed 6 percent of total expected investment in agriculture. The low status of marketing, both in policy statement and budgetary provision, could reflect two situations.

One might be a belief that the marketing problems would find their own solution more efficiently than if an attempt were made to solve them in the plan: that production developments aside from the main market demand would adjust themselves as discrepancies became evident; and that existing marketing enterprises would adapt, or new ones be formed, to meet the supply situation as it developed. This would be a traditional laissez-faire attitude. It would, however, be directly inconsistent with recognition of the need to plan production evidenced by the decision to formulate a plan in the first place. Moreover, there is little doubt that the market economy, left to itself in underdeveloped countries, often gives the wrong answers. Prices do not correctly reflect relative costs; opportunities for reducing risks through coordinated action are neglected; insufficient allowance is made for the value of knowledge acquired through unprofitable activities.[1] The striking growth of the maize export and kenaf industries in Thailand has been attributed to "a marketing system,

---

* United Nations Food and Agriculture Organization.

[1] W. A. Lewis, *Development Planning* (London: Allen & Unwin, Ltd., 1965), p. 18.

itself created in response to profit opportunities opened up by new external demands." However, it could go still further with specific assistance. In this context R. J. Muscat maintains that "A primary objective . . . of Thai economic policy should be to assist the marketing apparatus to function as aggressively and efficiently as possible. Such a policy should include measures to improve bulk transportation facilities and reduce transport costs, rationalization of the government's scattered agricultural information-gathering and dissemination agencies and improvement in their operation, encouragement of private investment in facilities that will improve processing and marketability (e.g., mechanical kenaf-decorticating equipment, maize-drying plants, maize bulk shipping), etc."[2]

The second possibility is that most of the present batch of development plans are drawn up by bodies with little interest in marketing, or inadequately briefed on it because they have not foreseen any need to seek specialized advice and assistance. One of the main themes of this paper is to demonstrate that this second situation is indeed widely prevalent, and to examine the consequences.

FORMULATION AND CONTENT OF NATIONAL DEVELOPMENT PLANS

Marketing participation in plan formulation

Review of the arrangements made for the preparation of some half-dozen area development plans in Mediterranean countries showed a participation by marketing specialists of only 3 to 5 percent.[3] These figures are based on man-months of service in the advisory team, with "marketing" construed very broadly to include work on cooperatives, storage, transport, and processing.

There is little to suggest that marketing is allocated a higher proportion of specialized time in the drawing up of most national plans. It certainly would not appear so from the requests received for international technical assistance, and resources of marketing "know-how" in the developing countries cannot be regarded as so strong relative to other professional fields as to support an assumption that local marketing specialists were filling the gap. The heads of the agricultural marketing departments in India and Pakistan for example, put in proposals over the

---

[2] R. J. Muscat, *Development Strategy in Thailand—a Study of Economic Growth* (New York, 1966), quoted in J. P. Gittinger, *Planning for Agricultural Development; the Iranian Experience* (Washington: National Planning Association, 1965), p. 36.

[3] J. C. Abbott, "Marketing and Area Development Studies," in *Toward Scientific Marketing*, Proceedings of the Ninth Conference of the American Marketing Association, Boston, December, 1963.

rather limited program areas of their departments and attend meetings of planning committees. Here they express *ad hoc* views on project propos- als which have proved valuable; but they cannot be said to participate in major planning decisions. In most other developing countries there is no such specialized internal representation of "marketing," and the extent of its consideration depends on the degree to which commerce or other ministries and general economic advisers are interested.

It is not even clear that the academic and professional authorities on planning allow a significant place for marketing studies. Arthur Lewis makes no mention of marketing when discussing the staffing of a plan- ning organization or the committees through which it would work.[4] He envisages committees established by industries, e.g., textiles, livestock; by institutions, e.g., company law, cooperatives; and by public services, e.g., roads, education—but not on marketing. The writings of Chenery, Hig- gins, and Waterston[5] show little marketing interest. Price Gittinger takes up marketing issues from time to time in his case study of planning in Iran, but investment in marketing got little priority in the eventual plan.[6]

Marketing content of plans

Increased awareness of the importance of marketing efficiency on the part of governments in the developing regions is evidenced over the last five years by a sharp increase in requests to FAO for assistance in advice and training. It has not yet, however, been reflected in their development planning.

Very few of the plans examined assigned a major heading to market- ing. The chapter on "communications and marketing" in the agricultural plan for Ethiopia comes nearest. Guaranteed prices, fruit and vegetable marketing, and fertilizer distribution receive fairly extensive treatment in the development proposals for Ceylon. Otherwise 4½ pages of text in the India plan out of 430 in total would be representative.

The need to improve quality to maintain sales on export markets is a preoccupation of almost all the plans, usually to be met by improved processing and quality control. Only in African countries such as Kenya and Chad do the nature and organizational links of the marketing enter- prise receive significant attention.

The requirements of domestic marketing receive relatively little atten- tion: the references in the Indian plan to minimum price programs, cooperatives, storage, and training of inspectors and public market

---

[4] Lewis, *op. cit.*, p. 247.

[5] A. Waterston, *Development Planning; Lessons of Experience* (Baltimore, Md.: Johns Hopkins Press, 1965).

[6] Gittinger, *op. cit.*

officials are more specific than in most. The Libya and Venezuela plans reflect ability and intention to mount substantial price stabilization and support operations, but do not discuss implementation. There is a definite tendency, as in Ecuador for example, to propose the establishment of a government department of marketing services, of a public trading enterprise to help stabilize prices, and possible export and milk marketing boards, without providing information either on the method of operation or the source of funds.

In Table 1 an attempt has been made to identify financial allocations for marketing and related development headings in a cross section of current plans. The median ratio of marketing outlays to outlays on agriculture as a whole is around 4 percent. The high figure for Libya includes an important element of agricultural price subsidization feasible because of the government's oil revenues. Ratios of 8–9 percent in Ceylon and Tanganyika reflect major public investment in storage and equipment for government and cooperative purchasing systems.

Planned investment in transport facilities and communications seems to be on a par with that in agriculture as a whole. Assessment of the proportion attributable to marketing has not been attempted for such a multiple-use investment. However, in countries with such immense distances between production and export or consumption centers as Ethiopia, Iran, and Tanganyika the benefits accruing to "marketing" will be substantial.

A number of plans also envisage major public and private investment in plants intended to process agricultural raw materials. These also contribute directly to marketing efficiency by creating a new intermediate market—though in the Korean plan, for example, they are seen primarily as meeting rising consumer demand. However, only in the plan for Chad does the total allocation to marketing and processing match the ratio to value of agricultural output considered desirable, for example, by L. Lorinez following his Latin American studies.[7]

Criteria for appraising the adequacy of investment in marketing, processing, and transport facilities have still to be developed. The volume of agricultural output will be a basic element, but the proportion available for sale, the number of independent producing enterprises, the nature of their output and of the markets to which it is to be directed, and the intensity of the need to earn foreign exchange are also critical variables. Insofar as the existing infrastructure in developing countries is weak and the need to offer incentives to increase output great, relatively

[7] His estimates of investment requirements in central and livestock auction markets, refrigerated and other storage, flour, rice, and oilseed mills, sugar processing, slaughterhouses, dairy plants, and fruit and vegetable packing and canning in five western Latin American countries amount to 2.6 percent of the annual value of agricultural output. L. Lorinez, "Marketing Western South America," unpublished contribution to FAO studies for the World Indicative Plan (Rome: FAO, 1966).

more attention to marketing would be appropriate there than in countries already more advanced.

Of the investment considered so far, almost all has been in fixed plant and facilities. While some advisory, extension, and training work conducive to marketing improvement may be carried out under other budgets plan, provision for organizational development in marketing is minor indeed.

Behind this apparently one-sided approach to development may lie a lack of effective tools to determine the factors strategic in output growth and the relative weight to be given them. Economic measurements such as cost-benefit ratios and the internal rate of return can be used in appraising alternative irrigation projects and a palm oil plantation project as against a fertilizer plant. They have not yet been developed to general use in determining priorities as between projects for physical inputs and extension and training services or measures to ensure economic incentives and improve marketing performance.

The problem lies not so much in assessing the effects of alternative measures. An increase in returns for certain produce because marketing costs have been reduced or sales methods are more effective, or ability to sell a larger quantity without reduction in price because of market development or price stabilization measures, can be measured. It can be set as an average increment in returns against increments in returns that result from security against drought because of irrigation facilities or higher yields because of fertilizer applications.

The difficulty lies in assessing how great an increase in returns will incur to the farmer from a given expenditure on market research, marketing extension, improvement of storage and packing methods, training of marketing management, sales promotion and advertisement, etc. Here there is little to go on except experience—examples where positive action has brought impressive results or situations where neglect of marketing considerations has led to great disappointments and wastage of investments in production resources. Pending the availability of more precise tools, this study is based perforce on a pragmatic analysis of experience in a cross section of developing countries in Africa, Asia, the Near East, and Latin America.

The form of a marketing system will depend largely on the national policies and economic structure of the country concerned including the socioeconomic structure of agriculture, landlord/tenant relationship, etc. These can vary between the extremes of central socialist direction and near laissez-faire. Nevertheless, the need for conscious consideration and clear decisions is there. Experience is accumulating with a number of approaches in the provision of marketing organizations, methods, and services adapted to the needs of development programs; they are consonant with a wide range of market situations and political preferences.

Table 1

FINANCIAL OUTLAYS RELATED TO MARKETING: SELECTED DEVELOPMENT PLANS

	Total Value Agricultural Output[a]	Total Investment	Total Agriculture[b]	Transport and Communications[c]	Plants Processing Ag. Products[d]
Ceylon					
1966–70	663,180		271,740		8,547
Chad					
1966–70	143,709	190,397	95,664	51,444	12,732
Ecuador					
1964–73	339,966	2,277,550	166,650	388,850	
Ethiopia					
1962–67			21,840		
India					
1965/66–1969/70	10,797,300	31,658,750	5,697,242	4,685,495	55,980
Iran					
1965/66–1969/70	1,222,320	2,510,640	533,333	497,640	59,453
Kenya					
1964–70	327,320	910,000	178,080	124,040	38,080
Korea					
1967–71	1,037,960	3,616,458	778,358	727,668	12,450
Libya					
1963–68		473,480	82,040	64,120	840
Madagascar					
1964–68	253,876	441,559	156,369	194,043	
Pakistan					
1965–70	4,200,000	10,920,000	1,820,700	1,472,310	147,000
Tanganyika					
1964/65–1968/69	393,680	688,800	103,600	74,480	3,360
Venezuela					
1965–68	483,062	6,381,584	1,553,622	843,027	

[a] GDP at factor cost from agriculture including fishing and forestry in most recent year for which data available. Source: *Year Book of National Accounts and Statistics,* UN, 1965.

[b] Public and private allocation for agriculture, fishing, and forestry plus amount shown for plants processing agricultural products where not already included under agriculture.

[c] Public and private allocations for road, rail and water transport facilities and equipment, and for telecommunications.

[d] Meat and fruit canning plants; rice, grain, and oilseed mills; sugar refineries, tanneries, and pickling plants, etc.

[e] Cotton ginneries, tobacco drying ovens, coffee pulperies, slaughterhouses, milk cooling and pasteurization plants, silos, refrigerated and other storage, etc.

National currencies converted into U.S. dollars at 1966 official exchange rates.

Plan references

Ceylon, Ministry of Agriculture and Food, *Agricultural Development Proposals, 1966–70,* Colombo, Ministry of Planning and Economic Affairs, 1966.

Chad, *Premier Plan Quinquennal de Développement Economique et Social 1966–70,* Fort Lamy, Ministère du Plan et de la Coopération.

Ecuador, *Programa de Desarrollo Agropecuario 1964–73,* Quito, Junta Nacional de Planificación y Coordinación, 1964.

	Marketing				Marketing as % Total Agriculture	Marketing in Average Yr. of Plan as % of Total Value of Ag. Output	Marketing & Processing in Av. Yr. as % of Total Value of Ag. Output
Fixed Facilities[e]	Services and Development	Cooperatives	Fertilizers, Seeds, etc.	Total			
Thousands of U.S. Dollars							
18,417		4,326	1,491	24,234	8.9	0.7	1.0
4,497	12			4,509	4.7	0.6	2.4
4,555	889			5,388	3.2	0.2	
872	260			1,132	5.2		
........145,297........		90,644		235,941	4.1	0.4	0.5
10,890	990		1,320	13,200	2.5	0.2	1.2
2,352	112			2,464	1.4	0.1	1.8
15,007				15,007	1.9	0.3	0.5
........11,480........				11,480	14.0		
6,239				6,239	4.0	0.5	
47,040	6,300			57,540	3.2	0.3	1.0
784	644	8,120		9,548	9.2	0.5	0.7
8,888	53,328			62,216	4.0	0.3	0.3

Ethiopia, Ministry of Agriculture, Second Five Year Plan 1962–67, Addis Ababa.
India, Fourth Five Year Plan: a Draft Outline, Delhi, Planning Commission, 1966.
Iran, Agriculture Third Plan Frame 1962–67, Teheran, Plan Organization, Division of Economic Affairs, 1961.
Kenya, Five Year Development Plan 1966–70, Nairobi, Ministry of Economics Planning and Development.
Korea, The Second Five Year Economic Development Plan 1967–71, Seoul, Economic Planning Board, 1966.
Libya, Five Year Econimic and Social Development Plan 1963–68, Ministry of Planning and Development, 1963.
Madagascar, Plan Quinquennal 1964–68, Tananarive, Commissariat Général au Plan, 1964.
Pakistan, The Third Five Year Plan 1965–70, Islamabad, Planning Commission, 1965.
Tanzania, Tanganyika Five Year Plan for Economic and Social Development, July 1964–June 1969, Dar-es-Salaam, Government Printer, 1964.
Venezuela, Plan de la Nación 1965–68, Caracas, Oficina Central de Coordinación y Planificación, 1965.

RELATION OF MARKETING ISSUES TO PLAN IMPLEMENTATION

Overestimation of prospective market for planned additional output

The first stage at which market considerations enter the planning process is forecasting probable demand as a basis for fixing production targets. While looking for potential resources to exploit is one of the first elements in any planning to accelerate economic growth, decisions on how to use these resources and at what pace to put their products on the market must depend on an appraisal of the demand. This includes both the demands of a growing domestic population and the demands on international markets in which a country hopes to sell as a means of earning the foreign exchange it needs for development.

As regards broad projections of domestic demand for grains, fats, sugar, etc., on the basis of population and income trends, the tendency in the developing countries has been towards under- rather than overestimation. Rice production in East Pakistan (1964–65)—10.3 million tons— exceeded the planned target by 1.7 million tons, but there was no surplus; population and population growth may have been underestimated; perhaps also under estimated may have been the tendency for consumption at low levels in rural areas to rise with yields and incomes. Stevens finds the "most likely" ranges for long-run income elasticity of food at the retail level to be "much higher than those seen in many studies" which "suggests a more rapid rate of growth in demand for retail food during development than is generally indicated."[8] However, even basic market data depend much on informed guesses in the developing countries and, quoting Lewis "we have had plenty of wild estimates of population growth, national income per head, etc."[9]

Where less familiar or more specialized crops enter a plan, careful attention to consumer tastes, preferences and habits is essential. Examples of misjudgments of the market on such grounds are common. A nationwide campaign to increase potato production in Colombia initiated in 1956–57 turned out to be based on a serious miscalculation of demand. In the face of a surplus in established markets an attempt was made to sell more potatoes in the tropical maritime provinces; but here most consumers preferred sweet potatoes, yams, and cassava. Apparent consumer reluctance to buy refrigerated and frozen meat in the Near East and some Southeast Asian cities has negated investments in processing and transport facilities and blocked programs to expand income from livestock raising. Many of the officially sponsored programs to introduce

---

[8] Robert D. Stevens, *Elasticity of Food Consumption Associated with Changes in Income in Developing Countries* (Foreign Agricultural Economic Report No. 23 [Washington, D.C.: U.S. Department of Agriculture, March 1965]).

[9] Lewis, *op. cit.*, p. 21.

nutritionally valuable foods based on oilseed and fish flour protein have foundered upon the same rock of consumer resistance.

Planners seeing good technical prospects for a new production line may easily underestimate competition from alternatives even on the domestic market. Assured of protection against imports, plans to develop substantial poultry industries in Nigeria and Dahomey still ran into marketing difficulties before attaining their targets because of the availability of relatively lower priced beef and fish. A tree fruit development in the Kassala area of Sudan was eventually largely abandoned, unable to cover its transport costs in competition with other supplies on the Khartoum wholesale market. So long as there are any alternative supplies it has proved difficult to sell home-produced tea in Iran.

Excessive variability in the quality and volume of supply is a characteristic problem for processors and market organizers in developing countries. Frequently it has blocked the successful outcome of a development project. A striking example is the abandonment of the Liebig meat-packing plant at Kosti in Sudan after only a few months of operation. Commercial juice extraction has been hampered in a number of Mediterranean countries by the range of citrus varieties grown and the fact that fruit only came on offer to juice plants when the fresh market was unfavorable.

Estimation of future sales on export markets, subject to international competition where there can be no resort to protective quotas and tariffs, is hazardous indeed. Inability to meet disease and pest control regulations for meat, fruit, and vegetables, low priority in obtaining quotas where entry is restricted by volume controls, lack of appeal to consumers of different habits and tastes, opposition by traders associated with other suppliers, difficulties in organizing shipments to arrive at the correct time and in avoiding quality deterioration without excessive cost have effectively cut off export possibilities viewed optimistically at the outset of such programs.

OVERESTIMATION OF INCENTIVES TO PRODUCERS

Scientific methods of farming in general use in the more advanced countries, properly applied to the conditions of those economically less developed, could lead to immense increases in output.[10] This would call, however, for extra effort and cash outlay by farm operators, which they are likely to make only if there is a clear prospect of benefit thereby. While adequate incentives at the farm level will not guarantee that all farmers will make the additional efforts needed to increase production,

---

[10] W. H. Pawley, *Possibilities of Increasing World Food Production* (FFHC Basic Study No. 10 [Rome: FAO, 1963]).

their absence will certainly mean that such efforts are unlikely to be made. Often the incentive is much less than expected because of difficulties in marketing.

Transport, storage and processing

One of the most obvious obstacles is inability to get produce to a market for lack of suitable means of transport. Excessively high-cost transport whether in the form of direct charges per unit volume moved, or losses and quality deterioration en route in the case of perishable produce such as fruit and vegetables, eggs, milk, livestock, etc., have the same effect in many producing areas of canceling out incentives apparent in prices at central markets. Plans for growing on the slopes of the Jebel Marra apples, potatoes, grapes, and other temperate zone crops which could replace imports into the Sudan, must await the construction of a good road or rail connection to the present railhead. It is claimed that the meat requirements of Lima, Trujillo, and Chiclayo in Peru could be met by intensive production in the Huallaga valley over the first crest of the Andes.[11] For lack of an access road at present only small quantities of meat are brought out by air, and imports are needed.

The reconstruction of about 25,000 miles of secondary roads in East Pakistan in 1963/64 had the effect both of increasing product prices and of reducing factor costs in many heretofore isolated villages. Thus, roads helped to provide incentives for greater efforts and for additional output on the part of substantial numbers of farmers.

The need for storage facilities to protect agricultural products against deterioration after harvest and to hold them until needed by consumers and other buyers is clear. It follows that producers are likely to be deterred from increasing their output if there is a danger that it will deteriorate before it can be sold for lack of adequate storage, or if suitable storage would cost so much as to make the crop unprofitable. Specific instances of such effects are many. The San Lorenzo irrigation and settlement project authority in Peru found it necessary to provide storage for settlers' grain while awaiting sale with the alternative that heavy wastage losses would discourage continued production.[12] Further plantings of mango trees in suitable areas of Colombia are being held up because 20 percent of the present crop is wasted for lack of enterprises to freeze the pulp of those which cannot be sold fresh at a profit.

Lacking, however, in current analyses of additional storage requirements is quantitative appraisal of the losses occurring under existing

---

[11] B. Ortolo, FAO Planning Adviser, Report, October, 1966.

[12] R. F. Burdette, *Agricultural Marketing with Special Reference to the San Lorenzo Irrigation Project*, FAO/EPTA report, Rome, 1963.

conditions, of those which could be eliminated by a particular storage investment, and of the effective costs. There are far too many statements like "losses of farm stored staples in Africa often amounted to 20–30 percent, and in extreme cases to more than 50 percent,"[13] without any indication of their representativeness and the feasibility of reducing them by alternative methods, including simple precautions requiring little financial outlay. In West Africa, for example, losses in maize are thought to occur mainly in wholesale channels: on the farm, where most storage takes place, they may not reach 10 percent.[14]

As a problem in implementing development plans, storage difficulties probably show up greatest in the form of low prices for sales immediately after harvest, and this is due mainly to scarcity of capital to hold produce rather than the physical means to do so. This would certainly be the case in Western Nigeria where the purchase of maize at harvest time for a 100 percent seasonal price rise is considered the best investment for a man who has cash in hand from cocoa sales.

Cooperatives and public agencies newly entering produce purchasing and obliged to buy varying quantities to meet obligations to members or under price guarantees, have also found that storage difficulties may cause them to lose the confidence of the farmers they serve. Several of the grain price regulating agencies in Latin America have found themselves in this situation. Most underdeveloped countries find the maintenance of long-term food reserves too expensive in relation to other uses of the capital,[15] and depend on international aid to help them out when need arises.

Most development plans lay considerable stress on the establishment of effective processing enterprises. The first gain is in the avoidance of physical wastage, simplification of transport requirements, spreading of the period of consumption, and greater convenience for the consumer. The second is the introduction in the marketing system of a concentration point which may constitute a focus for strategic improvements in both supply and distribution channels.

Generally there is no lack of initiative in the developing countries to set up small-scale processing operations—rice husking, flour milling, livestock slaughtering, soft drink preparation, and the like. The usual problem is that the operators lack the capital to purchase and maintain efficient equipment which would get the most out of the products they

---

[13] Statement made at FAO/ECA Expert Meeting on Government Measures to Promote the Transition from Subsistence to Market Agriculture in Africa, Addis Ababa, 1964.

[14] C. H. Caswell, Department of Agricultural Biology, University of Ibadan, statement, August 1964.

[15] F. Shorter, "Foodgrains Policy in East Pakistan" in *Public Policy* (Cambridge, Mass.: Harvard University Press, 1959), pp. 107–26.

are handling, or else they operate on too small a scale to justify the preservation and sale of potentially valuable by-products. Rice bran is generally wasted in Ceylon and India and much valuable vegetable oil and protein lost because of poor processing equipment. Hides and skins, export foreign exchange earners in the Middle East and Africa, lose much of their potential value to the countries of those regions because of careless flaying, curing and handling practices.

Many governments have intervened directly to set up large-scale processing installations and to create conditions favorable to their operation. Public bodies such as the Kenya Meat Commission and the Rhodesian Cold Storage Commission have been established with monopoly powers to ensure that their processing installations obtain supplies in line with their capacity. Tea factories have been set up on a similar basis in Kivu, Congo (Kinshasa). In Sudan a large-scale tannery and fruit-canning plant built with bilateral aid has been operated directly by the Government. It is with such enterprises that operating costs are only too commonly excessive, as evidenced specifically by the three last examples.

Monopsony pricing at the farm level

A common criticism of pricing systems in the developing countries is that prices sufficiently high at the retail level to restrict consumption do not reflect themselves at the producers' level in prices which stimulate them to grow and market more of what is needed. Published statistics may overstate the prices that producers actually receive for two reasons: (a) Economic pressures on producers of seasonal crops may cause them to sell most of their output at harvest time, so that the weighted price they receive is much lower than the average prevailing through the year in wholesale markets. This may constitute an effective brake on expansion of output. (b) Farmers part with their produce before it reaches the markets covered by price reports. They sell in their own villages, and to merchants from whom they have received credit advances, and with whom, for this or other reasons, they are in a poor bargaining position.

The extent to which monopsonistic pressure at the farm level due to lack of competition between buyers, weak bargaining power on the part of sellers, credit ties, lack of market information, etc., obstruct producer response to plan targets is an open question.[16] Statements on this subject from the developing countries uniformly declare that most farmers are small occasional sellers, ignorant of market values and too indebted to local shopkeepers and merchants to be able to bargain for a fair price.

---

[16] G. R. Wharton Jr., "Marketing, Merchandising and Moneylending: A Note on Middlemen Monopsony in Malaya," *Malayan Economic Review*, Vol. VII, No. 2 (October, 1962), pp. 22–44.

Chronic indebtedness of farmers to money lenders is reported specifically for new settlement areas in Indonesia and Thailand, for example.[17] On the other hand the existence of a relatively large number of small independent buying enterprises is on the face of it ground for assuming near atomistic competition. This is the foundation of P. T. Bauer's argument that monopsonistic pricing will be eroded away by farmers' enquiries concerning the prices—and credit terms where borrowing needs are a factor—obtainable in alternative outlets. At this point much empirical evidence can be marshaled to the contrary. There are associations of wholesale traders which explicitly prevent the use of alternative channels, and which fix prices, in West Africa[18] and the Copperbelt,[19] for example. The relative rise in prices to cotton farmers following the formation of the Victoria Cooperative Federation in Tanganyika is one of many examples where the entry of a new competitor under completely different direction has led to a reduction in margins.

Government requirements that sales by farmers must be made to a specified cooperative or other buying agency, can also lead to abuses which become a deterrent. Local managers are tempted to exploit their monopoly position. Case studies in Ceylon, for example, have revealed numerous instances of farmers bringing paddy to a cooperative to be told that it could not be accepted that day for lack of storage space or means of payment. Rather than take the paddy home the farmer sold at a discount of as much as 30 percent to a dealer who was standing ready to buy for cash. Even though the total volume sold in this way may not exceed 5 to 10 percent the possibility of such difficulties puts a brake on the planned incentive.

Instability of prices

Of special importance in assisting market demand to provide production incentives are reasonably stable prices, i.e., without discontinuous intra- or interseasonal changes, at a remunerative level. Unless farmers have confidence that prices will bear some minimum relationships to costs, they will hesitate before incurring additional work or expense to increase their output or raise its quality. Following, for example, successful experiments with the production and sale of artichokes in Libya, the Ministry of Agriculture sent an officer to persuade farmers to take up their cultivation. He quoted attractive prices in the market. The farmers'

---

[17] F. Shah, FAO Marketing Adviser, unpublished report, October, 1966.

[18] S. Comhaire-Sylvain, "Participation of Women in Industry and Commerce in African Towns South of the Sahara," mimeographed (Addis Ababa: ECA, 1963), p. 32.

[19] M. Miracle "African Markets and Trade in the Copperbelt" in *African Markets,* Bohannan and Dalton (eds.) (Evanston, Ill.: Northwestern University Press, 1962).

first question was what price could be guaranteed in the village. The officer's silence did not impress the villagers. They later said that if he could guarantee even one fourth of the price which he quoted, they would be prepared to undertake the cultivation of artichokes.[20]

Increases in prices, in excess of costs, after the bulk of a seasonal crop has moved into wholesale channels, bring no benefit for the producer, while discouraging consumers and export buyers. Farmers in the developing countries experience very sharp seasonal price fluctuations. Wide seasonal price fluctuations bear much of the responsibility for the failure to expand maize production in Ghana. Over the past 10 years, seasonal peak wholesale prices increased from about $140 per ton to $500 in 1966. Yet the price immediately post harvest rose only from $78 to $101 per ton. In consequence, maize production has become less attractive, except for the minority of farmers possessing the capital and storage which would enable them to postpone sales until later in the season.

Even when governments undertake price stabilization programs, it is often difficult to ensure that they are effective at the farm level. Although there was a minimum price for jute at which the authorized agents of the East Pakistan Jute Board were expected to buy under the buffer stock and repurchase scheme in 1964 and 1965, it is alleged that farmers received much less than the price entered in the agents' books. Similarly, the Colombian agricultural price support agency's undertakings to buy up any surpluses of wheat, rice, maize, beans, and potatoes could rarely be made good when really large crops were harvested, for lack of adequate storage space and purchasing funds—with obvious deterrent effects upon producers.

Marketing enterprises and organization

If the marketing system is to play its proper role in implementing a development plan, there should be specific enterprises which will undertake responsibility for locating firm foreign or domestic buyers for the various types and qualities of produce. They must be able to arrange assembly from farms, packing and presentation in appropriate containers, grading according to buyers' requirements, transport to buyers' depots or markets where they attend, storage where advantageous in spreading over time the supply to be put on the market, and processing if valuable in assisting conservation, reducing transport costs or opening up new outlets. Provision of the investment capital needed for fixed facilities and the working capital to carry purchases from farmers until resale proceeds are received is also required of them. Implicitly these enter-

---

[20] Shah, *op. cit.*

prises must possess the financial resources, qualified managerial, sales and technical personnel, initiative, and willingness to accept business risks needed to carry out these tasks efficiently. In export marketing or import substitution they must be able to compete successfully with similar enterprises in other countries.

How far have development planners been able to count on existing marketing firms to respond to such needs, collaborate in official programs and perform on the level required? Probably in most planned developments the existing enterprises were adequate to requirements; they could be depended upon to adopt the methods and provide the facilities likely to be needed to implement the plan. Publicity has usually been given to the occasions when they were not. Thus, it was envisaged that the marketing of the produce of the San Lorenzo irrigation area, Peru, would be undertaken by a Nestlé milk plant with unused capacity, by local investors experienced in canning fruit for export who were prepared to build a new plant in the area, and by existing traders who would purchase and transport the farmers' grain crop. The last group proved to a degree unreliable. With grain plentiful at the time of the settlers' first harvest, these traders prefer their normal suppliers. To obtain even the current average price for the settlers, the marketing advisers to the project were obliged to arrange for guarantee of availability of specific quantities and quality, and provision of storage.

The experience of the East Ghor project to settle farmers on 60,000 hectares of land in Jordan rams home the importance of marketing organization. A 1956 market survey of the Arab Near East favored expanded production of fruit and vegetables:

> In 1961, when the first 4,000 hectares came into production, the difficulties in marketing the additional produce from this small area were such as to create serious doubts about the feasibility of the whole project. In the absence of any marketing organization or facilities and of personnel with operational marketing experience, the new settlers had difficulty in finding satisfactory outlets for their produce. They became indifferent to assistance in improving cultivation practices and raising productivity, and reluctant to invest even small sums or to obtain credit for this purpose.[21]

An implicit problem in fitting large numbers of independent marketing enterprises into a planned development is their natural inclination to maximize profits—through whatever opportunities present themselves. The Indian grain wholesaler finds it difficult not to accumulate stocks in

---

[21] H. J. Louwes, FAO, "Organization of Markets and Marketing Procedures in Land Reform and Development Programs." Paper presented to the Mediterranean Social Sciences Research Council, General Assembly, Cairo, 1962.

face of an impending supply shortage and price rise, thus contributing to the impression of scarcity and prejudicing the reputation of the trading group in the eyes of a government trying to keep consumer prices stable. A government urgently needing foreign exchange for development will inevitably be critical of exporters who under-invoice hides and skins by an average of 30 percent to build up undeclared holdings in foreign banks, as was revealed in Sudan. Replacement of private citrus exporters in Morocco by a monopoly marketing board in 1965 was attributed to the discovery of similar currency manipulations. The administrator is tempted to settle for a possibly higher cost and less aggressive organization that he thinks he can trust, in place of those for which, in the situation his country faces, he must forever be devising controls and blocking loopholes.

A specific problem in fitting independent marketing enterprises into an incentive program for small farmers in the developing countries is the need for collecting repayments of credit at the time of marketing. This is most easily done by deduction from the proceeds of sale before they are handed over to the farmer. Traditionally, independent traders have done this when lending from their own resources. However, when acting as collecting agents for an agricultural bank, buyers of banan in Jamaica, for example, complained that it led farmers to seek other outlets, as well as involved onerous bookkeeping, etc. This has been a main reason why planners have been inclined to favor cooperatives which combined credit and marketing, or institutions such as the Gezira Board which could undertake a number of functions through its direct buying stations.

An important issue in the provision of appropriate marketing facilities is timing in relation to the phasing of production developments. Those responsible for the overall plan want marketing facilities established at the outset: they are concerned that farmers should not foresee a situation where they would have output with no one standing ready to buy it. On the other hand, private investors hesitate to set up expensive packing or processing plants or to undertake promotion in new markets until they are sure that there will be enough throughput for a profitable operation. It is often difficult to achieve marketing positions over the various stages of growth that are sufficiently favorable at each stage to sustain growth to the level of maximum economy. The solution in marketing slaughter stock in San Lorenzo (Peru) was seen as trucking live animals to urban markets until, after say 10 years, the offtake justified establishment of a slaughtering plant locally and refrigerated transport of meat. However, attainment of the potential high returns from producing fruit and vegetables for sale in distant markets offering important seasonal price advantages permits no such flexibility. Whatever is produced beyond the needs of limited local markets is likely to need a complete refrigerated marketing channel from the outset if it is to bring any return at all.

Distribution of consumer goods and production supplies

There is also substantial evidence that lack of access to consumer goods can be critical in slowing down planned development programs or distorting them from the lines originally envisaged. W. O. Jones sees as a pressing problem over most of tropical Africa the providing of useful and wanted goods with a greater diversity of prices which Africans can pay.[22] With their main concern for productive possibilities, planning economists have generally given little attention to this problem. Research is sparse and mainly anthropological in inspiration: the recent interest in incentives has tended to focus elsewhere. Obviously this is a difficult area for measurement.

The influence of the consumer goods incentive, and consequently of obstacles and inefficiencies in the distribution of such goods can be observed pragmatically at various levels of development. The most obvious is where population groups are sitting on potentially productive resources with no interest in exploiting them because they have not yet learned what they could do with the proceeds. In the Zande area of the Sudan the government's production plans made no progress until a trading unit was set up to display textiles, metal goods and cheap jewelry to give the population an interest in earning money.[23] In achieving desired output goals the Rhodesian Grain Board found it expedient to encourage the opening of general retail stores adjacent to its buying agencies, and sales on credit to stimulate farmers to bring in more supplies. Van der Meulen found poor distribution of consumer goods a limiting factor in the development of fishery activities in Papua and New Guinea.[24] In West Africa access to corrugated iron and cement for better housing has been an important incentive in production for the market.

Official plans to establish meat-packing plants in the important cattle raising Savannah belt of West Africa have been blocked by sharply differentiated consumer goods supply situations. Livestock have flowed steadily out of Niger into Nigeria because so much more could be bought there with the sales proceeds. A similar movement occurred between Upper Volta and Ghana, but a canning plant built on the Ghana side of the border to tap it was left without supplies when imports of consumer goods into that country were stopped around 1964.

Access on favorable terms to supplies of fertilizer, insecticides, and

---

[22] W. O. Jones, "Economic Man in Africa," *Food Research Institute Studies,* May, 1960.

[23] Statement by W. Habashi, FAO/UNDP Meeting on Savannah Development, Khartoum, October, 1966.

[24] J. Van der Meulen, *Fish Marketing in Papua and New Guinea* (Armidale University of New England, 1962).

improved seeds is particularly important for agricultural development. Most plans envisage increased imports or domestic production of such essential supplies. Yet many farmers are discouraged from using them by inadequate and too costly distribution arrangements.[25] Falcon and Gotsch report that the results in East Pakistan of the changeover from extension service to commercial distribution were "rather remarkable."[26] Plans for a detailed FAO study of the scope for reducing marketing costs and improving timeliness of local availability, credit purchasing terms, etc., in the developing countries are now under way.

INADEQUACY OR INAPPROPRIATENESS OF IMPROVEMENT MEASURES TAKEN

There is much evidence that of the measures taken to improve marketing, many have been misplaced or ineffective with consequent adverse effects upon plan implementation.

Reluctance to disturb existing structures

Fairly common is the situation where a clearly formulated program of improvement is put forward by the government, but is negated in practice by reluctance to disturb existing structures. The regulation of local assembly markets in India to ensure fair sales prices and protect producer-sellers against exploitation due to ignorance or weak bargaining power has been shown to have substantial incentive benefits.[27] Though this has been official government policy since 1935, there are still several states where it has never been applied, because the local legislatures have been unwilling to take the necessary initiative.

Effective support for measures to improve the pricing at the farm level of basic food grains in Sudan, where the "sheil" system of credit advances by local wholesalers is widespread, has never been forthcoming, though the urgency of the problem has frequently been stressed. In 1966, Sudan, with a population of 13.5 million for an agricultural land area of over 75 million acres, became a net importer of food grains principally for lack of market incentives to domestic producers.

---

[25] In one sample study in Pakistan 93 percent of the farmers wanted to undertake some technical innovation during 1962; nearly all who did not follow through indicated that their failure was due either to the lack of credit or the unavailability of materials. D. W. Sturt, "Producer Response to Technological Change in West Pakistan," *Journal of Farm Economics*, Vol. XLVII, pp. 625–33 (August, 1965).

[26] W. P. Falcon and C. H. Gotsch, *Agricultural Development in Pakistan; Lessons from the Second Plan Period* (Cambridge, Mass.: Harvard University Press, 1966).

[27] Savings to farmers from the regulation of 667 markets were estimated in 1960 at $18 million annually. N. P. Chatterji, "Agricultural Marketing in India," *Agricultural Marketing*, Vol. III, No. 1 (Nagpur, 1960), p. 7.

For many years plans to develop livestock production in the South of Chile by shipping beef to Santiago under refrigeration were blocked by official reluctance to upset an oligopolistic group of wholesalers who channelled live animals through the Santiago municipal slaughterhouse. Similar situations still prevail in Guayaquil, Quito and various other Latin American cities.

Discouragement of potentially efficient marketing enterprises

In their desire to modify patterns of ownership of marketing enterprises on political grounds many governments of developing countries are slowing down the realization of planned targets.

The role of the international private marketing enterprises in fostering development in the less advanced countries is relatively well known. They were able to recruit skilled technicians and administrators from the places where they were most plentiful, and could draw their capital from the lowest-cost sources. Because of their direct contact with buyers in destination markets, they were acutely conscious of competitive quality standards and supply costs, and ensured that local managers were trained to be aware of these factors. Ability to adapt to local techniques in developing supply and distribution networks was also developed. In consequence, the handling of commodities exported to the United States and Western Europe, such as tea, sugar, and rubber, has been relatively well organized. Frequently combined with this export business was the distribution of major lines of production supplies and consumer goods with economies in capital, transport and storage facilities and management.[28] In African and Asian countries such as Algeria, Tunisia, Ghana, Guinea, Senegal, Mali, Congo (Brazz.), Tanzania, Burma, Ceylon, and Indonesia, the opportunities to benefit from such marketing services have been subject to drastic restriction; in many other developing countries what has happened in the above has been a deterrent to new outside investment and initiative.

Even efficient locally based private enterprises are subject to continuing official attack where not operated by a member of the politically prevailing social group. Golay has shown how political power has been used in the Philippines to change the ownership of enterprises marketing strategic products, generally regardless of the cost in terms of efficiency.[29] Several newly independent African countries have assigned whole sec-

---

[28] W. A. Lewis argues that they will be hostile to import substitution because of the international export/import firms' interest in shipping and trade. *Op. cit.*, p. 42. However, there is also a substantial record of collaboration with governments of developing countries in establishing local processing facilities, assembly plants, etc.

[29] F. H. Golay, "Commercial Policy and Economic Nationalism," *Quarterly Journal of Economics,* Vol. LXXII (November, 1958), pp. 574–87.

tors of agricultural marketing to state or cooperative enterprises because they were dominated by aliens. . . . The point that such measures, though politically popular, are likely to result in a slower rate of economic growth, is implicit for the Philippines in Golay's analysis, and is brought out clearly for Tanzania.[30]

Even where certain types of enterprise have not been subject to an official barrier the knowledge that this is a political issue tends to hold back investment and induce them to look for ways of moving out their capital. Indecision where regulation and interference with existing interests would evoke opposition inevitably prejudices development.

Use of price controls, monopoly privileges, market regulations, licensing requirements with disincentive implications

The main disincentive to development applied through the marketing system is usually the fixing of low retail prices of food, etc., for other good reasons—to protect low-income consumers and contain inflation. Government preoccupation with measures to keep down food prices at the retail level has been at the root of the food problem in India over the last decade. In the face of these controls, backed up by releases of stocks from official sources, farmers turned from foodgrains to other more profitable crops—to sugar, for example, as shown in a case study for Uttar Pradesh.[31] Unwillingness to reflect the rising international prices for rice in internal price structures in Burma has held back expansion of output of a valuable export commodity in a country with generous land resources in relation to population.

Maintenance of municipal slaughterhouse and wholesale market monopolies, and the limitation by means of licensing of the retailing of a range of foods in one establishment has also been a development obstacle, particularly in the Latin countries of Europe and South America. In those countries it has slowed down the growth of supermarkets and of contractual arrangements between retailer and farmers for organized production and marketing programs. The consequent maintenance of higher marketing costs and blurred quality pricing procedures have constituted a continuing brake on development vis-à-vis countries with more open institutional environments for marketing. High export taxes, market charges, and cooperative society dues have also been effective disincentives in many developing countries.

A common tendency in developing countries eager to improve their

---

[30] G. Rutman, "State Trading in Tanzania," *South African Journal of Economics,* Vol. XXXIV, No. 2 (1966), pp. 148–57.

[31] S. Gupta and A. Majid, *Farmers' Response to Prices and Marketing Policies* (Bombay: Asia Publishing House, 1965).

marketing systems has been to *concentrate the greater part of their efforts upon the establishment of radically new organizations which proved difficult to operate in practice, or involved long delays and costs in attaining even a moderate level of efficiency.* The channeling of most government assistance to the support of a particular new form of marketing enterprise has been a feature of government policy in Ceylon, India, and many other countries.

The recent expansion of cooperative marketing systems in countries such as Ceylon, Tanzania, and Senegal reflects a shift away from the idealistic tradition of the Rochdale Pioneers to a more practical model seen in Japan. The cooperatives, which handle 70 to 80 percent of the rice marketed there, undertake only limited responsibilities as receivers and storage agents for a monopoly government food agency. They face little risk. For a number of years they were protected by a licensing system which made them the only official buyer in the area they served. The grain purchased is graded by government inspectors, who determine the price to be paid. With a secure base as sole assembling agency and earning a steady handler's commission, these cooperatives provide credit and sell fertilizer and other supplies to farmers on favorable terms with less risk than competing enterprises. Once capital had been accumulated from these low-risk operations they could, where the management was capable, take on additional functions, such as processing and the marketing of other crops.

In many of the developing countries, however, performance has been disappointing in spite of generous government expenditure on facilities, credit, and advisory personnel. Possible plans to promote the expansion of potato production in the Jebel Marra area of Sudan, where ecological conditions are fairly favorable, will be handicapped for a long time to come by farmers' experience with a government-promoted cooperative that was badly conceived and staffed.

When competing wholesalers ganged up against a new cooperative, governments have tended to give it monopoly purchasing privileges and then have had to face a different set of complaints—against poor service, corruption, and padding of marketing margins, as in Ceylon and Tanzania.

The main point here is: why rush at what is obviously a difficult task, before preparing the ground by training competent staff and working out the requirements for success of each specific cooperative endeavor? At the planning commission level it has often seemed that the assumption that marketing would be handled by planned, but as yet nonexistent, cooperative societies was a convenient way of disposing of a difficult problem.

Establishment of direct government marketing enterprises or of autonomous large-scale public enterprises such as marketing boards endowed with special powers has often seemed easier in the developing countries than the development of cooperatives with their rather complicated procedures. Again, attempting too much too quickly without the necessary trained and experienced staff has sometimes resulted in marketing conditions less favorable to producers than before. While a few of the Central and South American commodity boards have performed well, agencies established to handle several basic food products have usually been ineffectual, at great cost to taxpayers.[32] This is borne out in full by the import and export "comptoirs" set up in Guinea in 1960 and later replaced.

There is no doubt that the establishment of specialized packing, processing, storage, and wholesaling facilities to break out of the stagnation of a structure of interdependent, capital-starved, small-scale supply and distribution enterprises can be an effective instrument for marketing improvement. In some areas they have stimulated the development both of organized wholesale supply markets for meat animals, milk, etc., and of arrangements to distribute different types of finished products. *Unfortunately, governments have too often financed investments in physical structures for such purposes without working out the necessary complementary programs to ensure that they are used efficiently.*

Large public expenditures for physical marketing facilities are specifically induced by the financial and political conditions prevailing in many Latin American countries. A state governor in office for a limited time sees a large refrigerated abattoir (Lo Valledor, Santiago, Chile)[33] or complex of wholesale market buildings (CEASA project, Sao Paulo, Brazil)[34] as the most permanent potential monument to his term of office. Organizational studies cannot be allowed to hold up the pace of construction for fear that the funds available will lose their value.

In various countries 5,000- to 10,000-ton-capacity silos have remained 90 percent empty for a number of years. Partly this is due to lack of appropriate preparatory studies. However, the low storage utilization rate achieved by the Indian Central Warehousing Agency where locations were studied carefully, and the fumbling approaches to this problem of the Mediterranean area development agencies examined by Abbott in 1963,[35] suggest that reluctance of the planners to endorse coincidence of responsibility for operation of the plant and ownership of the produce passing through it is at the heart of the problem. In most cases this reflects embarrassment over the possibility that existing traders

[32] Lorinez, *op. cit.*

[33] P. Glaessner, Universidad de Chile, *Economic Appraisal Report on the Lo Valledor Meat Packing and Cold Storage Plant*, Santiago, May, 1959.

[34] E. Rascovich, *Planning and Organisation of the Wholesale Market of Sao Paulo* (FAO/EPTA Report No. 2054 [Rome: FAO, 1965]).

[35] Abbott, *op. cit.*

would be strengthened by access to public finance for facilities that would be used in close conjunction with their marketing operations, and generally in consequence with considerable efficiency.

Where new capital-intensive facilities are needed, there is much to recommend more general arrangements to furnish part of the capital in collaboration with enterprises equipped with management experience and valuable marketing contacts. Varying degrees of government supervision can be envisaged. Facilitation of easy credit for approved projects from certain banks is another healthy approach, provided there is always an adequate commitment of the borrower's own capital.[36] The loans program for small Kenyan business enterprises is one example. Returns from approved investments in marketing facilities may also be exempted from taxes for defined periods.

Lack of institutional support for integrated production and marketing organization

The hesitation to support private enterprises probably lies behind the slowness of many developing countries to develop the integrated arrangements necessary for maximization of benefits from perishable products or those requiring prompt processing before marketing. To have a good chance of success, an integrated plantation-processing-marketing enterprise, for example, must count on full government support in obtaining the use of suitable land on long leases, security against expropriation and a measure of market protection. The returns that can come from this are well illustrated by the Wonje sugar project in Ethiopia. A Dutch enterprise formerly in Indonesia built up its output to meet national requirements in seven years and is now preparing to export. Even in the cases of the Congo (Brazz.) and Kenya pineapple agreements with Libby, McNeill Libby, Inc., and California Packing Company respectively, where the advantages of bringing in a processor with an established distribution network and brand name have been recognized, direct support with government authority and services has been grudging. The Gezira Scheme and various banana export marketing arrangements also illustrate the effectiveness of collaboration between government and high-level private enterprises in this sphere. In the majority of countries planners now seem willing to conceive such an integrated structure only within a smallholder-cooperative-government corporation or board

---

[36] Plants erected by private or cooperative enterprises providing their own capital generally incur lower initial costs than equivalent publicly financed installations. J. C. Abbott and A. D. Goseco, "The Role of Government Financing Institutions in Developing Marketing Facilities," *FAO Monthly Bulletin of Agricultural Economics and Statistics,* Vol. VII, No. 1.

framework, as adopted for tea in Kenya, so augmenting the difficulties of administration, quality and cost control, etc.

As farmers in developing countries become more sophisticated and their farming more commercialized, there may well be scope for a move towards a more flexible and responsive system of producers' forward contracts with processors and merchants.[37] Guidance and supervision could be provided by an adequately staffed government agricultural economics and marketing service. The Taiwan jute, pineapple, and mushroom industries are characterized by contractual arrangements between large locally owned, independent processor wholesalers and small farmers with government mediation in annual price negotiations,[38] and periodical checking of weighing and quality definition procedures, etc.

Failure to establish essential services to initiate and implement marketing improvements

For maximization of returns from development efforts, systematic market news services, advisory programs for producers and handlers on choice of varieties, time of harvesting and selling, methods of storage, the organization and construction of supplementary marketing facilities, etc., strict control of quality standards and sales practices, and the training of operational marketing personnel are usually necessary. The benefits of informed coordination are especially notable where new products are marketed and where there are many suppliers, each offering small quantities. Yet failure to establish such services on an adequate basis, or at all, is general in the developing countries. Gittinger, for example, is struck by the almost complete lack of information on local processing and marketing operations, on margins and transport costs, etc.[39] Not enough is known about quantities of agricultural products reaching markets (apart from monopoly boards) nor the routes and means by which they get there. There is urgent need for data concerning effective prices at the farm level. Even where prices are said to be fixed, actual returns should be investigated. Information on the proportion of total agricultural output affected by indebtedness to buyers or by adverse pre-harvest sales is rarely available, leaving the aggregate impact on production without quantitative dimensions. Planners facing supply responsibilities would be aided by research to determine the proportion of total output originating from producers aiming only at low target incomes, its nature and loca-

---

[37] S. Taylor, who is undertaking a special study of contract farming in Africa, FAO, Rome.

[38] ECAFE, 1965, "Food Processing Industries," paper presented at Asian Conference on Industrialisation, Manila.

[39] J. P. Gittinger, *The Literature of Agricultural Planning*, p. 71.

tion, and details of the factors—particularly crop yields—affecting the producers' response to price changes.

Much of research undertaken in the developing countries is not directed to provide information useful for planning or to answer specific practical questions. Some official studies, including the Indian Agricultural Marketing Advisors report series, lose in relevance by endeavoring to be representative of too large and diverse an area. At another extreme, many of the market studies by anthropologists provide a wealth of local behavioral data but few constructive leads for marketing improvement policy. More penetrating economic analysis of the relationships within and between the various marketing channels in the developing countries is needed. Workmanlike research of the type required calls for a specific approach. General agricultural economists required to carry out studies on the establishment of canning plants, for example, have often been able to point only to the problems and principles; they either could not or would not assemble and analyze the data on which predictions of direction and magnitude could be based.

Central collection and dissemination of widely needed data reduce the area over which farmers, traders, and consumers must seek information themselves, and consequently are generally recognized as meriting the expenditure of public funds. Such services are very limited in the developing countries, as much one suspects, because of failure to present adequate justification for them as of ability to assemble and disseminate the information.

The returns from expenditures on marketing extension show up clearly, for example, in the unit value of hides and skins exported from Kenya during past years as compared with Ethiopia. Some of the African marketing boards have gone a long way in providing field staff to assist producers in clearing and grading produce, protecting it from insect infestation, etc. A national marketing extension service is now being established in India, and film and other instructional material have been prepared. In relation to the need, however, the scope of present services is still infinitesimal and many governments have shirked the issue by assigning the responsibility to already overloaded cooperative departments.

Most developing countries lose many market opportunities and have to accept less favorable terms for their products because of poor salesmanship. This handicap shows up both on export markets and in competing against imports in supplying high-income markets at home. The hotels of Montego Bay and the more discriminating retailers of Kuala Lumpur who demand imported fruit even when domestic supplies are plentiful at lower prices are not all exceptional. While basic commodities such as grain, and oilseeds can be sold on international exchanges at standard prices, processed products and more specialized fruits, etc., require careful selection to meet consumers' tastes, specialized presentation, and systematic advertising.[40] There are organizations which have met this challenge, such as the Ceylon Tea Propaganda Board which was so successful in promoting Ceylon tea as to provoke emulation by India, a much larger supplier;[41] unfortunately they are few.

The importance of quality controls on produce designed for exacting markets and to maintain a country's quality image in international channels has been recognized more widely. Most of the former British and French African countries had inspection services working effectively for major export commodities by 1950. Compulsory quality certification of wool exported from Pakistan, for example, is justified on the grounds of complaints received from buyers and the advantages of firm quality specifications in selling to distant markets where buyers' inspection before shipment is not practicable.[42] There is evidence that the expansion wool exports from Pakistan and improvement in prices received more than covers the direct cost of the service and its inconvenience for exporters.

The strengthening, during 1961–63, of the export quality control service operated by the Government of Libya, raised the average price earned for Libyan groundnut exports from $260 to $325 per ton, with steadily increasing buyer demand. In at least one other Mediterranean country, a poor reputation for quality because of ineffective inspection is a recognized handicap to development of continuing European outlets for its produce.

In most countries service work in marketing from research to regulation is hampered by lack of assigned responsibility to a particular government department. In the majority of Latin American, African, Near Eastern, and Far Eastern countries, elements of marketing services and controls are taken care of by different organizations without any coordination. Departments of agriculture as well as industries, cooperatives, agricultural banks, and municipalities are all involved. In India and Pakistan, where central agricultural marketing services were set up in the 1930s, the transfer elsewhere of some strategic functions, and salary scales inadequate for high-quality staff, have impeded full effectiveness. Yet without an adequate government service there is little hope of implementing any measures that require public initiative and continued action.

---

[40] Lewis, *op. cit.*, p. 50, attributes the failure of the developing countries to export more manufactured produce to poor salesmanship rather than high tariffs.

[41] See Abbott and Creupelandt, *The Establishment and Operation of Agricultural Marketing Boards* (Rome: FAO, 1966).

[42] Government of Pakistan, Cooperation and Marketing Adviser, *Report on the Marketing of Wool* (Karachi: Ministry of Agriculture, 1960).

Lack of trained personnel in marketing lies behind both weaknesses in the public services and in the operating performance of marketing enterprises. A seminar held in East Pakistan in 1966 showed that many government marketing officers with years of service had little or no training in marketing. While the public allocations made for agricultural marketing improvement in most of the developing countries are relatively small, the amounts actually used are still less. In Libya, for example, in 1963–64, it was only 0.03 percent of the total allocations. This was blamed on difficulties encountered in the construction of food grain storage and in the installation of processing and packing plants for vegetable oils and dates, indicating lack of trained personnel for conducting preinvestment studies and for the execution of plans.[43]

CONCLUSIONS AND RECOMMENDATIONS

1. *Planning units must be equipped to undertake two categories of marketing planning. The first is identification of probable markets for new output and estimation of the returns that can be expected. The second is determination of the appropriate marketing system to maximize these returns and formulation of measures to ensure that it is established.*

This implies that an adequate planning organization must have competent market research men on its staff from the beginning or have early access to their services. Later it will need specialists in the development of marketing enterprises to apply the necessary controls and inducements, provide advice and assistance at the enterprise level, and maintain continuing practical training facilities.

The direction and coordination of this work and the task of weaving its results into the different elements of a national development plan can be carried out effectively only by a member of the planning body who is himself competently trained and experienced in marketing.

Corresponding provision for specific treatment of marketing issues will be needed in the committee or other machinery through which a planning unit works. If committees are set up on a commodity or industry basis then there should be meetings specifically devoted to marketing aspects which would be attended by representatives of firms, boards, etc., with the appropriate marketing responsibilities and experience. A separate committee on marketing services will probably be needed to coordinate public action and take account of views of producers, traders, cooperatives, etc., on their performance in practice.

2. *Market research studies should be initiated in the earliest phase of the planning process: effective market studies require more time and resources than planners envisage.*

---

[43] Shah, *op. cit.*

Logically, market research precedes plan formulation. Production levels are planned to meet an assessed demand and price. Developing countries, in particular, cannot afford to support production for which there is not a market. Consequently, market studies should begin at the same time as identification of production expansion potentials. The closer the contact, the easier it will be to change the direction of production studies before too much has been spent if a seemingly attractive initial proposal offers limited market opportunities.

The volume and duration of the work involved in carrying out demand studies that will be specifically relevant should not be underestimated. Domestic market prospects cannot be based upon target overall growth rates. Only some of the data needed for reliable decisions on these markets issues are available in easily accessible publications. FAO provides commodity demand projections, for example, on the basis of high, medium, and low price alternatives. Planning groups must still make their own estimates of these price levels in the light of particular market situations.

Such estimates still do not provide very precise guidance on the share of the expected expansion in international demand which a particular producing area can expect to obtain. Information on the choice of varieties, quality levels, methods of presentation, forms of processing, and other market factors which determine the actual demand for particular lots of produce can be obtained only by detailed surveys of the wholesale and retail trade.

Since the additional output which a plan will endeavor to bring forth is not a fixed quantity, the plan will normally select that quantity at which marginal revenue will be maximized. This means that determination of probable market returns must be undertaken for a range of quantities of the commodities likely to be forthcoming under the production program feasible in the country concerned.

3. *Few national development plans face up to the need for efficient marketing enterprises and organization if implementation is to proceed satisfactorily. Yet many techniques and devices for inducing firms to follow desired procedures have been tried and shown effective.*

Experience shows that governments need not abandon hope of improving existing marketing enterprises nor incur other sets of difficulties by taking radical steps to introduce complete substitutes. Measures are available to strengthen farmers' bargaining power and competitive pricing. Fluctuations in supplies and prices of strategic food grains can be kept in bounds by a price stabilization agency equipped with a buffer stock.

Specific inducements such as expropriation of land for the site, privileges in obtaining construction materials and machinery, and guarantees of supplies of raw material up to agreed percentages of rated capacity can be used to secure investment by independent enterprises with established market outlets and sales organizations.

New marketing enterprises and systems under different ownership can be introduced. Where there are doubts as to whether the existing enterprises will respond adequately even with financial and technical assistance, because of conflicting interests, chronic managerial limitations, etc., marketing board structures can be used to rationalize produce movements and improve bargaining power by concentrating sales decisions. Cooperatives allow farmers to participate in combined credit and marketing operations once established. Limited responsibility as buying agent for a marketing board provides a favorable opportunity for cooperative growth where managerial talents are scarce.

4. *Financial allocations for marketing improvement are at present earmarked mainly for investment in fixed physical storage, processing, and public market facilities; provision for continuing marketing services including training would often be a better use of the money.*

Not merely are the public investments in marketing in most plans small in relation to its importance, the projects for which they are designed incur a high risk of wastage. Many of the physical marketing facilities built by governments in the developing countries have been criticized on grounds of location, design, and adaptability to practical marketing requirements. Subsequent utilization is often far below capacity because ownership of the plant is divorced from that of the produce going through the marketing channels the plant is intended to serve.

The basic difficulty seems to be reluctance to provide public financial assistance for the construction of facilities that will be in other than public or cooperative ownership. Yet, if the private sector is doing most of the trading in the channels a new plant should service, its full participation in the project is critically important for effective investment. A more general use of independent merchants to implement government marketing programs on agreed contract terms in developing countries might well be a cheaper alternative to direct public investment in large-scale installations. This is usually favored.

Public services to marketing—advising, training, quality control, and research—presently receive inadequate financial support. They constitute, however, a flexible instrument for improvement with prospects of considerable impact if well directed.

5. *A closer exchange of ideas is needed on the economics and practicalities of alternative forms of marketing enterprise between planning units and the originators of government policy.*

Plans allocate funds to construct physical facilities without making adequate arrangements for them to be fitted into the marketing system because their ownership is a political issue. Plans assume substantial private investment in marketing in setting their targets, but ministers make public statements likely to discourage such investment. Funds are lavished upon new forms of marketing enterprise which give disappointing results: alternatively the whole subject of marketing organization is given minimal attention in a plan for fear of implicit commitments that would meet criticism when it is published.

These problems can be solved only by a closer and deeper exchange of ideas between the planners and the government. If there is a confirmed policy to change certain institutions, agreement must be reached on what can be accomplished and what should not be disturbed during a particular plan period of 5 to 10 years. If the Government exercises extensive control over the private sector, it must develop a program for the private sector which will ensure that its decisions are efficient and mutually consistent.

A wide range of marketing systems exists from within which governments can select—from untrammeled private enterprise to complete cooperativization or state operation. It is the responsibility of marketing departments and planning bodies to inform ministers on ways of devising controls and combinations of ownership and management that will harness valuable experience and initiative to a government's development policies. The better equipped professionally the marketing staff concerned, the more confidence and conviction will go into their discussions with the authors of government policy, and the greater the likelihood of a favorable outcome. The waywardness of independent traders is a predictable factor with which planners in the developing countries must learn to deal, just as they must deal with the dreams and slogans of politicians and the tardy responsiveness of small-scale agriculture.

Lauchlin Currie raises some very serious questions about the transferability of developed country marketing institutions to the developing countries. Large-scale marketing and retailing institutions may be disadvantaged in the developing nations because of many considerations, including consumer service needs, differential labor costs, and legislative restrictions. But even if the capital-intensive distribution techniques prove more efficient, in a narrow sense, they may do little good unless adequate opportunities exist for the trade workers they displace.

LAUCHLIN CURRIE*

Marketing organization for underdeveloped countries

I. VARYING PATTERNS OF DEVELOPMENT

Some years ago Robert L. Heilbroner remarked that, in thinking of the problem of underdevelopment, most Americans make the mistake of conceiving of it as a global process of Americanization.[1] Putting the same thought in other words, and lulled by such insidious phrases as "developing" countries and "stages of growth," economists are prone to assume, mostly implicitly, that history will repeat itself and that the institutions and organizations appropriate for developed countries today will be equally appropriate for underdeveloped countries tomorrow. This need not be only an implicit assumption. The examples of such diverse, formerly underdeveloped countries as Japan and Puerto Rico, and the automobilization of Europe with all it implies and its obvious beginnings in all underdeveloped countries, all suggest the existence of a standard pattern. If such a pattern exists, the task of writers on marketing in underdeveloped regions is relatively simple; it is merely to apply the marketing organizations and techniques of the most economically advanced countries, with appropriate lags, to all less advanced countries. It is the purpose of this paper to raise some questions as to whether the task is really that simple.

Increasing attention in recent years has been paid to Puerto Rico, partly because it seems like such an obvious, and possibly significant link between two cultures and because the trends there, for example, in

---

* Simon Fraser University.
[1] *The Great Ascent* (New York: Harper & Row, Publishers, 1963), p. 12.

marketing surely foreshadow trends in less advanced Latin American countries.[2] Let's look briefly at marketing conditions there.

Although the commonwealth is Latin American in its cultural background, it is within the customs, monetary, exchange, and fiscal boundaries of the United States. Ocean transport is cheap, so that economically the commonwealth is an integral part of the United States with certain additional benefits in relation to taxes. The cultural and economic impact of this fact is obvious. The private automobile (though many may be third or fourth hand) determines more and more where people live and work. Under these conditions it is not surprising that supermarkets, chains, and wholesale organizations similar to those on the mainland are coming into existence. Of more interest and relevance to Latin America is the persistence of the neighborhood store, often combined with a cafe and/or a rudimentary delicatessen section. This reflects only in part cultural preferences, fewer cars, and a less concentrated population. It reflects also the ability of the family-type enterprise to compete with large organizations where the labor laws relating to overtime, minimum wages, etc. are "stringent" or "generous," depending on one's point of view. Such stores and their servicing may be of more interest and relevance to a country like Colombia than the giant trailers, whose cargoes are loaded on the mainland and discharged directly into units of supermarkets chains in Puerto Rico. These trailers are a characteristic feature of the Puerto Rican marketing organization.

In the discussion of marketing in Latin America probably too much stress has been laid on "cultural" and "traditional" patterns and not enough on basic economic factors. Only a few years ago it was repeatedly stated that people in Colombia liked to haggle and bargain, and for this reason fixed-price stores of the Woolworth type could not succeed, or that housewives (and their maids) liked the gregariousness of public marketplaces, and for this reason the more impersonal supermarkets also would fail. Both statements have proved to be mistaken. Colombia now has Woolworth-type chains and some supermarkets, to say nothing of Sears with its large volume of sales on credit. Evidently cultural patterns are not a barrier to innovations, if such innovations can justify themselves on economic grounds. Indeed, such innovations can count on an initial prestige or snob appeal as reflecting the way things are done in more advanced countries.

Another variety of the "cultural" argument is that ignorant rural people lack sufficient incentives to work. If, through advertising, wants can be created, then people will work harder to satisfy them. It is suggested, in a well-known article by Dr. Walt Rostow, that this might

---

[2] While this is doubtless true up to a point, it may be dangerous to read too much into the Puerto Rican experience.

be done by using traveling caravan trucks that would show the peasants the things they could buy if only they had the money. However, it would appear that in Colombia, at least, it is not the lack of felt wants that lead to low incomes (after all there are always the minor vices of smoking and drinking that require money to satisfy), but rather the overpopulation of the rural areas, the pervasiveness of intestinal parasites and amoebas that discourage initiative, and the general hopelessness that poverty itself induces. Even in larger cities as well as in the United States, the demonstration effect of conspicuous consumption appears to be of little relevance to large numbers of the urban poor.

But it is the underlying assumption of a standard pattern of development that this paper challenges. This view implicitly assumes that conditions in presently underdeveloped countries are not so different from those prevailing in the earlier stages of development of today's developed countries and assumes further that the dynamic process of growth will follow more or less the same course and produce the same changes in environment. This comfortable view rests in turn on the assumptions that the standards of the poorest will rise, that birth rates will fall, and that more and more people will own cars. I have elsewhere questioned the validity of these assumptions.[3] The mobility mechanism may be completely incapable of coping with the burden thrust upon it.[4] The lateness and the nature of the technology being introduced, the rapidity of the growth in population, the inadequacy of the measures to lessen the uneven distribution of wealth and income, the prevalence of imperfect competition and cost-push inflation, and other factors are creating an environment significantly different from that which confronted the developed countries in their earlier stages. If underdevelopment and poverty for the masses should happen to be self-perpetuating for most countries, this would mean that the high-income, car-owning, and suburban-living sector would remain a small proportion of the total, and rather violent upheavals and changes would appear likely.

If this should become the probable sequence, the proposed marketing organizations and techniques would have to be drastically revised if they were to serve the needs of the bulk of the people.

There is still another possibility. A strategy of development adequate

---

[3] *Accelerating Development* (New York: McGraw-Hill Book Co., 1966), and in my Royer Lectures delivered in 1966 and published by the University of California Press, Berkeley, under the title of *Governmental Planning and Political Economy,* 1967.

[4] By the mobility mechanism is meant the capacity of the system to absorb displaced or underemployed or poorly remunerated workers in better paying employment. This mechanism, which on the whole functions so smoothly and efficiently in developed countries, functions badly in all underdeveloped countries. The proof can be found in the gross inequality of incomes from work that characterizes such countries.

to deal with the diagnosis just presented would differ radically from the investment-output, trickle-down formula now in vogue (even with the accompanying frills of changes in land tenancy and intercontinent free-trade areas). It would call for massive aid to the badly functioning mobility mechanism, an incomes-prices policy, an induced change in the factor mix to combine technological advance with remunerative employment and a concentrated effort rapidly to raise the incomes of the poorest to provide, in turn, adequate motivation for family planning. These would imply a rather drastic induced change in the pattern of both investment and consumption with more emphasis on investment and employment in the construction of urban housing, in services and goods of mass consumption, and a consequent de-emphasis on luxury-type goods and especially on a private-automobile, suburban-living pattern of consumption, with its extravagant drain on savings to supply roads and dispersed public services.

It is possible that such a strategy would seek to minimize even further per capita expenditures on public services and urban transport through (a) large-scale renovation rehousing of people near the center of cities and places of work and (b) a national urban policy of decentralization of cities.

Such a strategy could, at least theoretically, be adopted either by a modified free enterprise system with planning and controls of a wartime type, or by a socialist, more direct, control system.

IMPLICATIONS FOR MARKETING ORGANIZATION AND POLICY

If, either as a result of the continuance of present trends, or as a result of a deliberate choice of a new-type strategy of development, the pattern of consumption varies widely from that of developed countries, it would be natural to expect that the appropriate marketing system and organization would also be very different.

In this section we will consider the possible differences.

We will consider retail marketing first, instead of last, as it is closest to the consumer. It is assumed that the overwhelming bulk of the consumers will continue to do its shopping on foot or, in the case of the rural dwellers, on foot with the help of horses or mules. This statement may be subject to some modification where mass means of transport are available in the larger cities, but such means are really not very suitable for carrying bulky and heavy foodstuffs. They simply permit occasional and smaller scale purchases in the central shopping districts of less bulky goods that can be carried by hand. This tends to limit the size of the most efficient or economic unit that caters to the poorer class of consumer, whether he moves on foot or by mass transport. This not only affects the size of the center as a shopping district but also greatly diminishes the number and size of individual units in the suburbs that can be reached most easily by automobile.

This tendency is reinforced by the consideration noted above in the case of Puerto Rico of stringent labor codes or individual trade-union agreements. In Colombia an employer, in addition to paying a legal minimum wage, is required by law to pay time and a half for overtime, a surcharge for nightwork not overtime, triple pay for work on the numerous holidays and Sundays, pay for medical expenses and time lost from sickness or accidents, bonuses every six months, vacations, quittance pay (so many days per year of employment calculated on the basis of the last salary), family allowances, 2 percent of the wage bill to support the vocational training system and various other charges. All this, in turn, entails a great amount of record keeping, typed reports to official agencies, the making of individual contracts with each worker and so forth. If, in addition, the worker belongs to a trade union, most of these fringe benefits will be even higher than the law requires, and there may be additional benefits as well. Consequently, the extra payment may equal or exceed the nominal wage.

The workers are keenly aware of their "rights," and there are lawyers who will take up their cases on a share basis and haul the employer into labor courts, which generally favor the worker. All larger organizations maintain full-time experts and a considerable personnel office to handle these problems. The small employer, into which class fall many retailers, is not only subjected to many charges and expenses of this nature but, if he is not careful and well informed, to occasional large charges for which no provision has been made in his accounts.

Protests are rarely made, because the labor code is sacrosanct and the larger employers, who might be expected to be the spokesmen of all employers, are often in a monopolistic or semimonopolistic position, and figure that they can pass along the charges in the price to consumers. Thus, in a fairly characteristic Latin way, energies are spent in "accommodating" to the law or in trying to find ways around it, rather than in opposing it.

In any case, all this gives a tremendous competitive advantage to the family store or the family enterprise and helps to explain the persistence of the neighborhood shop and the thousands of small artisan workshops. In furniture making, metalworking, automobile repairing, and a number of other activities, such workshops can compete with the large mechanized establishments, something that frequently puzzles visiting foreign experts.

Public markets, with their dirt and low volume of sales per seller, still remain an important feature of retailing, but it appears that as cities and distances grow, their market share declines. Their persistence is due not so much to cultural preferences as to their freedom from the labor codes and the absence of efficient distribution of perishable commodities through the small-store system. The higher income trade, where appearance and packaging are more important, tends to be served by supermarkets, larger private stores, or company stores run for employees' benefit. For this class of trade, traffic congestion, dirt, and haggling outweigh what advantages there may be in freshness and cheapness that can be offered by the public markets.

If we assume that, either by design or simply by continuance of existing trends, the neighborhood store will continue to play an important rôle in marketing, we should study how it might be improved, unattractive and uninteresting as it may appear to the student of modern marketing. One of the major problems appears to be that of securing supplies, especially of perishable commodities. Stocks are purchased from a number of suppliers and middlemen (they can hardly be called wholesalers). This entails a lot of movement to deliver, irregularly, very small individual quantities frequently poor or widely varying in quality.

The first answer to this problem that may occur to a student from a northern country is cooperatives. To say anything against cooperatives is almost like saying something against religion or motherhood. Nevertheless, the experience of many years is not too encouraging. The Latin culture is an extremely individualistic one, and the very existence of the neighborhood store is a manifestation of this individualism. The dedication that successful cooperation seems to require is missing. An able young manager is promptly enticed away by a larger private firm.

A more promising approach would be to explore the possibility of (a) a better organization of wholesale markets, (b) a new class of wholesalers to meet the needs of small shops, and/or (c) a better organization of middlemen again to supply the particular needs of a number of smaller shops. Today, in the large city of Bogotá with nearly two million people, the wholesale markets in grains and other agricultural products appear to be very disorganized. They are intermingled with retail operations, handle very few quality grades in the grains and none in fruits and vegetables, use no publicly recorded auctions, and indulge in a great deal of haggling. The purchase of many products whose quality cannot be determined by visual inspection is a gamble. Eggs may or may not be fresh; meat may or may not be tender; there is an unbelievable variation in the juiciness and flavor of all fruits.

Another solution that will occur to a foreign investigator is a chain of small but more or less uniform shops which could spread the per-unit costs of obtaining stocks of better quality. The difficulty would be that mentioned above—the high cost of labor to a larger employer in contrast to the individual family enterprise. This higher cost does not necessarily mean that employer organizations and greater productivity in physical terms cannot pay; what it does mean is that they must be more efficient and cost reducing than would otherwise be necessary to be able to compete.

Urgently needed is a fairly intensive study of the economics of neighborhood store-café retailing, especially as it relates to the sources of supply, ability to order by quality and grades, and the cost of distribution of generally small individual orders. While cooperation may not be the answer, there may be scope for licensing the use of a name with all that it implies for standarization of appearance, arrangement, and service. A guide for this may be found in the practice, already existing in Latin America, of financing and licensing uniform gasoline service stations that, while individually owned, appear to belong to a chain. In this way the flexibility of family enterprise may be combined with certain economies in distribution and uniformity in quality.

A particularly promising field for this type of marketing organization would seem to be in meat, where, at least in Colombia, the distribution system is chaotic. Retail distribution is in the hands of small butcher shops which acquire their supplies in the form of large cuts of animals which they in turn cut up. Apart from a few traditional cuts, there is an almost complete lack of standardization in quality, and crudely applied price controls militate against adequate price variations to reflect differences in quality. Larger vertical organizations, reaching back to the cattle growers and forward to the family butcher shop might, in these conditions, pave the way for modifications in the present system of price controls and for the inauguration of uniform cuts and qualities associated with brand names. The spectacular progress in the production and distribution of chickens and eggs in recent years suggests the progress that might also be possible in beef. In the former, the market in Bogotá has grown to the extent that producing units of 10,000 chicks in a batch are common, and deliveries from the hatcheries to the retail outlet in truckloads are economic. Thus the industry has progressed to a point where the market permits economies of scale, and these economies in turn favor the growth of the market at the expense of beef. In one case, competition favored the development of a relatively efficient marketing organization; in the other, competition, combined with sporadically applied price controls, has not been able to break through an inefficient marketing structure.

Milk is still another case where health regulations, price controls and a certain pattern of income distribution have together profoundly affected the marketing structure. The example is again drawn from Bogotá. The high-income market is catered to by a few relatively small pasteurizing plants selling high-quality milk at a high price. A middle-class market buys raw milk of widely varying quality at a lower controlled price. This milk is customarily delivered in bottles and is boiled by the buyers. Finally, the lower income market is supplied by a single pasteurizer with bottled milk of generally low protective value at a relatively low controlled price. Although tuberculosis of bovine origin is virtually unknown, as is also undulant fever, the emphasis is placed on health rather than protective food value. In terms of the latter quality, which should be the chief consideration, the cheap pasteurized milk is probably actually very expensive. This, then, is another case where the degree of competition that prevails is thwarted by price controls and health regulations from supplying the bulk market with milk of uniform and high quality.

BROADER CONSIDERATIONS

Writers on marketing, as on other economic activities, generally assume implicitly that greater sales per seller, or greater transport of ton-miles per person, or lower cost per unit handled, or better quality and packaging at the same time are all "good" and to be desired and to be striven for. If they thought it worth the while, they could doubtless say that for the sake of clarity in argument, a writer on marketing cannot be concerned with what happens to displaced workers, to total employment, or to the distribution of the work force. These considerations are in other economists' fields of study. The implicit assumption of a fluid labor market, of continuous "full" employment, and of an economic allocation of the work force is, however, frequently forgotten, and recommendations of marketing procedures and structures that depend for their validity on these assumptions are urged even where they do not hold. It is here argued that in dealing with underdeveloped countries, the writer on marketing should constantly be aware of his assumptions and be prepared to modify his recommendations when conditions do not accord with his assumptions.

I have elsewhere argued at some length[5] that a characteristic of Latin American countries is the continuing existence of an enormous mass of disguised unemployed or underemployed or, if one prefers to put the same thing in other terms, of a shockingly poor distribution of the work force. Under such conditions a release of manpower from marketing or distribution activities may not be an unmixed blessing. If, in real economic terms, the net gain from an improvement is measured by the value of what is produced by workers displaced by such an improvement, it may be nil. This, of course, is elementary, and the reader may impatiently say that such considerations are irrelevant to the discussion of a particular issue or improvement. A somewhat similar point might be made of the replacement of a number of stores with low sales per seller by a much larger and more "efficient" unit. Even if the displaced workers

---

[5] *Accelerating Development* (New York: McGraw-Hill Book Co., 1966).

are reabsorbed, the social costs of the necessary additional transport may outweigh the purely accounting savings.

The traditional reply that cost reductions lead to increased real demand, and hence employment, depends implicitly on the reabsorption of displaced labor. If this later does not occur, the increased real income of consomers is offset by the decreased real income of the displaced. This consideration should not stop us from trying to increase physical productivity; it merely suggests that we must beware of identifying such gains with gains for the whole community unless we are sure that the mobility mechanism is actually functioning.

When the mobility mechanism is functioning very badly, overcrowding of marketing activities may be only a reflection of this functioning and not the basic cause of low productivity and income.

For instance, it may be maintained that disguised unemployment in retail trade is a disguised form of poor relief which, by raising the price of food, is a tax on the poor, a large portion of whose income is spent on food. Disguised unemployment is undoubtedly an evil which impoverishes the society as a whole. But the blame is to be laid at the door of national policies and institutional factors which cause it. Given the lack of work, efforts of individuals to participate in retail distribution can hardly be said to *raise* the cost of distribution if competition prevails. The real cost is the opportunity cost of their not being able to work full time in more remunerative employment.

To what extent should a writer on marketing take such considerations into account? Does the horizon have to be expanded beyond the actual competitive cost and pricing process? If such a writer is to make his maximum contribution, it would seem that he should range further afield than is customary in weighing the possibilities. For example, with greater equality of worker incomes, what is "economic" in marketing becomes very different from what is economic when the economy is characterized by widespread disguised unemployment on the one hand, and highly "advanced" labor legislation on the other. In these conditions, what is economic has little to do with measures of physical productivity, and a great deal to do with structural or institutional factors. Consider the following: Some years ago there was a sudden decline in salary payments in the cotton textile industry in Colombia. It developed that following a marked gain by the union, the largest company found it would pay to import more rather costly office machinery and replace some of the salaried workers. This was no doubt economic in accounting terms. Whether it made sense in real or national economic terms is more doubtful.

This example suggests another limitation on the application of simple cost-benefit calculations. If foreign resources are strictly limited, as they usually are, and are rationed either through a high exchange rate or by the necessity to procure licenses, the apparently extravagant use of labor in distribution may be justified in terms of the opportunity cost of marketing equipment that may have to be imported. Equal sums spent on other imports may yield even higher national returns.

In developed countries, economic growth consists partly in producing better quality or new goods but mostly in producing goods with less and less units of labor. In underdeveloped countries, the main problem is putting idle manpower to work producing things for which there is effective demand. The emphasis, for some time, must be not so much on displacement of labor as on absorption in more remunerative work.

What is being suggested here probably will not be well received, as it tends to convert what may be a simple and elegant demonstration of cost-saving modifications in marketing (and in other activities) into a messy discussion of the repercussions and consequences of a host of institutional and even cultural factors. The advantages of supermarkets may depend, under these conditions, not so much on their superior efficiency in general as (a) on the size of the car-owning higher income groups and (b) the extent to which the greater efficiency can offset the higher costs imposed by the Labor Code or trade-union agreements. In other words, the particular marketing structure of highly developed and more egalitarian economies becomes more or less irrelevant to that appropriate in many underdeveloped economies if conditions vary widely. The structure that is appropriate can only be determined by calculations of costs and volumes of sales under actual conditions.

Even these considerations may, from a national or social accounting point of view, have to take account of shadow costs and prices. If once we bring ourselves to the point of saying that the private car-owning, suburban-living pattern can only be for the few and is in any case inappropriate in countries where the many lack the bare essentials of a decent existence, then our whole attitude toward city planning, urban transport, and marketing undergoes a change. What then may make sense may be securing greater densities with less traffic by renovating large blighted areas near working centers and by subsidizing high-rise apartments (or charging suburban dwellers properly with the urban transport and other social costs they entail). In such case, larger volume stores may become economic, not for the private car-owning class, but for the carless apartment dwellers. Even in this case, however, the undoubted economies of scale may have to contend with the lower wage costs and longer service hours of the neighborhood store.

In his *Essay on Development*,[6] Professor John Kenneth Galbraith spoke of the necessity of a new theory of consumption for poor, underdeveloped countries. Such a theory would call for a greatly increased emphasis

---

[6] (Cambridge, Mass.: Harvard University Press, 1962), pp. 43–45.

on the production and use of mass consumption goods. Actually, we seem to be committed to the Trickle-Down Theory, where a disproportionate amount of attention is given to the articles of consumption of the well-to-do and to such marketing innovations as supermarkets and Sears types of stores. It might be argued that marketing surveys and studies in underdeveloped countries should take as their point of reference the items and weights contained in the workers' cost of living indexes. Food and beverages constitute approximately 50 percent of the cost-of-living index for urban workers in Colombia. Clothing is another substantial item. Starting from this base, economies could undoubtedly be achieved that would lower significantly the relative cost of articles and services of mass consumption. The extent to which these economies would benefit the whole community, however, would depend on the efficiency of the economic system in providing remunerative work for those displaced from transport and marketing activities. Criteria of marketing efficiency based on customary accounting concepts are much too restricted to cover the field adequately in underdeveloped countries where massive, though disguised, unemployment is the rule.

In another aspect, writers on marketing from developed countries may be inclined to exaggerate the benefits of warehouse, silo, and general storage facilities. These are not economic in themselves but constitute a cost that is only justifiable to avoid waste and spoilage and to prevent the wide variation in prices that alternating gluts and surpluses occasion in commodities for which demand is inelastic. However, it must be borne in mind that most of the underdeveloped countries are in the tropic belt, and harvests are more frequent than in temperate zones. With two harvests a year, or harvests taking place at differing times during the year according to different climates and altitudes, the need and justification for storage facilities may be greatly lessened than appears at first sight. For Colombia, various studies recommended greatly increased storage facilities without laying the requisite theoretical and factual bases. It cannot be simply assumed, for example, that there exist greater seasonal and interregional fluctuation in prices than can be justified by the prevalent very high return on capital or by transport costs. A much less exciting but more rewarding (in social terms) study might be that of facilitating arbitrage operations on the part of persons owning and operating trucks. The establishment of wholesale markets with daily published transactions by grades and prices might be all that is necessary to even out the wider intercity price variations. Storage facilities and carry-overs can undoubtedly be justified in various crops to meet seasonal variations and those resulting from gluts and shortfalls of important harvests; however, it also would appear worthwhile to try to exert more influence on consumer habits by publicizing food values per unit of currency. The consumer demand for potatoes, for example, is so inelastic in Colombia that price swings from extremes of 30 to 300 pesos per unit have not been uncommon. Readily available starchy substitutes did not show comparable variations in prices at the same time.

It may not be fanciful to think that the consumer could bear part of the carry-over function. Home preserving is practically unknown and commercial canning is relatively expensive. Every year seasonal fruits at the height of the harvesting seasons sell on the streets at prices that must yield almost nothing to the producers. Most of these fruits could easily be preserved by consumers at small cost, as in former times in northern countries. For this change in habits, however, a considerable educational campaign would be necessary. This last case is an illustration of the tendency of both foreign and national technicians to look for inspiration to the practices appropriate to an economy like that of the United States, instead of looking to past practices in what are now developed countries, or to the development and improvement of existing practices in underdeveloped countries.

Another example of this tendency is the preference for expensively packaged goods instead of bulk sales, or for ready-made clothing instead of piece goods. The whole weight of advertising is on the side of the former, reinforced, of course, by snob appeal, natural indolence, and a great and growing lack of knowledge by girls of home crafts. The relative cheapness of maids and their natural and complete lack of interest in economic buying and utilization of food may be responsible for more waste than all the spoilage resulting from inefficient marketing procedures, which so concerns foreign observers. Making do with leftovers, a fine art in the United States and Canada 60 years ago, is an almost absent art in the middle- and upper-income classes in underdeveloped countries today. Maids customarily buy too much of the wrong things and throw away great quantities of food. They appear to be one of the more inefficient links in the distributing and processing chain, comparable to the great variety of foods offered even by comparatively small restaurants.

CONCLUSION

It would be a serious mistake to overstate the argument of this paper. Undoubtedly, laborsaving improvements in marketing as well as other types of improvements can and should be made in underdeveloped countries. The point of the paper, rather, is to warn against too easy an acceptance and recommendation of practices prevailing in developed countries without careful checking in each case. Various arguments can be adduced to cast doubt on the implicit assumption that American marketing organization and practices may be applied, with appropriate lags, to underdeveloped countries. These arguments rest on the possibility that underdevelopment is self-perpetuating, that certain modern American patterns and ways of life may be quite inappropriate for underdeveloped countries, that the appropriate strategies may also be inconsistent with the adoption of certain American patterns of living, that close attention must be paid to the early emergence of stringent labor requirements, and that storage facilities requirements differ in tropical regions where most underdeveloped countries are found. None of these is an unalterable condition, but may exist for some time to come. If so, this suggests the need for a new look at the neighborhood family store, together with ways and means of improving its efficiency—ways and means that may extend back to the producer. The assumption that all workers displaced by improvements will promptly be reabsorbed in the productive process, i.e., that the mobility mechanism is functioning smoothly, needs to be checked and, if not valid, its implications need to be weighed.

Finally, it is suggested that something can be done to improve quality and consumer education and to reduce wastage in the home. There may well be too much emphasis on preprocessing foods and in packaging in countries where poverty is the rule rather than the exception, and where labor is the superabundant factor.

Influence of MARKETING on the environment

In one of the preceding articles, Professor Bauer responds to often-voiced criticisms of the foreign firms operating in African markets. Under appropriate competitive conditions, Bauer points out, foreign marketers can be a source of considerable benefit to an economy. In this article, Dr. Adams shows how, under protected semimonopolistic conditions, the "alien" or "outside" traders can have dysfunctional as well as beneficial impacts. The concluding portion of the article indicates the resemblances between white-Indian relationships and other examples of culture contact in the marketplace.

WILLIAM Y. ADAMS*

The role of the Navajo trader in a changing economy[†]

The Navajo trading post, a general retail store serving a largely or purely Indian clientele, has been called "the best remaining example of frontier commerce."[1] Some 200 trading posts, all essentially similar in character, are scattered over the vast Navajo Indian Reservation in the "Four Corners" area of Arizona, New Mexico, Utah, and Colorado; until very recently they supplied nearly all of the commercial needs of about 90,000 Indians.[2] The trading post at Shonto, in northeastern Arizona, was the subject of an intensive anthropological and economic study between 1953 and 1956, from which the present chapter is drawn.[3] Information on

---

[*] University of Kentucky.

[†] Most of the material in this chapter is drawn from the author's *Shonto: A Study of the Role of the Trader in a Modern Navaho Community* (Bureau of American Ethnology Bulletin No. 188 [Washington, D.C.: Smithsonian Institution, 1963]), and especially from pp. 272–307 therein. The reader is referred to this work (hereinafter cited as *Shonto*) for full documentation of primary sources.

[1] C. Kluckhohn and D. Leighton, *The Navaho* (Cambridge, Mass.: Harvard University Press, 1946), p. 38.

[2] The institutions here described should not be confused with countless Indian curio shops which style themselves "trading posts" for the sake of local color. These latter are of course strictly cash-and-carry enterprises catering to the White tourist trade; Indians rarely set foot in them.

[3] The study was carried out by the present author during several periods when he was himself employed as trader at Shonto, and the behavior described is therefore largely his own. It was, of course, learned by imitation and precept from other traders, and was implicit in the role.

133

changes since 1955 was obtained in the course of a brief visit to Shonto and neighboring trading posts in July 1967.[4]

HISTORICAL BACKGROUND OF THE NAVAJO TRADE

Trading posts made their appearance in the Navajo country immediately after the Navajos were released from military control at Fort Sumner, just over a century ago. At this time, deprived alike of Government subsidy and of the power to raid their neighbors, the Navajos were obliged to take up a new way of life as settled farmers and pastoralists. They were aided in this transition by the earliest traders, who taught them to raise wool on a large scale for the commercial market, and who also encouraged their womenfolk to weave brightly colored blankets and rugs for the curio trade. At the same time, the traders instilled in the Navajos a taste for, and a dependence on, American manufactured goods, which very soon supplanted most of the native handicrafts. In the years between 1868 and 1900, no other agency of American society played so important a role in transforming the character of Navajo life as did the trading post.[5]

By the turn of the century, the interdependence of Navajo and trader was nearly complete. Trading posts, privately owned for the most part by local pioneer families, were scattered at intervals of 20 to 30 miles all through the Navajo country; for the great majority of Navajos they represented the only regular contact with the White Man's world. The trading post bought the Indian's wool and rugs, and in return provided him with most of the necessities of life which he could not produce for himself. It also provided him with his only real window on the world beyond the reservation. Other White Man's institutions—schools, hospitals, missions, and the like—were to be found only in a few administrative centers, and they hardly touched upon the daily life of the average Navajo. If someone had dealings with the Government, he generally went first to the trader, who acted as his intermediary. For their part, Government agents and missionaries alike sought the assistance of the trader in making contact with the Navajo. He was not only the sole White Man permanently resident in many districts of the reservation, he was also (as he remains today) the only one who spoke the Navajo language after a fashion. Thus he came to occupy a unique position as the principal avenue of communication and understanding between two cultural worlds.

The trader, then, enjoyed a comfortable and secure monopoly of commerce which lasted all through the early decades of the 20th century.

[4] I am grateful to the University of Kentucky Research Foundation for providing the necessary funds to carry out this inquiry.

[5] See especially Ruth Underhill, *The Navajos* (Norman: University of Oklahoma Press, 1956), pp. 177–95.

It was guaranteed alike by his territorial isolation, miles from the nearest competition; by the lack of mobility in his clientele, whose inability even to speak English condemned them to life on the reservation; and by the general Navajo ignorance of the White Man's ways, which made them culturally as well as economically dependent on the trader. The Navajos remained a primitive and an unassimilated people, and the reservation an undeveloped area. By and large, the White Man was content to have it so. The trader, having instituted and obtained control of a profitable economic exchange, was happy to let the process of assimilation stop at that point. The Indian Agent, nominally responsible for Navajo education and assimilation, was hampered by lack of funds and of public interest, and was satisfied with the status quo so long as the Indians did not become an economic or a political problem. Missionaries, although they worked tirelessly to educate the Navajos in a few areas, were few in number and were even more hampered by lack of funds.

Up to 1930 no more than 10% of Navajos had learned to speak English, and an even smaller number had actually been to school. Nearly all members of the tribe lived in earth-covered log huts (hogans) without benefit of furniture or modern conveniences, and there was not a mile of paved or even decently constructed road on the Navajo Reservation— an area half as large as New England. The same lack of progress was reflected in the trading post, which presented, as it still does to a large extent, the aspect of an old-fashioned country general store.

Until a generation ago the trading post genuinely deserved its name; very little cash was involved in the Navajo economy. Trading in the beginning had been a matter of straight barter, but the seasonal nature of lamb and wool production, as well as the absence of any concept of capital among the Indians, soon made the institution of credit essential. In the early 1900's the Navajo family lived chiefly on a combination of subsistence farming and credit against wool sales in the spring and lamb sales in the fall. Additional income was obtained from weaving rugs and from the exchange of commodities such as hides and pinyon nuts; these were paid for by the trader not in cash but with merchandise.

If the trader was obliged to carry the Navajo family on credit from season to season, the mercantile house from which he drew supplies was obliged to carry the trader on much the same terms. The trader had hardly more chance to accumulate capital than had the Navajo; his buildings and ground, situated as they were within the reservation, belonged by law to the tribe, and his accounts receivable were largely unsecured. His great hope was always to make a killing in the resale of wool, but his capital position seldom permitted him to hold it for any length of time while waiting for a better price. As one long-time trader expressed it, "In the old days we never kept accounts. We just sent our wool along to the 'merc,' and they told us whether we made a profit or a loss for the year." If trading in those days seldom offered opportunities for wealth, it was also at least largely free of the hazards of competition.

The 1930's ushered in an era of unrest and change. The Indian Bureau, alarmed at the rapid deterioration of the range through over-grazing, enforced a drastic reduction of Navajo livestock holdings which, in the eyes of the Indians, threatened their very basis of livelihood.[6] At the same time, and by way of economic compensation, there was insti-tuted a widespread program of road, school, and hospital construction, which for the first time made wage work available even in the most remote districts. The transformation thus begun was greatly accelerated by the onset of World War II, with its unlimited demand for unskilled labor. Navajos left the reservation in droves to work in mines, railroads, and ordnance depots; for many, it was the first real look at the outside world.

The demand for unskilled labor remained high during the long post-war boom, and Navajos continued to make the most of it. They sought out especially those types of work—agricultural labor and railroad track work—which would not take them away from their families and their livestock for more than a few months at a time. Thus an annual period of off-reservation employment became an accepted part of the seasonal round of life, and was expected of all of the younger men in each family. By 1955 off-reservation wage work was producing more than half of all Navajo income, while the value of all native industry (agriculture and livestock combined) had shrunk to less than a quarter.[7]

The trading post since 1955

The years since 1955 have brought further profound change to the Navajo country. Modern paved highways have been extended to many parts of the reservation; they have not only increased Navajo mobility, but have opened the area for the first time to an enormous volume of tourist travel. With it has come the growth of roadside business—service stations, cafes, motels, and curio shops—typical of modern America.

During the same period the Bureau of Indian Affairs and the state governments of Arizona and New Mexico have built innumerable new schools, hospitals, and other facilities on the Navajo Reservation. For the first time in history, nearly all Navajo children of grade-school age are now attending school relatively near their homes. On its part, the Navajo Tribal Government has made use of its substantial revenues from oil, gas, and mining leases to finance a series of public works projects designed to improve roads, trails, and range, and at the same time to provide short-term employment for Navajos. These projects, as well as the construction

---

[6] In actual fact Navajo income from livestock production increased consistently in the years following the stock reduction, although the quantity of fresh lamb and mutton consumed at home undoubtedly declined.

[7] *Shonto*, p. 146.

of new schools and other government installations, have very largely taken the place of off-reservation employment as the chief source of Navajo wage income.

Conspicuous and impressive as are the material advances in the Navajo country since 1955, a more potentially significant change is represented by the vastly increased number of non-Indians—both tourists and resident administrative personnel—who are now to be found in every part of the reservation. From a social standpoint, their presence has intensified the scale of Navajo-White contact and has further stimulated the Navajos' desire for the amenities of modern American life. Economically, they have contributed important new income to the reservation economy.

The total volume of cash in circulation on the Navajo Reservation has probably trebled since 1955. Several factors are responsible for the increase. First, as in America generally, there has been an absolute increase (amounting perhaps to 50%) in per capita income. Second, the rapid expansion of the Navajo population has added substantially to the number of wage earners. Third, the general replacement of off-reservation by on-reservation employment has meant that a much higher proportion of wage earnings find their way into the local economy. Finally, the increase in Navajo Reservation income from all three sources is probably equalled by the income now contributed by White residents and tourists.

In some respects, trading posts could hardly fail to benefit from the expansion of the reservation economy since 1955, and the actual volume of trade at most stores has certainly increased. At the same time operating costs have also increased significantly, and as a result profits are down in many areas. Most important, the trader's share of the Navajo cash dollar, in competition with town merchants and a few modern businesses which are beginning to appear on the reservation, has certainly declined. In the general economic expansion since 1955, the typical trading post has only just held its own, while town merchants and other modern retailers have reaped most of the profits. The underlying peculiarities and uncertainties of the Navajo trade remain to plague the traditional trading post and limit its capacity to change.

THE COMMUNITY OF SHONTO IN 1955

The Shonto region, a land of rugged mesas and deep canyons with an average elevation of 6,500 feet, remained one of the most remote and least developed parts of the Navajo Reservation. In 1955 it was still 132 miles from the nearest town and railroad, and 75 miles from the nearest paved road. The Government administrative center to which it was subject, including the nearest police, court, and hospital, was 55 miles away over a very rough road. Over 50% of Shonto adults still could not speak English, and fewer than 10% could read or write. The end of this condition was clearly in sight, however, for nearly all of the community's children were in school by this time.

In many respects, Shonto Navajos still lived as they had 50 years earlier. Their houses, their dress, and their material culture were hardly altered. Cars and trucks were few; light wagons and horses were the principal means of transport, and some parts of the region were inaccessible to vehicles. Above all, the traditional fabric of life, with its complex of social and ritual obligations, was still very much intact. Modern government, whether federal or tribal, was distant and impersonal, and affected the community chiefly insofar as it provided income in the form of jobs or relief. Christianity had not been introduced, and native religion continued to provide an important focus of interest and activity.

As might be expected in this relatively backward region, livestock, agriculture, weaving, and other native enterprises remained somewhat more important in the economic scheme than they did in other parts of the Navajo country. Even so, they accounted for only 22% of Shonto's income, while seasonal railroad work, with its concomitant unemployment compensation in the off-season, alone provided 52%. Other sources of income were agricultural and miscellaneous employment off the reservation (6%), wage work on the reservation (12%), and various forms of welfare payments (8%).[8]

Shonto Trading Post had a regular clientele of about 100 families (568 individuals), who lived widely scattered over an area extending some 30 miles from north to south and 20 miles from east to west. Within this territory the store enjoyed an absolute monopoly of trade. None of the families within the area traded to any extent, or received credit, at any other trading post, although they might of course make casual purchases when visiting in neighboring areas as well as in the course of infrequent shopping trips to off-reservation towns. Shonto Trading Post in return drew a certain amount of casual trade from other districts in the vicinity. In addition to its regular clientele, members of about 50 more families traded at Shonto often enough so that they were known personally to the trader, although they accounted for no more than 15% of sales. Itinerants unknown to the trader, both Indian and White, contributed another 5%. From the combination of these sources Shonto Trading Post in 1955 grossed about $150,000.

THE TRADING POST AND ITS OPERATION

The physical appearance of Shonto Trading Post was fairly typical of Navajo trading posts in the 1950's and had hardly changed since the store was built around 1918. The exterior was unprepossessing in the extreme:

[8] *Shonto,* p. 127.

a low building of rough-hewn native sandstone with a few small, heavily barred windows and a single door.

The interior of the trading post presented the typical cluttered appearance of the old country store. Merchandise of all sorts occupied every square inch of shelf space, hung all over the rafters, and stood here and there on the floor in the "bullpen." At any given time about 75% of the total inventory would probably be thus displayed; "they won't buy what they can't see" was a cardinal rule. Types of merchandise were essentially those found in any rural general store; they included groceries (mostly canned goods plus flour, sugar, and salt), drugs and sundries (chiefly packaged remedies), dry goods (ready-made work clothes for men, bolt goods for women, shoes for both), various kinds of hardware and utensils, camp furniture and manual appliances, harnessware and livestock equipment, fuels, and feeds.

Supplies were mostly obtained from two general mercantile houses located in towns adjacent to the Navajo Reservation, respectively 130 and 165 miles from Shonto. They were delivered by truck every two weeks, except when mud or snow made the roads impassable. High freight costs, as well as a high interest rate on his mercantile accounts, added substantially to the trader's overhead—a differential which was of course passed on to the Navajo consumer. Retail markups varied from about 35% on groceries, to 75% on dry goods, to 100% on hardware.

The normal staff of Shonto Trading Post comprised one or occasionally two White traders and a Navajo assistant. Additional temporary help was employed during the peak seasons of lamb and wool buying. Sales volume fluctuated enormously according to weather and season, but averaged out at about $500 per day. The store was open daily except Sunday from sunup to sundown, and was occasionally opened later, or on Sundays, for the benefit of customers from a distance. There were still a few Navajos, living in isolated areas, who did not keep track of the days of the week.

Business was transacted very largely in the Navajo language, or a pidgin derived from it. Traditionally it was a drawn-out ritual, with long pauses between purchases, and it was often punctuated by a good deal of verbal by-play. There was no serious haggling over prices, which were rigidly fixed and conspicuously marked. As a result of their trading experiences nearly all Navajos, literate or illiterate, had learned to read numbers, and they were always well aware if they had been overcharged or short-changed.

Day in and day out about 60% of sales were credit transactions, while 30% were cash sales and 10% involved direct exchange of merchandise —mostly Navajo rugs. Not more than one-third of credit sales were secured by pawn (native silver jewelry), which was kept in a locked vault at the back of the store. Other accounts were unsecured, since the assets of reservation Indians are legally exempt from attachment.

WIDER FUNCTIONS OF THE TRADING POST

Unlike many trading posts in even more remote areas, Shonto Trading Post was not, in 1955, the only representative of White America in the community. A small boarding school for younger children, built in 1935, occupied a plot of land adjacent to the store. It had an enrollment of 70, with a staff of two White teachers and four Navajo assistants. Ten miles away was the headquarters of Navajo National Monument, a tourist attraction which drew about 2,000 visitors annually, and which furnished employment for several Navajos. An itinerant missionary was active in the community during much of 1955, but did not succeed in setting up a permanent establishment.

Although it thus shared with the school, and national monument, and the missionary the responsibility of representing the outside world at Shonto, the trading post to a large extent retained its pre-eminence as the main focal point of culture contact. This role had of course been developed before the establishment of the other institutions, which were of more recent origin. The trader also remained the only member of the White community who could speak passable Navajo, and therefore the only one to whom a majority of adult Navajos could address themselves without having recourse to an interpreter. Above and beyond these practical considerations, however, the trader diligently maintained his traditional, protective interest in the community and all its doings.

Shonto's trader in 1955 remained far more than an entrepreneur. If anything, the complexities of modern life had increased the number and variety of functions which he was expected to perform on behalf of his clientele. As the official Claims Agent for the Railroad Retirement Board, he was responsible for recruiting men for railroad labor, and for obtaining their unemployment compensation during the off-season. He was officially delegated by the Navajo Tribal Government to distribute surplus commodities and emergency relief to the needy, by the Department of Agriculture to give out seedlings and pesticides, and by the Commodity Credit Corporation to arrange incentive payments to wool producers.

His unofficial functions were even more numerous and varied. He was universally expected to help the older people to get on relief and the younger people to find jobs; to help in securing veterans' benefits, back pay, and other financial rewards; to give advice and information on all manner of economic transactions; and to do everything in his power to assure a maximum income for each family in the community. He was also expected to protect individuals from the law if they got into trouble, by lending money to pay fines, by vouching for their character to the police, or, occasionally, by professing ignorance of their whereabouts. Having one of the only two telephones at Shonto, he was very often asked to make contact with police, schools, or hospitals outside the community. He was also asked to read and translate letters, and occasionally even to write them. Above and beyond all these things, he was constantly called upon to explain what was going on in the outside world in terms meaningful to Navajos.

The trading post itself served both officially and unofficially as a community center and a meeting place. It was the one place where every Navajo could sooner or later expect to encounter every other Navajo. News and gossip of the community were exchanged there, and the trader was expected to pass along the latest happenings on the outside, as obtained from the radio or from a recent trip to town. Officials of the Federal and Tribal Governments used the store as a place to hold meetings or to make contact with individual Navajos, and notices of importance to the community were posted on a bulletin board. All members of the community received their mail at the trading post.

ECONOMIC CHANGE AND THE TRADER

In 1955, then, the trading post remained a prominent and an indispensable community institution throughout the Navajo country. Nevertheless, the general pattern of change and development since 1930 had undoubtedly diminished its importance in Navajo life, and had begun to undermine its economic security as well. The development of wage work had introduced large amounts of cash into the reservation economy—income which could be spent at will and did not have to be marketed through an intermediary. At the same time the gradual penetration of roads and automobiles into the heart of the reservation increased Navajo mobility, and raised for the first time the specter of competition. The extension of schools, clinics, and other governmental facilities, as well as missions, throughout the reservation often meant that the trader was no longer the only White Man in the community, and some of the former dependence on him was transferred to others.

There was still very little competition between trading posts, except in the rare areas where they were located close together. By and large they shared the same conditions of isolation and limited resources, and few of them could offer inducements to trade which their neighbors could not duplicate. From the 1930's onward, however, there was always and increasingly the threat of competition from retail merchants in off-reservation towns. Situated close to railroads and highways, and dependent chiefly on high-volume, cash-and-carry trade, they could offer not only a wider selection of goods but also prices 15% to 20% lower than those obtaining on the reservation. Particularly in the postwar era, when an occasional trip to town became a regular part of life for most Navajo families, the trader had to resign himself to the loss of a certain proportion of cash trade to his off-reservation competitor.

Nevertheless, up to 1955 Shonto and most other Navajo trading posts had managed reasonably well to adjust to the changing times and to hold onto their markets. Territorial monopoly still largely insulated them from local competition, especially for the less mobile part of their clientele, and as marketing agents they could still count on nearly all of the trade for wool, lambs, and other commodities. It was only for the Navajo cash dollar that they had to compete with the town merchants.

Shonto's trader and his neighbors met this challenge very simply by minimizing the flow of available cash, through the technique of credit saturation. The key to their competitive position lay much less in territorial monopoly than in the fact that they were the only merchants close enough to the Navajo consumer, both literally and figuratively, so that they could afford to extend credit without security. This they proceeded to do up to the last dollar of predictable income—thereby insuring that whatever cash came into the community was encumbered in advance, and would not be free to flow out again into the hands of off-reservation competitors.

The seasonal nature of most Navajo income production—not only in livestock products but also in off-reservation wage work—insured a continuing high dependence on credit, and therefore on the trader. We have already observed that 60% of all transactions at Shonto in 1955 were credit sales, and the percentage in the case of the 100 families who traded regularly at Shonto Trading Post would have been considerably higher. There was no family in the community which did not live on credit during a considerable part of each year, and this circumstance more than anything else reinforced the trader's economic position.

In the practice of credit saturation the trader was aided in two ways by his wider role in the community. As intermediary in all sorts of financial dealings, he was able to predict Navajo income with considerable accuracy. He knew the size of every family's livestock holdings, and insofar as he could foretell commodity prices he could estimate the amount of income to be expected from lamb and wool sales. He knew from experience about how many rugs to expect from each weaver. His official position as Railroad Claims Agent gave him accurate information about each employee's railroad earnings, and also enabled him to foretell exactly how much unemployment compensation each man would draw during the winter. His unofficial dealings with the state welfare agencies on behalf of applicants and recipients furnished him with similar information in regard to welfare payments. He could and did obtain from his White neighbors information about the earnings of their Navajo employees.

Through his various channels of information, the trader could probably predict with 80% accuracy the income of almost any family in Shonto community. Credit limits were calculated accordingly, and were prominently marked on the cover of each family's account book. These figures represented something more than simply cutoff points; they represented an ideal level of indebtedness which the trader hoped would be achieved before the next income was received. The art of "filling up" credit so that an account reached its limit just before wool buying or before a check was due became one of the trader's essential skills. It was a practice fully comprehended by Navajos themselves; the more uneducated and more trusting members of the community actually expected the trader to "hold them down" and to manage their credit so that it would not be exhausted long before the next income was due.

A further advantage to the trader accrued from the fact that all Shonto families received their mail at the trading post, so that he generally knew when money, and especially checks, came in. The trader did not expect most of his customers to pay up without a good deal of prompting; he took it for granted that whenever they could they would take their money to town and spend it instead of settling their accounts. This made it essential for him to know when cash was actually received, and to assert his claim on it before it left the community. His task was greatly facilitated by the fact that nearly all cash income arrived in the form of checks, mailed in easily recognized envelopes, and sometimes with the face value visible through the transparent address window. The trader's normal practice when a check arrived was to deliver it to the recipient together with his account book, the unspoken assumption being that the whole of the check (or as much of it as was owed) would be applied on account.

Although of course the trader could not refuse to hand over a check to its intended recipient, he could and did refuse to cash it unless it was applied on account. The same stipulation was made in the case of money orders. If for any reason the recipient did not owe anything, the trader might refuse to cash a check or money order unless a certain part of its value (normally 50%) was taken in merchandise rather than in cash. Since it was 20 miles from Shonto to the next neighboring store, this sanction was effective enough in most cases. Moreover, checks for the illiterate majority of Shonto Navajos had to be thumbprinted and witnessed, and most merchants were unwilling to do this if they were not personally acquainted with the bearer.

The ultimate sanction which the Navajo trader could exercise over his indebted clientele was the threat of withdrawing credit. This would in fact be carried out whenever a family received income which it did not apply on account, and it would remain in effect until the account was paid. Since no Shonto family could afford to live entirely without credit, and since none could obtain credit anywhere except at Shonto Trading Post (except for very limited sums which could be raised by pawning silver jewelry), the trader could rest assured of ultimately collecting virtually all of his accounts. Over the years his credit losses were probably less than those of the average town merchant.

The trader used his position and influence in the community to competitive advantage in other ways. Insofar as he could, he discouraged or impeded mobility on the part of his clientele. He would not loan them money to buy cars, or furnish credit references to car dealers in town. Although obliged by the terms of his operating license to sell gasoline, he was often "temporarily out." Gasoline was sold for cash only; it was the only commodity handled by the store which could not be had on credit.

When he got the chance, the trader generally disparaged the town merchant and his goods. Low prices in town were probably a sign of inferior merchandise; also, they were "before taxes." (Retail sales tax was not charged on Indian reservations.) The trader did his best to prevent competitive advertising or mail-order catalogues from circulating in the community, and he would not give assistance in preparing mail orders.

Shonto's trader did not encourage Navajo economic activity which benefited his competitors more than himself. He was strongly opposed to seasonal agricultural labor, since in this case whole families left the reservation together, and little of what they earned found its way home in the form of cash. He also looked with disfavor on the permanent resettlement of families off the reservation. To him railroad track labor represented the ideal Navajo economic activity; it took the men away only intermittently, and did not bring them into close contact with disruptive influences on the outside. At the same time the women and children were left permanently on the reservation and in dependence on the trading post. Navajo familial responsibility was such that he could count on substantial sums being sent home by the absentee workers, even to the extent of granting credit against such earnings.

THE ROLE OF THE TRADER IN 1955

Up to 1955 Shonto and other Navajo trading posts had adapted themselves as best they could to the altered conditions of the postwar era, and continued to do a thriving business. Their adjustment was not notably in the direction of modernization; the physical plant, the inventory, and the operating methods of the stores had hardly changed in 50 years. Continuing isolation, undercapitalization, and high overhead condemned them to conditions of high markup and low turnover, and made it impossible for them to compete on even terms with the town merchant in a free market. They had, instead, retained their position by finding new ways of maintaining the Navajos' dependence on them.

At the same time it was clear that the process of social and economic change could not go very much farther without seriously threatening the livelihood of most trading posts. As Navajo mobility and financial independence increased, a few of the more favorably located stores might be able to transform themselves into a reasonable semblance of modern retail enterprises. The rest would inevitably go the way of the country general store elsewhere in America.

Alone among institutions of American society, the trading post had adapted itself to the special conditions of Indian life and culture, and had in its turn become dependent upon them. The trader thus found himself in the same situation as his most conservative and least educated Navajo clients. Of all the individuals and agencies involved in the contact of Indian and White Man, it was they who were least able to meet the challenge of a changing economy and society. In their respective ways they were both condemned to the reservation, and to the limitations of reservation life, by their inability to compete on the outside. They were in fact condemned to and by their dependence on one another.

Not surprisingly, then, by the middle of the 20th century the trading post had become a conservative force—perhaps the most powerful conservative force—in the Navajo community. The influence of the trader upon Navajo opinion and behavior remained, for the time being, greater than that of any other White Man. That influence, which extended far beyond the economic field, was used again and again, in subtle as well as direct ways, to reinforce the status quo. Above all, it was used to perpetuate Navajo dependence on the trading post.

The special relationship between the trader and his Navajo clientele could be summed up in the word "paternalism." It was this condition which ultimately gave the trader his competitive advantage over the town merchant, and which he sought in every way possible to maintain. He continued to perform all kinds of voluntary services for the community not merely because they often redounded to his profit or even because they created customer goodwill, but because in a larger sense they helped to perpetuate Navajo dependence on him.

The trader did not encourage Navajos to establish a similar relationship with other White Men. Of all the numerous functions of Government on the Navajo Reservation, only the schools and the hospitals were acknowledged as being wholly beneficial, and having a proper place beside the trading post. Other governmental programs—law enforcement, grazing control, resource development, and the like—were at best remote and impersonal, and at worst potentially detrimental to Navajo welfare. Insofar as community members were affected by such programs, it was best to deal with them through the intermediary of the trader, as the one man who could be counted upon to understand and to look out for their individual interests. From time to time the trader even went so far as to protect his clients from potentially detrimental effects of government action, by concealing his knowledge of excessive livestock holdings, by withholding information from the police, and by securing welfare benefits for individuals who were not technically eligible. In all of these ways he was able to emphasize the contrast between his own role as personal friend and adviser and the roles of most other White people, whose dealings with Navajos were necessarily more impersonal and governed by administrative protocol.

In short, the trader sought to maintain his historic position as the main avenue of communication between the Navajo and White worlds. He was still, in 1955, the only White Man to whom a Navajo could apply for advice or assistance on almost any subject without fear of being refused or referred to someone else, and he was the only White Man who could be addressed in the Navajo language. He was also still accepted by many of his fellow Whites as the best channel of communication with Navajos, as attested by his appointment as Claims Agent for the Railroad Retirement Board and his designation as local administrator for several government programs.

In addition to his function as an intermediary in communication, the trader sought also to maintain and to exploit his role as interpreter of the White Man's world and the place of Navajos in it. Here again his action was colored by self-interest. While he could hardly fail to pay lip service to the ideal of ultimate Navajo assimilation, he voiced the practical caution that most Navajos were not yet ready to make the break with age-old tradition, and that under the circumstances it was better to remain good Indians than to become poor imitation White Men. The truly educated Navajo, on the other hand, should not waste his time on the underdeveloped reservation, but should seek a permanent place in the outside world where there were opportunities commensurate with his abilities.

The trader's general attitude toward education suggested that there was no acceptable middle ground in the process of Navajo assimilation. The educated Indian should go forth and become to all intents and purposes a White Man, away from the temptations of traditional life. The uneducated should remain on the reservation and should remain Indians. This meant, for them, being content with life on the reservation, its facilities and its resources. For his part, the trader worked hard to see that as many as possible of the Navajo's needs were met within the community, and if possible through his instrumentality, and he sought to forestall the development of needs which could not be satisfied at home.

The off-reservation world, as the trader pictured it, was a hostile and dangerous place for uneducated Navajos. Merchants were cold and impersonal, took no interest in the individual welfare of customers and their families, and would not extend credit. The towns were full of gamblers, bootleggers, and prostitutes who preyed on the unsuspecting Navajo, and of police who were ever ready to jail them for disorderly conduct or loitering, and perhaps to steal their money and jewelry in the bargain. Once in jail there was no one to stand up for them or advance bail money as the trader did at home. Above all, there was no place in the system for the idler and the unemployed. If you weren't prepared to work hard you should stay at home. The easygoing security of life on the reservation, with the trader standing as a buffer against the disruptive forces of the modern world, was thus contrasted with the dangers and uncertainties of life on the outside.

However much they may incidentally have benefited from it, most traders were perfectly sincere in this conception of their role in Navajo life. Nor was it by any means an inaccurate one. For the uneducated majority of Shonto Navajos the trading post, for all its coercive sanctions, really did offer an indispensable measure of security and a protection against the disruptive influences of the 20th century. Alone among the bewildering array of the White Man's institutions, it overtly assisted Navajos in maintaining many elements of their traditional way of life.

Thus what had been, a hundred years earlier, the most active force for change in the Navajo world had become instead a source of stability and a buffer against change. The still paramount influence of the trading post in Navajo-White relations was now exerted to retard, to divert, and to prevent cultural change rather than to promote it. This had become more essential to the trader than to many of the Navajos themselves.

In their 40 years of operation up to 1955,[9] the traders at Shonto had consistently sought to increase the community's material standard of living without disturbing the traditional framework of Navajo life, with its implicit condition of dependence on the trading post. From the vast complex of 20th century American life they had selected and introduced only those needs which they themselves could satisfy. They had endeavored to confine the impact of American culture on Navajo culture to those economic and material fields which would directly benefit the trading post, while minimizing or forestalling a more general assimilation which would weaken Navajo dependence on them. The external impulses which had passed through them from the White world to the Navajo world had been selected, modified, and reinterpreted for their own purposes, and they had presented Navajos with a picture of American life and their place in it which was largely of their own devising. In 1955, they had become a focal point of resistance to further cultural assimilation of the Navajo.

---

[9] Trading at Shonto actually began in 1915 when a trader from a neighboring district brought in a wagonload of supplies which he sold out of a tent. The permanent store was built three years later. The business had had five owners up to 1955, and was sold again in 1958.

Traders were often criticized by Navajos and Whites alike for their conservative influence and their unwillingness to accept change. In a way, and to a large extent unwittingly, they were nevertheless performing a vital service to the Navajo people. In the contact of tribal peoples with western civilization, social disintegration and cultural demoralization have very often resulted from a too-rapid process of change, when traditional life-ways have been abandoned before there were any satisfactory alternatives. Up to 1955 this had not, in general, been true of the Navajo. Traders had played their part in restricting the scope of culture contact and in slowing down the process of culture change so that the integrity of native society was preserved. Most significantly, they had managed the process of economic change so that it did not, as among many other tribal peoples, have disastrous repercussions in other areas of life. However self-interested their motives, the Navajo traders were helping to keep alive an archaic but still necessary social and economic order even while a new one was taking shape around them. In so doing they were once again helping to smooth the Navajos' road from the past to the present.

THE SHONTO TRADING POST IN THE LAST DECADE

To a very large extent, the amount of change observable in Navajo trading posts over the last decade can be measured in terms of the volume of White trade which they are able to attract. Some stores, located close to the new highway, have become essentially roadside businesses, and now rely on the casual tourist for a good part of their income. Some of the larger administrative centers on the reservation now offer most of the amenities of full-fledged towns, and here are to be found modern self-service stores fully competitive with those off the reservation. These enterprises have dispensed altogether with credit and commodity trade, and are content to rely instead upon the substantial White cash-and-carry trade in their communities, and on the very considerable Navajo cash trade which their lower prices and wide selection can attract.

At the opposite extreme, trading posts which remain "off the beaten path" have changed hardly at all since 1955. Lacking the advantages of a White clientele, they are obliged to continue the old practice of credit saturation as the only hope of hanging onto their consumer markets. In spite of the increasing hazards of collection, resulting from much greater Navajo mobility, the number of credit accounts based upon livestock production, and the amount outstanding on them, has actually increased since 1955. To some extent, the greater risk in the livestock trade is offset by an increase of between 200% and 300% in the number of welfare accounts. Since relief checks continue to be sent through the trading posts, these represent the only credit accounts which are still "captive"; they are becoming the cornerstone of trade at some of the more backward stores. One trader of many years' experience flatly stated in 1967 that "it's the relief that's keeping these places going."

In 1967 Shonto Trading Post found itself in a position somewhere between the two extremes described above. The store was still 10 miles from the nearest pavement, and was not attracting any appreciable amount of tourist trade. On the other hand, the construction of a large boarding school in the community offered potentially a vast new source of income. In 1967, its first full year of operation, the school had a staff of 40 teachers and 128 full-time employees; its annual payroll was probably equal to the entire income of Shonto Navajos ten years earlier.

In an effort to attract the trade of the school personnel, Shonto Trading Post in 1966 underwent its first significant modification in 30 years. Although the old building was retained, the trading area was considerably enlarged, and groceries were put on self-service counters. Several refrigerated cases were installed, and the store carried some fresh fruits and vegetables, as well as bread and other bakery products. Hardware and dry goods were sold over the counter, as before, in the older part of the store.

The attempt at modernization appeared to have relatively little effect on trade. Although the school personnel were doing some "fill-in" shopping at Shonto, and their trade was undoubtedly important to the store, it was clear that they were doing the bulk of their shopping in town or in a larger center 50 miles away, where they could find lower prices and a wider selection. To a large extent it was the same with the Navajo clientele; self-service alone was not enough to draw them, although it was undoubtedly appreciated by many of the younger members of the community. In general, however, their cash trade went where lower prices were offered.

As a result, the basic operation of Shonto Trading Post was little changed between 1955 and 1967. The store continued to rely heavily on credit accounts based on livestock, relief checks, and local payrolls. The volume of lamb and wool purchases had declined slightly, but had been partly offset by an increase in rug production. Credit accounts based on local wage earnings, at the school and at Navajo National Monument, had largely taken the place of the older railroad accounts.

The situation of Shonto Trading Post seemed typical of the dilemma of many traders in 1967. There were now two almost unrelated economic systems on the Navajo Reservation: the older, essentially seasonal economy involving an annual round of livestock production and temporary wage work, sustained largely on credit, and the new year-round cash economy in which credit could be sacrificed in the interest of low-price, high-volume trade. The more remote trading posts were still inextricably tied to the former, while the most favorably located stores could devote themselves wholly to the latter. Shonto and many other stores, however, faced an immediate practical problem in attempting to bridge the gap between the two systems so as to make the most of both of them.

As of 1967, they had apparently not found a satisfactory solution to the problem. They seemed to face a choice between sticking to traditional methods of operation, with a continual decline in their share of the Navajo consumer market, or undergoing a drastic modernization which was probably beyond their means, and for which a large part of their clientele was in any case unprepared. Whatever might be the cost in terms of economic backwardness, it was still true in 1967 that there was no other institution either within or beyond the community which was prepared to take over the complex of functions which the trading post had traditionally performed in Navajo life for the better part of a century.

THE ENTREPRENEUR IN CULTURE CONTACT: SOME GENERAL REFLECTIONS

The role of the trader as a preserver of traditional culture in the modern world is by no means restricted to the Navajo country. It has parallels wherever entrepreneurs are in contact with native economies: in South America, in Africa, in Southeast Asia, and in Oceania. In each of these areas the trader entered the scene as a powerful force for change, and has ended as a defender of traditional ways of life.[10]

This recurring transformation of the trader's role has significant implications for the study of developmental change in general. It points up the obvious fact that the various representatives of western civilization—soldiers, administrators, missionaries, and traders—have quite different motives for making contact with primitive peoples, and these motives in turn condition the response which they expect of the natives. Probably all of them today subscribe at least nominally to the ideal of assimilation, but it is also clear that they define "assimilation" in very different and sometimes conflicting terms.

To the soldier, assimilation perhaps means no more than disarmament and pacification. At that point his work is done, and he therefore seldom remains a permanent factor on the scene. To the trader, assimilation means articulation into a commercial economy, through production of raw materials and consumption of manufactured goods. At this point his ideal of assimilation is likewise satisfied; any further development of the

---

[10] See *Shonto*, pp. 298–307, for specific references to the role of traders in other parts of the world.

process might bring with it a degree of economic self-sufficiency which would be detrimental to the trader's interest. To the missionary, assimilation means the adoption of Christianity as well as of a wide variety of ethical standards and interpersonal responsibilities, and the abandonment of any native beliefs and practices which are inconsistent with them. It does not, however, mean the adoption of the less desirable characteristics of modern complex society, and consequently the missionary usually discourages any degree of intermixing with civilized westerners. To the Government administrator, assimilation may mean the attainment of full citizenship or independent self-government, but not to the extent of eliminating the existing bureaucratic structure.

In their different ways the soldier, the trader, the missionary, and the administrator each adopts a limited definition of native assimilation. If the trader's is more conservative than those of his colleagues, it differs in degree rather than in kind. No one in practice wants the process of assimilation to go so far that his own livelihood is endangered. In 1849 the U.S. Army strenuously objected to surrendering control of Indian affairs to the newly created Indian Bureau, arguing (as military authorities have in the case of more recent projected pullbacks) that the danger of hostilities was not yet past. In its turn the Indian Bureau in the 1950's opposed the idea of a general Federal withdrawal from the Indian reservations, again arguing that the time was not ripe. Like the trader, each of these institutions revealed itself as a conservative force when its continued operation was threatened. If the trader is more often and more overtly conservative, it is because he is more immediately threatened.

The history of economic contacts between western civilization and tribal peoples would probably reveal a fairly consistent pattern of development. Except where military conquest was involved, the earliest contacts would probably have been made by entrepreneurs of one sort or another. In some parts of the world they would have found a market economy already flourishing; for the most part, however, they would only have encountered some form of subsistence economy. Initial trade would necessarily be a matter of barter. However, if the natives could produce any commodity for which there was a general market, the entrepreneur would soon organize commercial production, in exchange for a regular supply of European manufactured goods. Credit could be introduced as soon as the trade became institutionalized.

Predictably, the pioneer trader would soon be followed by missionaries, administrators, and, in circumstances favorable to commercial agriculture, by settlers. In the latter case the natives would eventually be dispossessed of their best land, and a plantation economy under European management would emerge. The native subsistence base would then be largely destroyed, and the native himself would become a wage or indentured laborer. The trader's function would be absorbed by the planter and his company store.

An independent native economy would be likely to survive only in areas unfavorable to commercial agriculture, or where, as in the case of Indian reservations, it was artificially protected. In these areas the role of the trader, as connecting link between native economic production and the modern market economy, would become institutionalized.

In the beginning the trader, no less than the missionary and the administrator, would have a strong interest in promoting change in the native culture. His particular objective, however, would simply be to develop a maximum volume of trade without disrupting other areas of native life. Once trade was fully developed he would have no interest in further assimilative change, which might tend toward the creation of a free market economy and thus undermine his own position. At a certain point, therefore, he might find himself at odds with the missionary and the administrator, who would continue to work toward a greater degree of native assimilation.

When education had reached a certain level of development the native himself would recognize the advantages of assimilation, and would work actively to promote it. The trader would then be left with a stronger interest in the status quo than any other individual, either native or western, and would become the most powerful force in the community for the preservation of traditional culture and society. This was what was happening at Shonto in 1955.

Professors Glade and Udell argue that the marketing concept is as appropriate a business orientation in the developing countries as it is in the
developed ones. They judge the behavior of Peruvian industrialists against
the standards inherent in the marketing concept and find much room for
improvement. The Peruvian economy has suffered, they find, because of
the businessmen's failure to study, to appreciate, and to serve the available
market potential.

WILLIAM GLADE and JON G. UDELL*

The marketing behavior of Peruvian firms:
obstacles and contributions to
economic development

INTRODUCTION[1]

In the literature of development, it is recognized that the possibilities for
economic growth are strongly conditioned by prevailing institutional
patterns. To date, this recognition has led to studies of a variety of social
organizations which influence the economic process at one point or
another: e.g., trade unions, financial intermediaries, land tenure systems,
and governments. Yet only a beginning has been made in clarifying
many aspects of business behavior in the newly industrializing countries,
notwithstanding the likelihood that the development process implies
considerable alterations in the structure and functioning of business units
no less than in other socioeconomic organizations.[2]

---

* University of Wisconsin.

[1] The material which follows is related to a field research project conducted in
Peru between February and July, 1966, under the joint auspices of the Center for
International Business Research of the University of Wisconsin and the Universidad
del Pacífico of Lima.

[2] This comparative "underdevelopment" of business research in underdeveloped
areas is probably attributable to a variety of factors. Among them are: the immediate
need to develop sectoral and macroeconomic measurements for planning purposes; the
belief that the policies of the public sector (which may be viewed as the leading
sector in development) are more susceptible to change; the tradition of business
secrecy in underdeveloped countries; and the lesser interest of trained business
researchers in the problems of these countries (given the abundance of researchable
topics closer at hand).

The focus of this article is one aspect of business behavior, the marketing practices of industrial sector firms, in Peru, a country which is currently well into the initial stages of industrialization.[3] The selection of this particular behavioral aspect was based upon the assumption that the activities of marketing constitute an integral part of a dynamic economy, for it would appear that a modern type of economic system cannot operate effectively without fairly massive and efficient marketing efforts. Witness, for example, the recent policy changes which have been made in the centrally planned economies. It is the contention of this article, however, that improved marketing performance is also crucial to the economic modernization of less developed countries.

Though the importance of the market (as distinct from the marketing process) was recognized in such early works as the *Wealth of Nations,* the mainstream of economic analysis has concentrated on the production of goods and services and the participation of production factors in the income stream. Insofar as the market has been considered, it has been included in the observation that aggregate demand constitutes a principal limiting condition in development.[4] Market size, in turn, has commonly been taken as a given condition, determined primarily by the volume and distribution of purchasing power,[5] with occasional references to the effects of transport costs on the extent of the market. Less frequently, except in studies of agricultural market organization, has market size been viewed as a partial function of the marketing behavior of business firms. Notwithstanding Schumpeter's recognition of market development as an important form of entrepreneurial endeavor, the marketing process has been largely relegated to a distinctly subordinate position in the field of development analysis.

To fill part of this gap, the present essay seeks: (*a*) to offer an explanation of the marketing behavior observed to be prevalent in Peru, and (*b*) to indicate, by projecting this behavior against a performance

---

[3] According to the latest revision of Peruvian product and income statistics prepared by Mr. Richard Webb of the Banco Central de Reserva del Peru, between 1950 and 1964, real GNP grew at an average annual rate of 5.7 percent while the average growth rate for the manufacturing sector during this period was 7.8 percent. Productivity, or output per worker, rose at an average annual rate of 3.5 percent during these years, but the annual rate of improvement in productivity in the manufacturing sector was 5.1 percent on the average. As yet, however, manufacturing contributes only 17 percent of national income, compared with 16 percent for commerce and 22 percent for agriculture.

[4] This, for example, is the way in which the market is treated in well-known works of Rosenstein-Rodan, Nurkse, and Mosk.

[5] The income-distribution effects on the character of market demand, discussed several years ago by W. P. Strassmann in "Economic Growth and Income Distribution," *Quarterly Journal of Economics,* Vol. LXX (August, 1956), pp. 425–40, have been applied to the Brazilian case in "The Growth and Decline of Import Substitution in Brazil," *Economic Bulletin For Latin America,* Vol. IX, No. 1 (March, 1964), pp. 1–59.

criterion called the "marketing concept," the impact with shortcomings in marketing practices have on the development process of that country. The performance criterion is drawn from recent developments in the field of marketing in the United States. While it incorporates a certain normative value, it appears to derive this (at least to judge from the context of current discussions of the subject) experientially. In this sense, the marketing concept designates an orientation in business behavior which is functionally appropriate to an industrialized setting, somewhat as the familiar Parsonian schema of pattern alternatives has often been employed to describe the social relationships characteristic of (and functional to) a modernized setting. Given the objective of development, it is almost unavoidable that normative values tend to be associated with the relationships and behavioral orientations which predominate in industrialized societies.

For purposes of this paper, we have taken "marketing" to include the planning, promotion, distribution, and servicing of the products used by consumers (broadly defined to include both households and industrial and institutional users). The term, the marketing concept, identifies the focal point or source of direction for the conduct of these and related functions in the enterprise: the perception that a consumer orientation, supported by market research and consequent innovations in products and distribution strategy, should be central to the operations of the enterprise. It contrasts with a managerial orientation in which production decisions tend to set the pace of the firm, with the marketing functions being relegated to the task of disposing of that which has been produced. The difference between the two approaches may be viewed as one of emphasis, but it does serve to distinguish the area of business activity in which the "leading decisions" are taken.

Theoretically, of course, the exercise of consumer sovereignty and Adam Smith's "invisible hand" of competition direct the allocation of resources in a free market economy. However, from a social point of view, optimum allocation may not occur when industry is not competitive in the classical meaning of the term. Instead, a conscious effort by management to determine and cater to the changing needs and desires of consumers is necessary to derive maximum social benefit from a nation's private-sector resources.

Fortunately, this conscious effort, which is really another way of expressing the marketing concept, also relates to consumer sovereignty and provides a basis for differential success in the area of business rivalry. It is undoubtedly this private reward, not public considerations, which is prompting the adoption of the marketing concept in American industry. Thus, that the marketing concept should emerge as functionally appropriate in a high-income society is understandable. With the more elemental consumer needs already met, at least insofar as these are registered in patterns of market demand, and with interproduct substitution an increasing possibility, competitive success often rests importantly on skill in ferreting out less obvious consumer fancies. For rather different reasons, the marketing concept would seem to have decided relevance as a performance criterion in the industrialization process of low-income countries.

ORIGINS OF THE PERUVIAN INDUSTRIAL SECTOR MARKETING SYSTEM

Many believe, not altogether without justification, that Peru is a bastion of traditionalism in Latin America. Since the mid-19th century, however, there has been a distinct change in the economic organization of the nation which grew out of the old Spanish viceroyalty. For over a century this transformation has centered upon the growth of the export sector. Led, at first, by the exploitation of guano deposits, export-induced development has brought also the commercialization of coastal agriculture (primarily cotton and sugar), the initiation of highly capitalized mining ventures in the highlands, and most recently, the rapid growth of the fishing industry. Though the importance of guano exports eventually dwindled considerably, as did a short-lived boom in natural rubber around the turn of the century, the other export industries have remained as significant props of the national economy, giving Peru a more diversified set of comparative international advantages than any other Latin American nation except Mexico.

In the process, the nation acquired railways, port facilities, and communications systems, all of which facilitated the flow of goods to foreign markets. Meanwhile, earnings from the growth of exports financed a counterflow of imports, mainly to Lima and a few other, quite secondary, population centers. These centers emerged, therefore, as an accessible nucleus of domestic markets whose consumers drew their livelihood from employment in foreign-trade businesses, government, the professions, various domestic financial and commercial enterprises, and, owing to the institution of absentee ownership, from provincial agricultural estates as well. This domestic market growth was not, however, widespread; as recently as 1961, according to the Banco Central de Reserva, the Lima-Callao departments, which contain less than a quarter of the national population, received 42 percent of the national income. Gradually, even before the turn of the present century, local production serving these markets came into being: e.g., an assortment of food and beverage firms, textile mills, and woodworking enterprises. Here and there, machine shops were established, initially for repair and maintenance functions, but in time some of these began to fabricate a variety of comparatively simple producer goods needed by the economy. Virtually all of these early firms were small-scale operations; and since their customers were ordinarily close at hand, their marketing activities tended to be quite simple.

From this period of incipient national development, there sprang a number of features of lasting consequence for the subsequent course of Peruvian growth. However rudimentary it was at the time, a newer type of distributional network came into being which served primarily the coastal markets and, to a lesser extent, scattered portions of the highlands. Based upon the handling of exports and imports, it differed considerably from the traditional segmented market organization which served the provincial and rural regions of the nation, although there were occasional points of contact between the two types of structures. Thanks to the rising volume and value of exports and imports, the mercantile enterprises active in the external sector emerged as major focal points of domestic capital accumulation. Frequently established by immigrant entrepreneurs, typical firms which date from this period are those which bear the names of Ferreyros, Berckemeyer, Piaggio, Weise, Gildemeister, and Custer. Moreover, these same firms were often linked with new banking institutions which they had helped establish to provide the local financial services required for the conduct of foreign trade. In the 20th century, as conditions became appropriate for the initiation of a greater variety of local production enterprises—in part due to internal changes such as growing urbanization and rising income levels, but also because of exogenous events such as two world wars and the interwar depression —these firms played a leading role in the process.

For several reasons, in fact, the foreign-trade houses were uniquely advantaged to enter domestic manufacturing. In the course of handling imports, they had gained considerable knowledge of modern product specifications, had accumulated capital internally, and had acquired established lines of credit both in Peru and abroad. Moreover, through the marketing of imports such firms had developed the best knowledge available concerning the existing local markets as well as the distributional networks which gave them access to these markets. Although there were risks and uncertainties involved, the nature of their Peruvian business experience had prepared these firms to overcome many of the obstacles which commonly afflict the new entrepreneur in a less developed environment. Whereas, for example, the environment was still foreign-trade oriented and generally deficient in external economies, the scale and ramifications of the mercantile firms generated internal economies which encouraged the vertical and horizontal integration of an expanding array of business ventures. Thus, the historic precedent of the early European industrial revolution which witnessed the transformation of mercantile capital into industrial capital was partially replicated in Peru.

Both deliberately and unintentionally, public policy during the past three decades or so has facilitated the transformation: through protective tariffs and other commercial policies which modified the composition of imports and promoted local industrialization, and through public spending programs which boosted aggregate demand in these by-now partially closed local markets. On occasion, for instance, protection was a by-product of measures aimed at strengthening the balance-of-payments position; at other times it resulted from the rise of revenue tariffs to quasi-protective levels.[6]

In all of this, little resembling the marketing concept was involved. Relatively passive forms of marketing efforts sufficed for the captive local market, in which the range of buying alternatives was severely limited by protective tariffs and a scarcity of domestic competitors. On the basis of the market cultivated previously through importing activity, a certain demand was practically assured for local manufacturers. In addition, the captive demand was subject to further expansion because of population growth, accelerated urbanization, and the rising incomes generated by the growth of exports and public and private investment activity. Given this setting, it is not surprising that the chief focus of private business attention was on the investment and production aspects of development.

Public policy, meanwhile, had a very similar orientation, although, in this, Peruvian policy makers were merely conforming to the dominant counsel of the times. With few exceptions, the theorizing of development economists and the policy recommendations of various advisors placed an emphasis on such matters as capital formation, investment priorities, and the fiscal and monetary policies deemed appropriate for raising national investment and production levels while reducing strains on the external economic position of a country. For the most part, and particularly in respect of industrialization, it seems to have been generally assumed that marketing progress would automatically accompany progress in production and the provision of physical distribution elements such as roads.[7] Therefore, changes in market structures and marketing

---

[6] It should be noted that, in Peru, governmental encouragement of import-substituting industrialization has not been so deliberate or systematic a feature of public policy as it has been in many other Latin American countries; and the general level of tariffs has been lower than in these other countries as well. See, on this point, the Economic Commission for Latin America, *Analyses and Projections of Economic Development, VI, The Industrial Development of Peru* (Mexico: United Nations Department of Economic and Social Affairs, 1959), pp. 152–54; and Santiago Macario, "Protectionism and Industrialization in Latin America," *United Nations Economic Bulletin for Latin America,* March, 1964, p. 75. On the other hand, the lack of a consistent and comprehensive policy in this regard has not meant that fairly high levels of protection have been denied specific industries. The result has been, according to a recent study, a rather haphazard and dispersed development of the industrial structure. Comisión de Industrias, *Diagnóstico del Sector Industrial* (Documento Preliminar para Discusión [Lima: January, 1966]), p. 26.

[7] For example, the case for "unbalanced growth" (meaning the deliberate development of "strategic imbalances"), presented several years ago by A. O. Hirschman in

policies were treated as derivative or induced aspects of economic development, not as initiating or possibly autonomous sources of growth and higher productivity.

DYSFUNCTIONALITY IN ENTERPRISE BEHAVIOR

In a somewhat different context, Alfred Marshall observed long ago that "the struggle for survival tends to make those methods of organization prevail, which are best fitted to thrive in their environment; but not necessarily those best fitted to benefit their environment. . . ."[8] The point is pertinent to the present conduct of industrial marketing in Peru. In the light of the evolutionary situation which conditioned the industrialization of that country, the marketing traits which are common to a large portion of the firms studied are understandable, being an outgrowth of the economic milieu in which these firms have operated. At the same time, however, it is questionable that this marketing behavior—oriented, as it has been, to exploitation of a captive market—represents the most promising basis for sustaining the industrial momentum already achieved, if, indeed, it ever was instrumentally valid from a social standpoint except on a *faute de mieux* basis. For that matter, it is probably not even functional from a private point of view insofar as it tends to lower the marginal efficiency of the capital invested in the private sector. At any rate, given the present national commitment to accelerated development within the framework of a mixed economy, the modal type of marketing behavior observed, particularly among domestically owned and managed firms, appears clearly dysfunctional.

The degree of protection accorded certain industrial lines, while certainly justifiable up to a point, has nevertheless permitted a fairly high level of costs to develop. Partly a result of the simple managerial and labor inexperience which is unavoidable in a newly industrializing society, the high cost level is also a function of a variety of other factors, including public policy. As the E.C.L.A. study of Peruvian development noted,[9] the fiscal system (including tariffs) long remained geared primarily to revenue considerations, resulting in relatively stiff taxes on raw materials and intermediate goods imports (and even some capital goods

his *The Strategy of Economic Development* (New Haven, Conn.: Yale University Press, 1959), makes heroic assumptions in this regard, for it posits an elasticity of supply response of a very high order, despite the author's recognition (*ibid.*, p. 154) that administrative or office operations are likely to lag substantially behind production operations in efficiency. Of the two chief sources of development advice for Latin America, E.C.L.A. and and the World Bank, the latter has generally taken greater cognizance of the relevance of the marketing process than the former.

[8] A. Marshall, *Principles of Economics* (New York: Macmillan Co., 1949), pp. 596–97.

[9] E.C.L.A., *loc. cit.*

imports) for which substitute domestic supplies were not likely to be available for a considerable length of time. Consequently, production costs are raised, while the costs to the ultimate consumer go up even more from pricing policies based on a high unit markup and low sales volume principle. The cost-price situation is not helped, to say the least, by what appears to be a generally casual approach to the selection and development of efficient distribution channels. Comparatively few firms, in fact, seem to have given much explicit consideration to possible alternative means of placing their output in the hands of the final consumers with minimal intermediary charges.

Moreover, perhaps from a desire to avoid the troubles associated with dealing with a larger labor force as well as for want of sufficient local engineering competence to adapt imported techniques, the choice of capital-intensive production technologies and of industrial lines with this characteristic has led to the familiar dilemma of selecting between high-cost suboptimal scale plants and more nearly optimal-sized facilities used at less than capacity and, therefore, at high cost.[10] The aforementioned distribution and pricing policies tend, of course, to aggravate the situation by contracting the marketable volume. The result is a final product price level so high that the potential market, small enough to begin with, is reduced even further.

Beyond this, however, both the production technologies and the products these technologies are designed to turn out have often been borrowed from abroad with scant regard for the question of whether or not either is the most appropriate choice for the Peruvian situation. Indeed, there is remarkably little evidence in the survey of over one hundred industrial firms that much systematic market research has ever been made to identify consumer needs and preferences among alternative product types, as these preferences might be expressed if the range of effective buying options were broader. In practice, the range of consumer choice is very limited. A seller's market often prevails, and, from the standpoint of those consumers who are not priced out of the market, the offering of goods is, in many instances, on a "take it or leave it" basis.

In regard to the prevailing nonexperimental approach to the determination of product suitability, recent experience in Chile is perhaps instructive. There, at the suggestion of the late Jorge Ahumada, the Banco del Estado surveyed domestic manufacturers for their interest in developing new economy-lines of bicycles and stoves for sale to low-income

---

[10] Certain public policies, such as the financing of welfare services out of payroll taxes, rather than taxes on profits, have tended to inflate the cost to firms of labor factors, while low-interest-rate loans to finance the importation of fixed capital and certain tax concessions such as exemptions on profits reinvested in plant and equipment have tended to lower the cost of the firms' capital inputs. Domestic inflation, which affects wage rates, combined with stability in the foreign exchange rate, has further favored the substitution of capital inputs for labor inputs.

groups. Manufacturers doubted the feasibility of the proposal, mainly on the grounds that there was little market for such items. The Bank then placed a sizable order for both, undertaking to act as the marketing intermediary. At the same time it initiated a savings account campaign in low-income districts (where, it was widely believed, there was little savings potential), employing the inducement that savers depositing a certain amount would be eligible to purchase the stoves and bicycles through the Bank. Within a short time, both the savings were elicited in encouraging volume and the new economy-line products were sold. Thus, through governmental marketing initiative, a new market was opened up for private "enterprise."

On the whole, Peruvian firms seem no more innovationally inclined than their Chilean counterparts, so that it does not appear that business activities in Peru are, in any very meaningful sense, geared to the real needs and desires of the national market. Indeed, there is evidence that even some firms which are relatively large by Peruvian standards may not know much about the market they already reach,[11] while still less is known of the marketing possibilities outside of the principal metropolitan centers. Practically all of the very limited market research which is conducted seems to be devoted to advertising problems and is confined to the two largest urban market areas. The whole production-distribution complex, in fact, exhibits the traits which one might expect in a situation in which a partial shelter from foreign competition is combined with a weakness in domestic competition. With limited access to capital supplies, a lack of effective legal safeguards on collusive and monopolistic behavior,[12] and the inability of the small domestic market to support more than a handful of firms in particular lines of production,[13] the situation permits production and distribution to be carried on without a constant effort to reduce costs. Inflation, though less rapid in Peru (about 8 percent annually from 1950 to 1965) than in certain other South American countries, has been still another factor associated with a lack of cost consciousness on the part of producers.

As will be seen, the result of the foregoing is a paradox. On the one

---

[11] When, only a few years back, a large nationally owned manufacturing enterprise was purchased by a foreign holding company, it was discovered that the firm had no records of the sales volumes of its different product lines and no information on where its several products had been sold. Neither had it developed cost accounting procedures to determine the costs and, hence, the relative profitability, of its various activities. Little basis existed, therefore, for planning the company's marketing strategy.

[12] Vertical integration has, in all likelihood, been encouraged further by the turnover tax which gives an advantage to goods fabricated through several stages of processing by one enterprise as contrasted with goods whose several processing stages are handled independently.

[13] According to the previously cited *Diagnóstico*, 50 percent of the gross value of industrial production is generated in only 155 firms.

hand, the impression is widespread in the business community that the total market size is relatively static or fixed, that there are no more than 3 million or so active consumers in the market of a nation with 12 million people. The large majority of the inhabitants are simply not participating, or not thought to be participating, in the national economic development process. Insofar as the market for national production is thought to be subject to expansion, it is largely through a process of import displacement that involves selling the same set of consumers a wider range of locally manufactured goods. While the national market does expand somewhat, to the extent that income and employment multiplier effects may accompany the process of domestic investment, these expansionary influences are limited by the high cost and price levels of national production, which tend to reduce effective demand by eliminating the lower-income groups from the market. Therefore, the perception of a comparatively fixed total market tends, apparently, to be confirmed.

On the other hand, it will presently be clear that the market size described by this set of conditions is partly a function of prevailing business practice itself. To the degree that business behavior is predicated on the assumption of a relatively inelastic market, a situation arises which approximates the so-called self-fulfilling prophecy.

MARKET SIZE AS A FUNCTION OF BUSINESS BEHAVIOR

Economists, it must be admitted, may bear some share of the blame for this predicament; for, more often than not, they have described economies such as that of Peru as dual economies consisting of a modern sector and a subsistence sector. The latter term designates the population of the sierra,[14] which is viewed as not being a part of the consumer market of the nation. In one sense, the "subsistence" label could indicate a level of living which, for the majority in the sierra (and for many on the coast), is scarcely above the level necessary for survival. However, it is likely that another connotation of the term often influences the general perception of the subsistence sector. From this point of view, "subsistence" defines a system of production and consumption in which households are almost entirely self-contained units, producing most of that which they consume. In such a system, there is at best a meager scope for trade and monetized exchanges, which means that the process of commercialization has not developed very far.

Of these two connotations of subsistence, there can be little doubt that the former is indeed an accurate characterization of the life of many

---

[14] The Peruvian sierra, consisting of the Andean mountains and intermontane valleys, includes the majority of the indigenous population, many of whom do not even speak Spanish. Some 70 percent of the total national population lives either in the sierra, nearly 60 percent, or in eastern Peru, about 12 percent.

Peruvians, especially in the sierra but also on the coast. But to hold that the latter connotation of subsistence is equally accurate would be misleading; as the colorful indigenous fairs and markets attest, there is a striking amount of exchange occurring within and among the villages and regions of the highlands. Some of this trade is conducted by barter, but in many instances money is used, particularly in effecting exchanges of highland goods (foodstuffs and handicraft items) for manufactures (chiefly from the coastal region). Moreover, the experience of the credit cooperative movement in mobilizing substantial savings from the low-income groups of the sierra suggests that the amount of hoarded money (i.e., latent spending power) in the highland economy may be considerably larger than one might expect from the conventional description of the area as a subsistence sector. When, for example, one of the earliest credit unions was established in 1955 in the impoverished town of Puno, there were many who expected it to fail for want of resources and interest. Its beginning, with 23 members and a capital of $30 (U.S. currency), was not auspicious. Yet only six years later it had attracted well over 3,000 members and a capital of $400,000, the largest of any credit union in the country. For that matter, credit unions catering chiefly to the lower-middle and lower classes so increased their activity in the country generally that from 1961 to the end of 1964 their share of total savings in financial institutions rose from 2.8 to 8.1 percent. In short, although conventional business practice implies as much, it is a distinct exaggeration and misstatement to treat the poorer portions of the Peruvian economy as a nonmarket segment altogether divorced from the centers of economic modernization.

Nevertheless, even though there are links between the modern sector and the less affluent sectors, they are tenuous and rather rudimentary in nature—a circumstance for which there are several explanations besides the low level of popular income, the cultural isolation of the indigenous populace, and the shortcomings of the transport system. The customary pricing policies and the production and distribution costs of the modern sector place much of its output beyond the economic reach of would-be purchasers both in the hinterland and the coastal region. Developmental, or penetration, pricing as a means of market cultivation seems seldom to have been considered or utilized as a means of tapping the purchasing power of this unexplored market. In addition, the distribution practices of the modern sector's firms have paid slight attention to the possibilities of devising newer, more economical means for placing coastal products in the diverse marketing channels of the provincial regions.

Further, as noted earlier in another connection, it appears that comparatively few firms of the modern sector have ever made any systematic study of the actual and potential needs and buying preferences of the participants in either the traditional or the modern sector of the economy, particularly the former, to ascertain what products might be most fitting for the various conditions of life which prevail. Since, however, most of the decision makers in domestic Peruvian business come from the coast and from social strata quite removed from the day-to-day living patterns of the majority of the population, it cannot be assumed that firsthand knowledge of market characteristics is common among those in charge of preparing marketing programs.[15] Accordingly, there is little market research basis for either modifying existing products or developing new ones in order to render output more appropriate for the needs of consumers in the forgotten three fourths of the nation. Meanwhile, although political parties have done better in this respect, only modest attention has been given by business firms to the matter of communicating effectively with the non-Spanish-speaking population. Whereas consumer education or instruction is an important aspect of marketing communication in situations in which large numbers of people are abandoning traditional life styles for more modern buying habits, there is little reflection of this need in the marketing communications of most Peruvian firms. Few companies even do much to train their sales force, although the lack of trained sales personnel is a common lament among business firms.

Undoubtedly the underdeveloped state of provincial financial institutions and the limited range of investment options in the highlands help to account for the aforementioned money hoards which the credit cooperatives have begun to tap. But one strongly suspects that the failure of the modern sector to supply the traditional sector, through effective marketing, with either an adequate range of incentive consumer goods or suitable types of producer goods must be another important factor in explaining the existence of these funds. The lack of effective marketing also helps to explain the low level of aggregate regional income out of which these savings have been accumulated over the years. As Rostow has emphasized, ". . . archaic marketing arrangements make it unprofitable for the farmer to engage in higher productivity, agricultural production, and they thereby reduce not only agricultural output but also the size of the market for manufactured goods."[16]

---

[15] One of the lasting benefits of the recently inaugurated Cooperación Popular program, a national community development effort somewhat similar to the Peace Corps operations, may be its role in familiarizing the educated youth of the coast with the highland ways of life. Never before has Peruvian industry been able to draw upon such a reservoir of personnel so well acquainted, through direct experience, with the highland markets.

[16] W. W. Rostow, "The Concept of a National Market and Its Economic Growth Implications," *Proceedings of the American Marketing Association, 1965 Fall Conference,* p. 16. It is interesting to reflect that, as early as the eighteenth century, Spanish mercantilist writers were calling attention to the developmental advantages to be gained from encouraging a shift in indigenous consumption patterns to more modern styles. See, for example, Bernardo Ward, *Proyecto económico, en que se proponen*

The result of this situation, therefore, leads one to reexamine the validity of the widespread assumption that there are only about 3 million active consumers in Peru. It is clear that the assumption is valid only to the extent that definition of the market is based on prevailing pricing policies, the kinds of goods currently manufactured, the degree of skill presently employed in detecting consumer demand patterns and in operating marketing communications systems, and the existing distributional network. To assume further that the market size is static is to assume also: that income and other co-determinants of the market must remain constant, that the distribution system must continue to be unresponsive to the interests and needs of the populace, and that there will be no development of improved marketing structures.

THE COSTS OF MARKETING DYSFUNCTIONALITY

Inasmuch as the present performance of the Peruvian industrial sector, in its preoccupation with production, leads to business policies which are, from a national development point of view, poorly conceived and executed, there is some advantage in specifying the nature of the resulting costs to the economy, however impossible it may be to quantify these costs with any reasonable degree of accuracy. The reason for so doing is to suggest the value of adopting policies more in line with the marketing concept, although it is not implied that these are the sole requisites of advance in business performance. On the contrary, our research has turned up considerable evidence that such matters as improved industrial relations, personnel management, and the more effective use of cost accounting as a basis for managerial decisions are also areas in which current practice falls far short of what would be desirable in the interests of economic efficiency.

In the first place, given the current scarcity of aggregate national resources (a scarcity which can only be relaxed over a protracted period) and the enormous development needs of the economy, it is evident that the prime social task of the business sector is to devise means for relating resource use as closely as possible to the particular needs of the market. In so doing, the value generated by resource transformation will be enhanced and, in the process, consumer welfare will be better served within the constraints laid down by resource availability. Under the present production orientation, with its rather cavalier disregard of consumer requirements, available resources are not being stretched to meet the unfulfilled needs of the populace. Instead, consumers are forced by

---

varias providencias dirigidas á promover los intereses de España, con los medios y fondos necesarios para su plantificación, 4th printing, first written in 1762 (Madrid, 1787), pp. 266–84, and Joseph del Campillo y Cosio, *Nuevo sistema de gobierno economico para la América* (Madrid, 1789), pp. 112 ff.

public and private business policy to select from what happens to be offered (at high prices), while the needs of many consumers are ignored altogether. Under the circumstances, it is patent that a misallocation has occurred which involves a substantial sacrifice of consumer welfare, one which is especially costly since the marginal value of a given volume of misdirected resources tends to be great at lower levels of income. Since aggregate consumption must necessarily be restrained in the interest of national capital formation, a painful process in view of the prevailing low income levels, it is essential, if the development process is to be socially tolerable, to organize the output of consumer goods to minimize the sacrifice of short-term consumer welfare.

Indeed, considering the politically explosive situation which exists in Peru, as elsewhere in the underdeveloped world, this could be taken as a prerequisite of systems maintenance. The ability of the mixed economy to survive may well depend on its capacity to attain high standards of exactitude in supplying the consumers what they need.[17]

Secondly, an allocation of resources which is made without close attention to market preferences not only diminishes consumer welfare by supplying unwanted products or the provision of second or third choices rather than first choices. It also implies a waste of scarce capital and cooperant resources. To some extent, this resource wastage is present throughout broad portions of the captive domestic market, but at times the disregard of market demand possibilities has gone so far as to result in outright failure of crucial investment projects.

The fertilizer plant near Cuzco, for example, was established almost purely on the basis of production-oriented criteria: for example, the availability of a considerable supply of unused electric power which, in turn, derived from a previous miscalculation of potential market demand. After a brief period of capacity operation, which was intended to lower the unit production costs but which rapidly filled its warehouses to overflowing with unsold output, the plant management was brought forcefully, if belatedly, to the realization that marketing considerations

---

[17] This assignment of social validity to the set of needs expressed in the market is not, of course, absolute. To further long-run national development not all possible demands registered freely in the market should necessarily be ratified by corresponding shifts in the pattern of production. Indeed, clearly a good many should not be: e.g., pandering to an antisocial degree of conspicuous consumption is hardly supportable on any grounds while more urgent claims on resource use go unmet. In this, the operations of the public sector are of paramount social value, provided that private waste is not simply replaced by public waste as has unfortunately happened in some parts of the world. Similarly, there may be harmful products for which a demand might conceivably exist or be cultivated (for example, narcotics), the free production of which would not be proposed by even the most ardent classical liberals. These cases aside, and with all due recognition of the social validity of certain contraventions of the market mechanism, it remains true that effective marketing can play a valuable part in reducing the manifold market imperfections which have long held the efficiency of resource use to such low, and inhumane, levels in many parts of the globe.

are as important as production considerations in achieving an efficient use of capital. After only a few months of operation, in February, 1966, production was suspended, amid the embarrassing glare of national publicity. Although agriculture in the region served by the plant is, for the most part, notoriously primitive, the company evidently expected that the advantages of fertilizer would be so obvious that the product would sell itself. Virtually nothing was invested in developing a sales force, in advertising and consumer education, in setting up a distribution network, or in consumer service facilities.

A third category of cost relates to the charge that the deliberate fostering of national manufacturing development involves uneconomic departures from the pattern of resource use which would be dictated by comparative international advantages in production. Without entering into the cases for and against industrial protectionism, one may nevertheless observe that the presumed sacrifice of comparative advantage involved is certainly enhanced to the extent that national producers are careless in their production and marketing practices. Yet, with their potentially more intimate knowledge of domestic market requirements and with their firsthand knowledge of domestic marketing structures, and lower final-product transport and labor costs,[18] domestic manufacturers may realize, at least in certain lines, comparative advantages in designing, producing, and marketing goods specifically for the needs of the Peruvian market. In contrast, foreign-located firms selling in a variety of overseas markets, each differing in a multitude of ways from the others, must often seek their advantage in economies of scale, by producing and marketing relatively uniform products on a worldwide scale.[19] Thus, in their present production and marketing policies, local firms may well be forefeiting their latent competitive advantage in being able to gear their product development decisions more closely to the special requirements of their home market.

Moreover, to the extent that the smaller, less bureaucratized firms which predominate outside of the United States may possess, potentially, a greater flexibility in responding to changes, this last mentioned possibility becomes particularly important.[20] The accelerated social and eco-

---

[18] Few Peruvian manufacturers report substantial difficulties in imparting industrial skills to their work force, so that labor costs tend to be low, though not as low as the wage level might imply.

[19] Significantly, one of the difficulties which has been encountered in the current U.S. drive for export expansion is the predisposition of U.S. based manufacturers to neglect to adapt their products (often designed mainly for the conditions of the U.S. domestic market) to the requirements of overseas customers in a particular area.

[20] Edward A. McCreary, *The Americanization of Europe* (Garden City, N.Y.: Doubleday & Co., Inc., 1964), chap. xv. The book, while a popular, rather than a scholarly work, contains suggestive insights on this point. See also, Jon G. Udell, "Taking Advantage of Changing Markets," *Selected Proceedings of the First Annual Wisconsin Small Business Management Conference,* Madison, Wis., March, 1962.

nomic development being attempted in Peru should present a valuable competitive advantage over imports to the domestic firm practicing a skillful marketing management which is responsive to a rapidly changing market situation.

By anticipating these shifts in the needs of the economy, through careful market research, by planning investment and production programs accordingly, and by undertaking an unrelenting search for more economical means of moving goods from production sites to consumers, domestic producers could contribute far more strongly than they have been doing to the productivity of national resource use. Such would seem to be the chief hope for enlarging the market served in order to attain a more efficient scale of production, more favorable capital-output ratios, and ultimately, higher levels of real income and employment. To be sure, the process of import displacement has hitherto sufficed to expand the volume of industrial investment, but as the import-substitution possibilities are used up, new market development will become increasingly essential for maintaining the rate of capital formation in the industrial sector and absorbing the growing labor force productively.

Furthermore, if more efficient marketing is a prerequisite for developing the domestic market, it is no less so for reaching out to adjacent and somewhat similar export markets—or to export markets in general. Given the state of marketing behavior which prevails among Peruvian firms, the objectives sought in the United Nations Conference on Trade and Development are not likely to be realized even if the advanced countries were to reduce the barriers to imports of manufactures from the underdeveloped countries. Notwithstanding the economy's probable potential comparative advantages in manufacturing production,[21] Peruvian firms could hardly expect to do well in the much more competitive international scene where few or no captive markets would exist for them to exploit.

Finally, insofar as marketing-oriented business behavior involves consumer items which represent incentive goods, the availability of which at a reasonable price tends to encourage a greater expenditure of effort on the part of would-be consumers, the expansionary effect of constructive marketing strategies are multiplied. This is of particularly vital developmental importance in the rural sector where the marketing of incentive goods also has a positive role to play in fostering social integration. In addition, the utilization of modern marketing techniques in the distribution of producer goods such as agricultural implements, fertilizers, pesticides, and improved varieties of seeds can scarcely be overemphasized as a means of effecting agricultural modernization, another of Peru's major

---

[21] In view of its easily trainable labor force, its varied endowment of industrial raw materials, its abundant reserves of cheap electric power, and the littoral location of its industries, Peru would seem to have a good base for developing export-oriented manufacturing.

development objectives. In this connection, it should be recalled that only part of the agricultural advancement of the United States and Western Europe can be attributed to the work of schools of agriculture and to governmental agricultural extension services, important though these have been. All along, the dissemination of innovations from these institutions has been supplemented and extended by a multitude of salesman "extension agents" and a communications system of impressive size and effectiveness, all operated as part of the marketing activity of private producers of agricultural requisites. For that matter, the same holds true for the sources of productive innovation in the industrial sector itself where the marketing of machine tools and other producer goods has been a major element in elevating technological efficiency in industry at large.

Considering the magnitude of the need of the Peruvian economy for greater output in agriculture and manufacturing, the challenge presented to the marketing abilities of the private sector is enormous. The social and economic benefits of successfully meeting the challenge—in terms of the potential for better resource allocation and increased productivity—are also substantial, from both the public and private points of view. The types of marketing behavior which predominate at present, however, suggest that the national development program should give considerably more attention than it has in the past to improving this particular aspect of enterprise performance in order to increase the return on other program inputs.

Because of a number of considerations outlined in this article, the growth process in the developing countries of today differs substantially from the historic process of industrialization in Western Europe. Nevertheless, Professor Mintz points out, peasant traders in developing countries may be the closest available counterpart in entrepreneurial spirit to the trading bourgeoisie who revolutionized the European feudal economy. In contrast, large-scale merchants may exhibit the same lack of aggressiveness that Glade and Udell found among Peruvian industrialists. Consequently, Mintz argues that development plans should try to enlist, rather than ignore, the small traders' entrepreneurial drive and talents even though those traders are severely handicapped in any attempt to expand their activities.

SIDNEY W. MINTZ*

Peasant market places and economic development in Latin America[†]

It seems to be generally accepted in this country that our international obligations, as well as our practical and strategic necessities, require a policy of economic aid to less developed countries, perhaps particularly those of the western hemisphere. Though opinions vary widely regarding this policy, it will be treated here as a given: the United States is officially undertaking to raise the productivity (and, hopefully, by this means the living standards) of the economically retarded countries of Latin America, and is doing so deliberately, and professedly in its own best interests.

DIFFERENCES BETWEEN EUROPEAN AND LATIN AMERICAN DEVELOPMENT PATTERNS

The immense concern with economic aid for development in recent years has led some observers to ask whether the experiences of the underdeveloped countries, as they change, will parallel those of the countries of western Europe at an earlier time. This question is a fascinating one. In the sixteenth century, western Europe itself was economi-

---

* Yale University.

† This article originally appeared, in slightly modified form, as Occasional Paper No. 4, published by the Graduate Center for Latin American Studies, Vanderbilt University, whose permission to publish the article is gratefully acknowledged.

cally backward; it might even be argued that some of the underdeveloped lands of today stand roughly where the nations of western Europe stood at that time. But such a view justifiably stirs skepticism.[1] The West, after all, did not develop in a vacuum; its lands and peoples had specific kinds of economic relationships to the non-western world. This was of course true even before the sixteenth century, and it would be reinforced much more strikingly after the eighteenth. Following the discovery of the New World and of the sea route to India, there was a rapid increase in the outward probing by Spain and Portugal; and northern Europe was not far behind. The Europeans "discovered" and conquered non-western peoples ranging in scale and in political complexity from tiny migratory hunting bands to great literate civilizations. In spite of occasional political and military setbacks, the history of the West from 1500 to 1900 was one of progressive territorial expansion, so far as the outside world was concerned. The relationships between the western countries and the lands they dominated were based on the military, political, and economic mastery of the West, and the nature of these relationships meant that the *primary* uses to which the non-western lands and peoples would be put would be in the service of the western world.

In contrast, today's underdeveloped nations do not have a large "external" world to explore, conquer, and make use of, almost at will. Moreover, today's underdeveloped nations—yesterday's colonies, in many cases—were not merely peripheral to the West's economic development. They have not been standing still since the sixteenth or since the eighteenth century, but were instead being transformed themselves, and in ways which the West found to its liking.

Yet there is at least one sense in which the economically backward nations do resemble western Europe of earlier times and there is one regard, at least, in which they must expect to parallel that past. Western Europe before the rise of capitalism was capital-poor, and it lacked the means by which pooled wealth could be thrown into use so that development could result. Similarly, the less developed countries of today appear to lack the basic aggregation of capital required to make self-sustained economic growth possible; they, too, lack the means to employ effectively such wealth in achieving rapid economic growth.[2] And one thing is

---

[1] See, for instance, Peter T. Bauer, *Economic Analysis and Policy in Underdeveloped Countries* (Durham, N.C.: Duke University Press, 1957), pp. 44–49, *et seq.*

[2] The search for the single prerequisite—as Albert O. Hirschman puts it, "the *primum mobile*"—of economic development has been rather empty. To speak of the need for capital, and for institutional means to invest it, as I have done here, is commonplace; but the lack of agreement among economists on the essentials is striking. W. Arthur Lewis, *The Theory of Economic Growth* (Homewood, Ill.: Richard D. Irwin, Inc., 1955), p. 23, speaks of the three "proximate causes of economic growth": economic activity, increasing knowledge, and increasing capital. Albert Hirschman, *The Strategy of Economic Development* (New Haven, Conn.:

certain: *without* effective capital accumulation, the expected and sought-after development will not come. To put it crudely, there is no "easy way" to economic development.

On the whole, the needed saving or capital-building which today's economically backward lands must undertake is likely to be a much more centralized and governmentally-sponsored process than was ever true in the history of western Europe. The likelihood of greater reliance on "forced saving" (command), rather than on the operation of the market for this aggregation of capital will probably not diminish, even in the face of United States unenthusiasm or displeasure. Governmentally-exacted saving will mean, in turn, that investment in development will also be much more a governmental matter than was true in the history of western Europe. All the more reason, perhaps, why North Americans may well reflect on opportunities to assist development in ways which seem consonant with the United States' proclaimed ideology of free choice, the open market, and the moral and economic superiority of private initiative over centralized planning.

As background to such reflection, it may be useful to review very briefly the rise of western industrialism, and the growth of capitalism which underlay it. The economic growth of the modern western world was difficult and painful. The spread and consolidation of an economic system which tore asunder the traditional restrictions on economic activity established by church, guild, feudal aristocracy, obligations of kinship, and powerful local traditions, resulted in an entire transformation of the societies within which it occurred. Relationships among men, among the groups which claimed and exercised power, and among whole peoples, were completely remade. The serfs were driven violently from the land; the craftsmen were separated from their tools; customary prices, conventional standards of quality and workmanship, and the traditional and religious barriers to completely untrammeled economic activity were crushed. Step by step, the forces which had restricted economic change or growth, and which had also maintained the ancient protections of the European peasantry and artisans against the open market, were driven back. And all of these steps, as Marx, Dobb, Polanyi, Heilbroner, and many others have dramatically recounted,[3] were in the

Yale University Press, 1958), pp. 1–28, emphasizes the relationships between factors rather than the factors themselves in seeking the preconditions of development. Peter T. Bauer and B. S. Yamey, *The Economics of Under-Developed Countries* (Chicago: University of Chicago Press, 1957), pp. 127–46, criticize well the idea that capital alone is enough. In the absence of a commonly accepted description of essential preconditions, I have stated the case very generally.

[3] Karl Marx, *Capital* (London: Sonnenschein, Lowerey & Co., 1887), Vol. I, pp. 736–74; Maurice Dobb, *Studies in the Development of Capitalism* (London: International Publishers Co., 1946), pp. 221–34; Karl Polanyi, *The Great Transformation* (New York: Rinehart & Co., 1944), pp. 43–76; Robert A. Heilbroner, *The Worldly Philosophers* (New York: Simon & Schuster, Inc., 1953), pp. 9–32.

direction of making the Law of Supply and Demand—that is, the law of the self-regulating market—the economic law of the land.

So far as the common man was concerned, the immediate effects of these changes were disastrous. The Acts of Enclosure—of which everyone has read, even if their significance in European economic history is too little reflected upon—are but one part of the convulsive changes by which emergent capitalism strangled European feudalism. Countless thousands of rural agricultural folk, secured in their tenure on the land by centuries-old feudal rights, were driven off at spearpoint, to wander the roads or to collect in the newly-forming towns and cities, starving, defenseless, untrained, psychically destroyed. The alienation of man from the land; the conversion of land and labor into commodities; the enshrining of impersonal, market-determined price as the sole determinant of what should be produced, and how much—each step was part of a lengthy and profoundly disturbing metamorphosis.

One of the most interesting features of the destruction of European feudalism by a new economic system was the way in which this process opened up, widened, and unified channels of trade. The traditional restrictions which had kept the products of craftsmen limited in quantity and fixed in price, which had immobilized vast stretches of unused land, which had kept agriculture and industry backward, and which had limited interest on loans or forbidden it entirely, also severely restricted the conduct of trade. For instance, the prices in the town market places and fairs of medieval Europe were mostly established by custom by the municipal councils, as those for the products of artisans were set by the guilds. Merchants' activities were limited by the ordinances of church and town, and by the ideology of the aristocracy; the merchants themselves, by virtue of their profession, were considered incapable of pleasing God. Money-making, in fact, was regarded as altogether contemptible both by the Church and by the feudal aristocracy. Those who sold but did not "produce," it was felt, really contributed nothing to the value of the product. They had no place in a stable society; motivated by lust for gain, they were immoral, as well as parasitic.[4]

But the same forces which transformed land, labor, and tools into commodities, and freed them to be employed as capital, gave new impetus to the traders, and created new settings for economic maneuver. Local market places grew as centers of exchange for imports from far-off lands. The network of trade uniting the countryside and the towns proliferated, especially as the number of non-food-producers increased. New consumption needs arose, and those with money sought to satisfy them. More was being traded and sold and, as the older power groups

---

[4] This theme, especially as it applies to the modern world, is dealt with eloquently and well in Abba P. Lerner, "The Myth of the Parasitic Middleman," *Commentary,* Vol. VIII (July, 1949), pp. 45–51.

lost their ability to keep the market immobile, new opportunities for intermediation appeared. It is not possible to examine here how and why these kinds of changes occurred. But as they did, more and more persons had an opportunity to enter trade. As traders, they made their livings by uniting those who had to sell with those who wished to buy; by accumulating quantities of a desired item which could then be carried to another place for resale; by subdividing the bulk of a good so that it could then be sold in desired, smaller quantities; by processing crude products (such as unhusked grain) in order to resell them, one step closer to use, wholesale or retail; by packaging items which were fragile, and preserving those which were perishable; by providing producers with access to distant market places; and so on.[5] They were able to sell their services because those services were needed by others, and they competed with each other for customers. Eventually, many such traders became wealthy. And ultimately they married into the impoverished aristocracies which had once spurned them, and gave charity to the churches which had once condemned them.

Some features of this rather familiar success story are of interest in the present connection. First, the trading bourgeoisie often had humble beginnings. Many began their profession as *déclassé* or *déraciné* persons, perhaps even as erstwhile serfs who had lost their claims on some feudal lord. The scale of their operations was often minuscule; but many of them succeeded in improving their economic position over time, and in acquiring more and more skill in trade. Their poverty, together with their lack of social position, might be supposed to have worked against their immediate success; but the truth is that poverty and lowly social status

---

[5] Dobb, a careful student and severe critic of capitalism, insists that trade alone could not have generated the primitive accumulation of the early European capitalist merchant, and emphasizes the role of plunder and monopoly in multiplying gains during the rise of the traders. Yet Dobb is careful to pay real respect to the creative, capital-building activities of the merchant capitalists: "Commerce, by widening markets and making supplies, in greater variety, available in places or at seasons where they were never available before, served to raise the standard of life of the producer, and so derived its gains as a share of this general increase and not as an encroachment on an unchanged standard of consumption. It is true enough that the spread of commerce had an effect in raising the standard of communities that were previously confined within the narrow limits of a local market, just as at a later stage it created the conditions within production itself for an extended division of labour and hence a greatly enhanced productivity of labor. . . . By bringing salt and spices from a distance it enabled flesh to be eaten that might otherwise have rotted or been unpalatable; by fetching raw materials from afar it enhanced the quality of local cloth or even enabled cloth to be spun and woven where this was previously unobtainable; by finding an outlet for crops when the season was bountiful and filling the hollows of an unfavourable year with outside supplies, it often helped to spare the cultivator the alternate tragedy of a glutted local market and of famine" (Dobb, *op. cit.*, 1946, pp. 87–88). It is not surprising that this list of useful activities is almost identical with that characterizing the modest local entrepreneurs of many contemporary underdeveloped societies.

can prove advantageous to traders under certain conditions. Second, the stakes of these traders in the newly-emerging capitalist society of western Europe were new stakes, and had to be struggled for against other, competing interest groups. The political objectives of the bourgeoisie were intimately related to their economic objectives; and at times these objectives differed sharply from those of the aristocracy, or of the Church, or of the representatives of political absolutism. For the bourgeoisie, as for each other competing group, economic and political aspirations were but different aspects of the same struggle.

With these points in mind, it is useful to turn back to the underdeveloped countries of Latin America. As has been stressed, those countries, while economically backward, are not in the position of the countries of western Europe of a few centuries ago. Instead, they developed, in Heilbroner's telling phrase, ". . . as immense supply dumps to be attached to the mother countries' industrial economies."[6] Their institutional apparatuses, their occupational groupings, their technology and ideology are neither wholly like those of the western world of today, nor like those of that world three or five centuries past. In some ways, these are *developed* societies—but not in the ways which can provide their populations with the economic freedom of action, the productivity, and thus, the levels of life, regarded today as the legitimate objectives of the world's peoples. In view of what has been said so far concerning the role of traders in the rise of western European society, one may now ask whether traders may be able to play any comparable role in the development of Latin America. The question asked this broadly is unanswerable. There are many sorts of traders, after all, operating on different levels and in relation to different markets. Little useful can be said which treats a supermarket owner in Rio, an itinerant Indian peddler in Guatemala, and a coffee export buyer in Haiti as if they were members of a single economic category.

LATIN AMERICAN INTERNAL MARKET SYSTEMS

However, some insight may result from restricting the analysis to a somewhat less general category of traders and trading situations. In order to attempt this, the following treatment presupposes the presence of an internal market system, and will be concerned with certain kinds of traders who operate within such a system. The term "internal market system," as it is used here, does not refer to "the market" in the economist's sense, which would cover such diverse phenomena as the stock exchange, commodity markets, and numerous other supply-demand sit-

---

[6] Robert A. Heilbroner, *The Making of Economic Society* (Englewood Cliffs, N.J.: Prentice-Hall, Inc., 1962), p. 207.

uations of various sorts. Rather "internal market system" means here a system of exchange which includes concrete centers of commerce—market places—where crowds of sellers with their wares meet crowds of buyers in order to trade.

Market places

Such market places are usually open-air centers, often filled with perishable or semi-perishable crops, livestock, and craft products of the countryside. They accommodate large numbers of buyers and sellers relative to the total supply of stock, and the sellers frequently carry small quantities. In many cases buyers and sellers cannot be distinguished; often the buyer is also a seller. Market places of this sort are variably distributed in the New World; the best-known in this hemisphere, perhaps, are those of Mexico and Guatemala. They are common as well in the oldest sphere of western European colonialism in the New World, the Caribbean islands, and they are important in the Guianas and in Brazil. In Mexico such market places have a pre-Columbian past. Cortés wrote of a market place in Tenochtitlán, the capital city of the Aztecs, where 60,000 traders are reported to have assembled daily.[7] In the Andes, by contrast, the market places are certainly post-Columbian; the early chroniclers give no indication of market places in pre-Pizarro Peru or Bolivia. In the Caribbean, internal market systems are vigorous in the non-Hispanic areas—that is, in most of the islands except for Puerto Rico, Cuba, and eastern Hispaniola (the Dominican Republic). Since the market systems of the Caribbean, the Guianas and Brazil co-occur with populations largely descended from African slaves, it is easy to attribute such systems to the African past. But it is worth noting that the slave populations of Cuba, Puerto Rico, and the Dominican Republic did not, apparently, develop strong internal market systems; and of course the market systems of Mexico and Guatemala, vigorous as these are, could hardly have originated in Africa, since there is good evidence of their pre-Columbian importance. Again, in the case of the Andes, the market systems which flourish there today were a late development, quite unrelated to any African tradition.

The presence of market places is a comment on the nature of local economic activity. Where they are present, the outsider can see the transmission of local products to other rural centers and to the cities, and of foreign imports and regional specialties from the cities to the countryside, before his very eyes. In this way the market system is, among other

---

[7] Eric R. Wolf, *Sons of the Shaking Earth* (Chicago: University of Chicago Press, 1959), p. 40.

things, a useful device for the scholar in getting at an important aspect of the rural economy.[8]

But to walk into a market place within such a system is to wonder how one can really go about studying it. The market place itself is often large and amorphous; buyers and sellers look alike; the products are probably mostly unfamiliar, and the measures of quantity and the means for calculating value unusual; the process of exchange may either be so rapid as to be almost incomprehensible, or very slow, but with little to clarify the rationale of negotiation. There is a strong temptation to view much of the activity as erratic and pointless, particularly if one is unfamiliar with the premises of value which underlie local trade. But of course there is order in such market places, and those who buy and sell are engaging in these activities for fully comprehensible reasons. Over time, the rationale which underlies exchange in such settings comes into view, and the sequence of exchange in specific instances becomes more predictable. As this understanding grows, the ability to view the market place as part of a system increases; one comes to see it as a part within an arrangement of parts, the total nature of which depends on one sort of structure rather than on another.[9]

One of the keys to this understanding is the obvious notion of equivalency. The market place is a venue for exchange. Whether or not there be a generally accepted medium of exchange—money or some other counter of value—items will not be exchanged without reference to quality and quantity. One of the procedures in observing market place activity scientifically is that of recording conventional criteria and measures of quality and quantity, insofar as these can be studied and recorded in any way.[10] There is seeming arbitrariness behind all such standards. For instance, why North American society measures salad oil by volume, sugar by weight, grapefruit by number, cloth by length, and so on, only becomes a

[8] Sidney W. Mintz, "Peasant Markets," *Scientific American*, Vol. CCIII (September 1960), p. 112; Mintz, "Markets in Haiti," *New Society*, Vol. I (March 28, 1963), pp. 18–19; Mintz, "Market Systems and Whole Societies," *Economic Development and Cultural Change*, Vol. XII (July, 1964), pp. 444–48.

[9] Descriptions of internal market systems are rare. See, for instance, Alice G. Dewey, *Peasant Marketing in Java* (New York: Free Press of Glencoe, 1962); Bronislaw Malinowski y Julio de la Fuente, "La Economía de un Sistema de Mercados en México," *Acta Anthropologica* (Época 2), Vol. I (1957); Sidney W. Mintz, "A Tentative Typology of Eight Haitian Market Places," *Revista de Ciencias Sociales*, Vol. IV (March, 1960), pp. 15–57. See also Paul Bohannan and George Dalton (eds.), *Markets in Africa* (Evanston, Ill.: Northwestern University Press, 1963), for a number of interesting reports on African marketing. A complete bibliography of published works and research in progress on such systems will be offered by the author in a future publication.

[10] Sidney W. Mintz, "Standards of Value and Units of Measure in the Fond-des-Nègres Market Place, Haiti," *Journal of the Royal Anthropological Institute,* Vol. XCI (1961), pp. 23–38.

real question when the rationale for doing such things differently, within different systems, comes into view.

The notion of equivalency—of equalness and non-equalness—makes possible the description of unitary acts of exchange. It also permits, by the observation of sequential acts over time, the documentation of the range of permissible variation in similar acts. Thus, for instance, it may be discovered that the cost (in some other good, or in some kind of money) of the same quantity of a product may vary, 5 or 10 or even 20 percent in the course of the market day. This variation, once it can be determined, facilitates the asking of new questions. To begin with, to what is the variation attributable—are the goods of approximately the same quality or does the variation reflect quality differences? Do all buyers and sellers stand in the same relationship, or does the variation reflect status differences among buyers or sellers? Has the supply-demand situation remained approximately the same during the course of the day, or do price variations faithfully reflect that situation?

Queries concerning the relationships between goods and goods, and between goods and money, lead inevitably to further queries—this time about the relationships between goods and people, and between people and people. That is, within the market place human beings are dealing with each other through the instrumentality of things—agricultural products, handicrafts, food and drink, the measures of quality and quantity employed in establishing equivalences, etc.—and a map of the people as sociological "persons" is essential to an understanding of the market system as such. This assertion brings the argument to the traders themselves. In Latin American internal market systems, these traders are of many sorts. The extent to which an analysis of their economic significance can be penetrating depends on the care and completeness with which they and their economic operations are described; and such trading groups are somewhat different in each country in which they are found. For the purposes of this paper, however, several general characteristics of the internal market systems themselves can be used to give background to the character of the trading groups. In Haiti, Guatemala, and Jamaica, and in Mexico and the Andean countries (perhaps particularly Peru and Bolivia), internal market systems operate in somewhat analogous ways. Until more data are available, it is difficult to state the degree of similarity among these systems; but they do share important features. Elsewhere,[11] eight features of such systems are set down, which hold for the first three countries named, to a lesser extent for the fourth, and possibly to some degree for the Andean nations as well. These

---

[11] Sidney W. Mintz, "Internal Market Systems as Mechanisms of Social Articulation," *Proceedings of the 1959 Annual Spring Meetings of the American Ethnological Society,* pp. 20–30.

include the use of a national currency in most if not all transactions; a concentration in market place trade of transactions among class equals (that is, among rural and urban poor); a partial flow of imports through the market places, from city importers through retailers and bulk-breakers, down to the rural and urban poor; a flow of agricultural products, especially perishables, and utilitarian-artistic craft objects, from the rural and urban poor to the middle and upper classes, especially in the towns and cities; a largely or completely separate marketing channel for export commodities (such as coffee, sisal, and essential oils), employing specialized licensed intermediaries outside the market places; a heavy concentration of very small-scale intermediaries, usually women, within the internal market system, who render economic services of various kinds; and a dichotomy between peasant agriculture and marketing in that marketing practices are generally less bound by traditionalism and more capitalistic in ideology and practice, while peasant agriculture tends to remain more conservative and with more vested interest in backwardness. Finally, exchange is typified by important institutionalized personal economic relationships, through which small favors, concessions, and credit are employed to protect the traders' competitive positions.[12]

In these systems, as in the trading patterns of early capitalist Europe, the intermediaries render specific services for which they charge a price. On the whole, that price is determined by supply-demand considerations. The services are not imposed on customers; they are salable because buyers and sellers require them. Intermediaries transport, process, accumulate stock, break stock, grant credit to agricultural producers and to urban consumers, pay taxes, keep truckers employed, and contribute much to the ready functioning of the economy. Since they are usually very numerous, due to the chronic lack of alternative employment opportunities, they compete fiercely to protect their rights to serve their customers. Generally, this competition keeps the prices for their services at relatively low levels; the same competition helps to assure primary producers of prices consonant with the demand situation, and to protect the consumers from disproportionate charges. It is important to stress a connection (admittedly, neither invariant nor absolute) between the large number of intermediaries and the cost of the services they provide. If the numbers of such middlemen were reduced, the change would not

---

[12] On this final point, see Margaret Katzin, "Higglers of Jamaica" (unpublished Ph.D. dissertation, Northwestern University); Katzin, "The Business of Higgling in Jamaica," *Social and Economic Studies,* Vol. IX (September, 1960), pp. 297–331; Sidney W. Mintz, "Pratik: Haitian Personal Economic Relationships," *Proceedings of the 1960 Annual Spring Meetings of the American Ethnological Society,* pp. 54–63; and Edwin R. Dean, "Social Determinants of Price in Several African Markets," *Economic Development and Cultural Change,* Vol. XI (April, 1963), pp. 239–56.

necessarily disadvantage customers, since there are so many middlemen competing altogether; but neither would a reduction in numbers necessarily help the customers, since it is by the competition for their business that prices and middleman profits are kept low.[13]

The intermediaries, or middlemen—in most Latin American internal market systems, they are more likely to be "middlewomen"—are of many sorts. Many will be the wives of small-scale cultivators, who carry the produce of their husbands' holdings to the nearest market place, mainly to get needed cash to buy that minimum of imported or regionally specialized items considered part of essential consumption by local people. Such women have their roots in the countryside, and identify themselves with the interests of their husbands, so far as the outside world is concerned.[14] Other intermediaries will be city women, but operating on a minuscule scale—those who buy small quantities of food which they cook and sell for immediate consumption; or who sell their services as carriers; or who locate small quantities of stock carried to the city by country folk, and buy it up as agents for wealthier traders. These women, though urban, may have meaningful rural ties, and may continue to see their life-stakes in terms of the countryside.

However, there are other categories of market place trader whose scale of operations and whose values are different. These include persons who have built up their businesses from a few pennies to a capital of thousands of dollars.[15] Though their own class position and identity in some ways remain quite unchanged, they often "aspire vicariously"—and their wealth may enable them to secure mobility opportunities for their

---

[13] W. Arthur Lewis, "Economic Development with Unlimited Supplies of Labour," in A. N. Agarwala and S. P. Singh (eds.), *The Economics of Underdevelopment* (Bombay: Oxford University Press, 1958), pp. 400–449, supposes that the supply of labor in petty trade is so large that substantial reductions in numbers would do no harm, and might even improve the consumer's position. He writes: "Petty retail trading is also exactly of the [oversupplied] type; it is enormously expanded in over-populated economies; each trader makes only a few sales; markets are crowded with stalls, and if the number of stalls were greatly reduced the consumers would be no whit worse off—they might even be better off since retail margins might fall." It is true that in some cases retail margins might fall and the consumer's position might improve. However, the opposite is also quite possible—which is to say that each case of this kind should probably be analyzed independently. Comments on this question are found in C. Shephard, "The Small Scale Farmer: Marketing and Processing Problems," *Caribbean Commission Monthly Information Bulletin*, Vol. VIII (October, 1954), p. 61; P. T. Bauer, *West African Trade* (Cambridge: Cambridge University Press, 1954), pp. 26–27; Katzin, *op. cit.*, 1960; Sidney W. Mintz, "The Role of the Middleman in the Internal Distribution System of a Caribbean Peasant Economy," *Human Organization*, Vol. XV (1957), pp. 18–23; and especially P. T. Bauer and B. S. Yamey, "The Economics of Marketing Reform," *Journal of Political Economy*, Vol. LXII (June, 1954), pp. 210–35.

[14] See, for instance, Margaret Katzin, "The Jamaican Country Higgler," *Social and Economic Studies*, Vol. VIII (December, 1959), pp. 421–40.

[15] See Bauer, *op. cit.*, 1957, pp. 75–76; Sidney W. Mintz, "Nana of Duverget: A Haitian Market Woman," *Haiti Sun* (May 3, 1959), pp. 4, 13.

children, especially through education.[16] Vigorous and successful traders
may feel themselves to be in league in some way with the city, and
detached from rural values. But they are often openly (or secretly)
hostile to "the government," particularly if they feel that legal rigidities
of various kinds interfere with their opportunities for trade.[17] At the same
time, their opposition to bureaucratic control does not necessarily make
them friends of the peasantry. Sometimes they are moneylenders, whose
activities underwrite the dealings of many lesser marketers. Or they may
be the creditors of the peasantry, supporting and stimulating commercial
agriculture in their quest for stock to be drawn from a future harvest.[18]

The trade and investment opportunities available to intermediaries of
these sorts vary significantly with the particular economic circumstances
in each region or nation. Matters of crop perishability, the quality and
quantity of roads and motor transport, the scale and reliability of consumer demand in the cities, and many other considerations also affect the
nature and extent of intermediary activities. In turn, such activities may
stimulate development in specific ways, such as supporting the growth
and political demands of the trucking profession; giving a voice to
subsistence cultivators being drawn for the first time into production for
sale; supplying credit to producers and to lesser traders; and otherwise.
Attacks on such intermediaries (which claim either that they overcharge
for their services, or that they shut out competition by charging too
little) must be examined carefully in each case and judged according to
specific circumstances.[19] Indeed middlemen of this sort may hamper the
economy if their position in intermediation is artificially protected—that
is, if they can control prices by interdicting the accesses of buyers and
sellers to each other, or by combination in buying and selling. In most
cases, however, their large numbers and the sharp competition among
them tend to reduce the costs of the services they offer, and to support
activities leading to further economic growth, such as road-building, the
introduction of new crop choices, the integration of isolated rural regions, and the provision of credit.[20]

---

[16] See C. J. Legerman, "Kin Groups in a Haitian Market," *Man*, Vol. LXII
(October, 1962), pp. 145–49; Mintz, *op. cit.*, 1959.

[17] See, for instance, *Time* (January 3, 1964), pp. 52–53. An adequate study of the
political views of market women in a Latin American market system has never been
made.

[18] Different sorts of trader are described in Katzin, *op. cit.*, 1960; Dewey, *op. cit.*,
1962, pp. 76–77, *et seq.*; and Mintz, *op. cit.*, 1957. On the whole, this subject has not
been dealt with adequately in the literature.

[19] Mintz, *op. cit.*, 1957.

[20] Economies stemming from the presence of a multiplicity of traders are eloquently summarized in Bauer, *op. cit.*, 1954, pp. 22–27; the positive economic effects
of the efforts of traders are noted in Bauer, *Economic Analysis and Policy in
Underdeveloped Countries* (Durham, N.C.: Duke University Press, 1957), pp.
70–71.

Large-scale merchants

The emphasis in this description so far has deliberately been on small-scale traders, rather than on those who buy up agricultural commodities for export, engage in the wholesaling of imports, or carry on large-scale retailing and storekeeping. Traders and merchants of these kinds, while they may superficially resemble small-scale intermediaries because of some features of their economic activity, are much more different from petty traders than they are like them. Such merchants, wholesalers, importers, and export buyers generally reside in the cities and larger towns; they often employ bookkeeping and hire agents in the conduct of their businesses; and they will handle some or all of their credit arrangements through the use of banks; above all, they have substantial capital holdings, and operate on a relatively grand scale.

In many instances, the merchant sector of this sort to be found in an underdeveloped country consists of two distinguishable segments, one of which is "native" and the other "foreign." In Haiti, for instance, there is an important Syrian and Lebanese sub-group engaged in town trade; in Jamaica, the Chinese carry out a somewhat similar role; in other underdeveloped countries, the "alien" group may consist of Jews, Palestine Arabs, Indians, and so on. If the members of such a group are immigrants or the recent descendants of immigrants, they are likely to live in uneasy accommodation to the majority, politically exposed (and often surprisingly defenseless) because they may be viewed and manipulated as "foreigners" by nationalist politicians. Their separateness may be based on ethnic self-consciousness (sometimes with chauvinistic overtones), on external pressure from the majority, or on both.

So common are these ethnic enclaves in the commercial life of the underdeveloped nations that an eminent economist, Hla Myint, has singled out their very presence as an important *indicium* of underdevelopment.[21] Myint has stressed the importance of such groups in bringing the populations of technically retarded lands into contact with the world market and modern economy, and Bauer has dramatically underlined the same point.[22] But Myint also supposes that these merchants have *limited* the extent to which local people have been able to familiarize themselves

---

[21] H. Myint, "An Interpretation of Economic Backwardness," in Agarwala and Singh, *op. cit.*, 1958, pp. 122–23.

[22] "In West Africa, for instance, almost all successful African industrial entrepreneurs or transport contractors are, or have been, traders or their employees. This is not surprising, since such experience acquaints people with the working of a money economy, and especially with the habitual and orderly management of business affairs, besides providing contacts and a knowledge of the market." Bauer, *op. cit.*, 1957, pp. 71–72, *et seq.*

with the outer world, by their presence. Myint's view, in this instance, calls to mind Wolf's insightful characterization of the "cultural broker," who ties the local community to the outer world but at the same time may limit the acculturation of outsider and "native" to each other.[23] Actually, the history of ethnic enclaves in underdeveloped countries suggests that their roles in the economic life of such countries can change rapidly over time. In many instances, immigrant minorities are able to improve their social and economic position by shifting from wage labor to petty commerce and intermediation and gradually acquiring greater wealth. In time, such groups may take on the social and economic orientation of the "native" middle classes, and eventually engage in essentially the same kinds of economic activities. But in the process, they may forfeit, by changing, special developmental contributions to the local economy which they were able to make at an earlier point. They may shift, for instance, from investment in petty trade and small-scale agriculture to investment in importing; from business travel in the country-side to a permanent location in the city; from small-scale moneylend-ing and brokerage to investment in slum real estate; and so on. In so doing, such groups may remain ethnically distinct while becoming eco-nomically (and ideologically) similar to the "native" middle-class groups; thereby, some part of their unique contribution (both potential and realized) to local economic growth may well be lost.[24]

At the same time, it turns out that the small-scale intermediation and market place activity which are of central concern in this paper are rarely if ever in the hands of "foreigners"; rather, such trade is almost always conducted exclusively by "natives." Furthermore, the economic and social distance between these "natives" and the mercantile middle class, *native or not,* is considerable.

---

[23] Eric R. Wolf, "Aspects of Group Relations in a Complex Society: Mexico," *American Anthropologist,* Vol. LVIII (December, 1956), pp. 1065–78.

[24] The extent to which this "acculturation to economic conservatism" may occur will vary greatly with local social and economic conditions; admittedly, in many instances it may not occur at all. Bauer has convincingly stressed the role of migrant enclaves in speeding economic growth in underdeveloped countries. However, few studies contrast the activities of migrants and native bourgeoisie in such situations, or indicate to what extent the migrants may shift to "safer" investment over time. The very fact that ethnic enclaves are frequently in political limbo may incline them away from those investment opportunities taken up by the native bourgeoisie; but it may also lead them more toward reinvestment outside the underdeveloped country. I know of no clear case where intermarriage and mutual acculturation has resulted in the movement of native capital into developmentally more effective enterprise. Useful contrasts, too little elucidated to permit generalizations, are offered for the case of natives vs. migrants (in Indonesia) in Dewey, *op. cit.,* 1962, and in Clifford Geertz, *Peddlers and Princes* (Chicago: University of Chicago Press, 1963), *passim.* No work known to me deals adequately with data of these kinds for a Latin American country.

THE MARKET TRADERS' ENTREPRENEURIAL POTENTIAL

Stress on the foregoing facts is necessary. These facts mean that small-scale intermediation is probably the principal way in which the poorest segments of the national population can acquire knowledge of commerce and of entrepreneurialism—knowledge of a kind which could be of great importance in creating or speeding economic development.[25] The nature of petty trade, when undertaken by a multiplicity of traders, evokes sharp competition, and rewards individual intelligence, energy, and daring. Whereas import-export enterprises in the cities, and export-commodity buyers' posts in the towns and country, are often operated in the absence of substantial competition—sometimes even with prices fixed by governmental fiat—the small-scale entrepreneurs of market place trade must usually conduct their businesses under extreme pressure on many fronts. It might well be argued that capitalism—in the sense of a free market and perfect competition—is realized more fully in the activities of Haitian or Guatemalan market women, than it is in those of the owners of export-import houses, electrical appliance stores, and tourist junk studios in the capital cities of those countries.[26]

If true, this suggestion raises a curious fact concerning economic development activity in technically backward countries. It is commonly believed (even if it is not always made explicit) that the crucial social group in development is "the middle class." This belief raises many conceptual and definitional problems because it is often extremely diffi-

---

[25] This claim admittedly raises serious questions. Those who question it are inclined to regard petty trading as no more than an expression of rural under-employment (See Lewis, as cited in footnote 13, for instance). So viewed, petty trading by numerous competitors can be considered as an obstacle to development, rather than as an economic use of scarce resources (capital) as opposed to plentiful resources (labor). Hereupon hinges the somewhat paradoxical assertion that the low price of intermediary services as provided by the poorest classes interferes with the economic growth of the middle classes, who would (presumably) charge more for the same services. Geertz (*op. cit.*, 1963, p. 11) describes how: ". . . the market was flooded by hundreds of small-scale traders eking out a marginal living where before a few large-scale merchants had made a handsome one"; and again, (*ibid.*, p. 17) how: ". . . the few outstanding efforts by members of the old merchant class to create *more efficient* productive and distributive institutions in the town are nearly swamped by the hundreds of small-scale petty traders trying to squeeze a marginal living out of traditional commerce" (italics added. S.W.M.). The economic reasoning behind this view is not entirely clear, and the case is anything but proved.

[26] Which is to say that the merchant groups in underdeveloped countries frequently enjoy the benefits of certain kinds of restrictionism, achieved through political influence or resulting from the limited numbers of potential competitors with enough capital to be rivals. The "pure" competitive capitalist ethic of the petty trader can be corrupted as readily as anyone's, of course. All that maintains it is the petty trader's inability to monopolize or restrict the market in the face of numerous competitors. But this inability, in turn, was apparently an important developmental aspect of early capitalism.

cult to formulate satisfactory criteria of middle-class membership. In
most underdeveloped countries, foreign visitors perceive "the middle
class" as consisting largely of the native urban export-import merchants;
their class equals in any newly-established, ethnically distinct minorities;
and the bureaucratic, professional and military cohorts and kinsmen of
these groups. Surely no foreign visitors to such countries ever conclude
that the crowds of poor and ragged market women who throng the city
streets might be regarded as members of "the middle class." Yet it can be
argued tellingly that such women are more convincingly middle class in
certain regards than those wealthier than they, and that the term "middle
class" really does not apply effectively to their class superiors in the less
developed nations.

Two sources of confusion in this connection should be noted. First,
there is the misperception inhering in the use of the term "middle class."
From the point of view of its consumption ideals and its living standards,
a social group may be "middle class," even when its ideology (and
perhaps its economic activities) may be, or may have become, quite alien
to the historical western European implications of that label. Second,
there is the misperception resulting from the way the minuscule scale of
market place intermediation is seen by outsiders, especially those coming
from a much more developed economy such as that of the United States.
Bauer and Yamey write:

Local entrepreneurship necessarily begins in a small way because technical
and administrative skills as well as capital are at a low level; its manifestations
may easily be overlooked by those who equate entrepreneurship with the
launching on a massive scale of a new industry or product, and who forget that
large industries and firms have almost invariably sprung from small beginnings.[27]

Because North American thinking is heavily colored by the scale of
enterprise in the United States, foreign small-scale intermediary activity
is often viewed with amused contempt, at best. It is, unfortunately, not
surprising that a *Time* article on the "matriarchs of the market," while it
lauded the commercial zeal of the market women of Latin America,
almost entirely ignored the economic and political significance of their
activities and ideology, and dwelt instead on their picturesqueness and
doubtful morals.[28] Sears, *Time* magazine's twentieth-century model of
entrepreneurial verve and daring in Latin America, can be so precisely
because the United States equivalent of the small-scale Latin American
intermediary is almost as extinct as the bison. Of course, programming
economic development is much more congenial for North American
technicians when the representatives of the host country are themselves

---

[27] Bauer and Yamey, *op. cit.*, 1957, pp. 104–5.
[28] *Time, loc. cit.*

Iowa-trained agronomists, Columbia-educated doctors, and others who "talk our language," figuratively and, perhaps, literally as well. But what is being ignored in so comfortable a rationalization is the crucial difference between middle-class behavioral norms, especially of consumption, on the one hand, and the ideology of entrepreneurialism on the other.

Earlier, the point was made that some of the underdeveloped nations were actually developed by foreign powers, but that these developments were not primarily in line with local (national) needs. One distinguished economist likens the economy of the labor-rich underdeveloped countries to a "sea" of subsistence, in which there are many scattered "islands" (plantations, mines, modern shops).[29] Such development, clearly, is a product of external capital and power. The importers and exporters, with their array of commodity buying posts, processing depots, and city stores, were a "natural" accompaniment to a particular kind of unevenness of growth. The competition which characterized comparable types of intermediary and service-rendering activity in western Europe and in the United States was much more exigent, both because the economies in these cases were so differently composed, and because they enjoyed important advantages in institutional and human-capital factors. But this means that some of the potential forces for development in the underdeveloped countries of Latin America today may not be found where they are being looked for, precisely because of the essentially colonial economic history of these countries.[30]

If development is being sought or thought of in terms of the play of the open market—which is the North American preference—rather than in terms of the aggregation of development capital by governmental decree, this point should be borne in mind. Something must be said, then, of the development potential of the small-scale entrepreneurs of the countryside and market place, since the emphasis here has been on the way these specialists have been ignored in planning. To begin with, the economic contribution such groups will be able to make to development is likely to be severely restricted.[31] Such a statement is surely anti-climac-

---

[29] Lewis, *op. cit.*, 1958, p. 408.

[30] Myint writes (*op. cit.*, 1958, p. 116): "Measures for 'economic development' then consisted mainly in attempts to persuade or force the backward people into the news ways of life represented by the money economy—for example, by stimulating their demand for imports and by taxing them so that they were obliged to turn to cash crops or work in the newly opened mines or plantations. Whether it was meaningful or not to the people, the accepted yardstick of economic development of a 'country' was its export and taxable capacity."

[31] For instance, I have written of Haiti's economy: "That economy seems to have considerable resiliency because of the readiness of intermediaries swiftly to change their mode of operation, and otherwise to show verve and originality in investing capital productively. Such daring and skill cannot communicate their consequences more effectively to the agricultural sector because of the overall limitations upon the economy, particularly in its lack of a secure or an expanding market." Sidney W.

tic; but the stress here must be on the word "likely." Since their own capital holdings are in most cases very small, market women cannot easily expand the scale of their operations. However, there are cases in which such expansion has occurred in spectacular fashion. In Nigeria and Ghana, the "market mammies" have often enlarged their enterprises, and have contributed significantly to economic growth; and even in economies such as those of Haiti and Jamaica,[32] market women may build their fortunes and also contribute to economic growth in the ways referred to earlier. Whether that contribution can be importantly increased in the internal market systems of Latin America is not certain. Questions of the scale of the market and national terms of trade must be kept in mind, and cannot be dealt with here; but several more immediate problems can be instanced. One limitation on the operations of petty traders is the scarcity and high cost of capital. For example, in Jamaica, a market woman may pay up to five per cent on capital which she borrows for three days' use.[33] While such women substitute labor for capital at every opportunity, and invest prodigious effort to conserve scarce resources, their ability to improve their own positions in commerce is sharply confined by the lack of capital and of credit. Though this may be due at times to an absolute scarcity of capital, it also can be caused by the lack of means for organizing the distribution of credit.[34] The need for modest credit may well be one of the major obstacles to successful integration of petty traders and small-scale agricultural producers into development programs. But the absence of such means may come from insufficient attention by planners to the potential of very petty capitalists for contributing to economic growth. And this, in turn, may come from the tendency to concentrate on what are superficially the most "middle-class" sectors in development planning.

Whether small-scale traders may be able to invest capital in other sectors of the economy besides commerce is also problematic. In some instances, such traders invent means for the short-term use of liquid funds in agriculture itself during slack trading periods, concentrating on activities which allow for rapid turnover.[35] They aim to be able to transform stock into liquid capital once more, in time for the start of the next harvest, and may occasionally innovate as they contrive solutions to this problem. But it is not known whether such innovations have any

---

Mintz, "The Employment of Capital by Market Women in Haiti," in Raymond Firth and B. S. Yamey (eds.), *Capital, Saving and Credit in Peasant Societies* (Chicago: Aldine Publishing Co., 1964), p. 286.

[32] See Bauer, *op. cit.*, 1957, pp. 56, 75–76; Mintz, *op. cit.*, 1964.

[33] See Katzin, *op. cit.*, 1960; Mintz, "The Jamaican Internal Marketing Pattern," *Social and Economic Studies,* Vol. IV (March, 1955), pp. 95–103.

[34] Myint, *op. cit.*, 1958, p. 126.

[35] Mintz, *op. cit.*, 1964.

significant long-term beneficial effect on the agricultural patterns themselves. That attractive alternatives for investment are not available to
small-scale intermediaries is of course a comment on the backwardness of
the economies within which they function. The very limited opportunities to invest in other than agricultural production is a profound difficulty
to the solution of which petty traders may not be able to contribute. But
so far as is known, no attempt has ever been made by planners to explore
the entrepreneurial talents of these traders at all.

Finally, a comment is in order here concerning the ideology of the
petty trader, particularly in view of the doubts expressed earlier about
the entrepreneurial orientation of the large-scale export-import houses
and factor groups of the cities. To suppose that middle-class levels of life
and consumption standards are naturally accompanied by commercial
drive and entrepreneurial intrepidity is surely questionable. And to assume that the ideology of the very poor is shaped more by the general
nature of their poverty than by the specific nature of their economic
activity is likewise open to question. Myint writes:

> The fundamental assumption of liberal economics is that the free play of
> economic forces would lead to the maximum development of *individual*
> talents and abilities; whereas in practice the free play of economic forces in
> backward countries has resulted, not in a division of labour according to
> individual abilities, but in a division of labour according to stratified groups.[36]

In less developed economies with internal market systems, economic
individuality (insofar as its utility for development is concerned) is
probably more plentiful among lower-class petty traders than it is among
their store-owning class betters. Certainly there are aspects of the economic history of Europe and the United States which are suggestive in
this connection. And it is very worthwhile, at the same time, to reflect
upon the possible political outlook of those who, poor but hard-working,
must live by their skill and daring at a level and in a commercial setting
where every penny counts. Such folk know that it is in a situation of
maximum freedom of economic alternatives that their excellence and
industry will be rewarded. That their aspirations may be ignored by
those planners who believe in decree-solutions to economic problems is
nothing less than could be expected.[37] That they should be cruelly

---

[36] Myint, *op. cit.*, 1958, p. 129.

[37] In this connection, it is useful to make reference to the farmers' markets in the
Soviet Union. It seems quite clear that an embarrassingly large proportion of the
Soviet Union's total agricultural output continues to come from the numerically and
really insignificant "private plots" which still exist. Most such production, other than
that for immediate subsistence needs, is sold through the farmers' (*Kolkhoz*) markets.
A recent (1961) decree was aimed at ending individual participation in these
markets, ostensibly to help the peasantry: "Thanks to this, the collective farmers will
be relieved of the necessity of transporting surplus farm products long distances in
order to sell them and will not be taken from productive work on the collective

ignored as well in programs of economic development launched by the supposedly ardent defenders of unfettered free enterprise may one day turn out to be one of the neater ironies in modern Latin American economic and political history.

farms." But the markets were one of the few institutions in Soviet society which were able to function without the dominant participation of Party officials—and surely the sole legal opportunity for individual economic maneuver. As one writer puts it, ". . . the markets, next to the family, must have been the major leak in the Soviet totalitarian dike." See Roy D. Laird, "Khrushchev and Stalin's Unfinished Revolution," *Your Government,* Vol. XVII (February 15, 1962), pp. 3–4. The political—and not just economic—implications of this situation should be kept in mind when dwelling on the "inefficiency" of internal market systems in underdeveloped countries, particularly when modern supermarkets receive official protection to enable them to drive petty traders out of the market.

As the preceding articles have suggested, one of the arguments for expanding marketing activities in developing countries is that marketing may be a spawning ground for entrepreneurial talent. Professor Alexander examines the extent to which industrial enterprisers in four developing nations emerged from marketing and other backgrounds. He also examines the way in which marketing, and other origins, may influence industrial decision making and behavior.

ALEC P. ALEXANDER*

Merchants and the recruitment of industrialists

The critical importance of industrial entrepreneurship in developing economies directs attention to several questions which are as difficult to answer as they are important to the development process. Questions such as the following are of legitimate concern to economists and to other social scientists interested in the problem of economic development: Where do industrialists come from? What influences a person to become an industrialist? What determines the overall supply of industrialists? Among those who have become industrialists, why do some pursue policies which are conservative and passive while others are innovating and aggressive? These and similar questions deal with the very mainsprings of economic development.

Research on these topics has been limited but growing.[1] The questions raised are inherently difficult to answer, in part because researchers are sooner or later compelled to cut across the boundaries of several social science disciplines. The available research includes case studies of entrepreneurial development in a small number of countries. The findings of these studies suggest certain common themes regarding the development of industrial entrepreneurship in some of the presently low-income economies. One of these underscores the importance of merchants as a source of recruitment of industrial entrepreneurs and of mercantile profits as the source of initial industrial investment. Merchants have in fact emerged as the single most important source of recruitment of industrialists.

---

* University of California, Santa Barbara.

[1] Academic interest in this area is illustrated by the existence of the quarterly journal, *Explorations in Entrepreneurial History*, Second Series.

The purpose of this paper is to further explore this theme. An attempt will be made to assess the importance of merchants as contributors to the supply of industrialists, to offer explanations for their contribution and to inquire whether industrialists with a trading background demonstrate any particular performance characteristics. Inevitably however, these objectives must become even broader. First, the contribution of merchants to the supply of industrialists must be weighed in relation to the contribution of other economic-occupational groups. Therefore, to the extent that data are available, the overall pattern of industrial entrepreneurial recruitment must be examined. Second, the reasons for the merchants' special contribution must be compared to the reasons for the contribution of other groups. But there are also general conditions which inhibit or encourage the transition of members of all economic-occupational groups into industry. Therefore, the analysis will gain from the presentation of a more generalized framework of conditions affecting the supply of industrial entrepreneurship. Third, if a possibly distinct pattern of performance of industrialists with a trading background can be discerned from the available data, it can best be described by comparing it to the pattern of performance of industrialists of other backgrounds.

The three sections of this paper will deal correspondingly with these broad topics. The empirical data will be drawn from four of the country studies which are relatively well documented for our purposes. These countries are Greece, Philippines, Pakistan, and Turkey. Even though these studies present difficult problems of comparability of data, a number of important conclusions can still be drawn. The recruitment pattern of industrialists in the four countries will first be summarized.

EMPIRICAL STUDIES IN FOUR COUNTRIES

Greece[2]

Some of the findings on the recruitment of industrialists in Greece are summarized in Table 1.

Column (2) shows that the origins of Greek industrialists are rather diverse but that merchants, craftsmen, and second-generation industrialists account for about three fourths of the Greek industrialists. Merchants were the single most important group from which first-generation industrialists were recruited. One quarter of all industrialists (and one third of first-generation industrialists) had formerly been big or small merchants, about 20 percent had formerly been craftsmen, while smaller

---

[2] Alec P. Alexander, "Industrial Entrepreneurship in Contemporary Greece: Origin and Growth," *Explorations in Entrepreneurial History,* Vol. III, No. 2 (Winter, 1966), pp. 101–20.

proportions were recruited from the ranks of business executives and professional men.

A measure of the contribution of each economic-occupational group to the supply of industrialists in terms of its relative size in the working population is provided by a comparison of columns (2) and (3). The higher the ratio in column (4) the greater is a given group's productivity in industrialists. In this sense, the group of big merchants is by far the most productive in industrialists; less than 1 percent of the working population produced more than 20 percent of the Greek industrialists.

Table 1

ORIGINS OF GREEK INDUSTRIALISTS

Economic Occupational Activity	Distribution of Father's Activity (1)	Distribution of Industrialist's Former Activity (2)	Distribution of Greek Working Populations (3)	Ratio of Columns (2) ÷ (3) (4)
Craftsmen	17%	19%	8.0%	2.4
Big merchant	16	21	0.8	26.3
Small merchant	13	4	4.0	1.0
Industrialist	30	(30)*	...	...
Professional man	3	5	0.7	7.1
Business executive	1	8	1.0	8
Farmer	11	...†	50.0	...
Other	9	13	35.5	...
Total	100	100	100.0	

* Second-generation industrialists; no activity prior to entry into industry.
† Insignificant.
Source: Alec P. Alexander, "Industrial Entrepreneurship in Contemporary Greece: Origin and Growth," *Explorations in Entrepreneurial History*, Vol. III, No. 2 (Winter, 1966).
Sampling basis: approximately 56 percent of a population of 635 industrialists.
Definition of industrialist: manufacturer employing at least 50 workers.
Approximate date of survey: 1962–63.

Entry into the industrial entrepreneurial group is part of a mobility process involving more than one generation. A study of entrepreneurial recruitment therefore must be extended further back in time. As a first approximation, the activities of industrialists prior to their entry into industry may be compared with those of their fathers (column 1). Present-day Greek industrialists have fathers whose economic-occupational activities had also been diverse. Thirty percent of these fathers had been industrialists themselves, nearly 30 percent had been big or small merchants, while the remainder had mostly been craftsmen or farmers. Excluding those who were industrialists, more fathers had been engaged in trade than in any other activity.

There is much discontinuity between the economic-occupational activities of fathers and those of their sons before they became industrialists.

Overall, most sons moved out of their fathers' activities and into something else before becoming industrialists. This discontinuity, combined with the diversity in the activities of the industrialists' fathers as well as in their own before entering industry, reflects the high degree of mobility which went into the formation of the Greek industrial entrepreneurial group. The one major exception to the intergeneration discontinuity in economic-occupational activities occurred in the field of trade. Nearly 70 percent of the industrialists who were formerly big merchants had fathers who were either big or small merchants (45 and 24 percent respectively). The trading background of a significant proportion of Greek industrialists therefore goes back to at least one generation. Finally, when the fathers' activities are compared with those of their sons prior to their entry into industry, a trend is observed from "lower" to "higher" status activities: there are increases in the proportions of big merchants and business executives and decreases in the proportions of small merchants and especially of farmers.

There are practically no industrialists in Greece whose main preceding activity was farming. At least part of this can be explained by the virtual absence of large landowners in Greece who might have been in a more advantageous position to enter industry than the presently typical very small proprietor. The farmers' sons who moved out of farming moved into several other fields before they became industrialists, but the largest group first became merchants. To this extent, there is an intergeneration movement from farming to trade and then to industry.

Finally, even though big merchants were the most important single group from which present-day Greek industrialists were recruited, there is evidence that the first industrialists in Greece around the turn of the century and later had been recruited primarily from the ranks of craftsmen. This is also confirmed by the finding that of the 30 percent of the fathers of industrialists who had been industrialists themselves one half had formerly been craftsmen.

Philippines[3]

Table 2 summarizes some of the available information on the sources of industrial entrepreneurial recruitment in the Philippines.

The distribution of activities immediately preceding entry into the industrial entrepreneurial group (column 4) shows that trade, even more than was the case in Greece, was the most important source of recruitment of industrialists. A second major source was "manufacturing." This term is somewhat misleading. To a very large extent it refers to very

---

[3] John J. Carroll, *The Filipino Manufacturing Entrepreneur* (Ithaca, N.Y.: Cornell University Press, 1965).

small enterprises whose owners can more accurately be described as craftsmen. Thus merchants and craftsmen account for the immediate backgrounds of nearly three fourths of the Philippino industrialists. Other activities in which industrialists were engaged immediately prior to their entry into industry include government and the professions.

Other data in the Philippine study show, as in the case of Greece, that there is much discontinuity of activities intergenerationally, suggesting that the formation of the industrial entrepreneurial group in this country is also the result of a great deal of mobility. The highest incidence of

Table 2

ORIGINS OF PHILIPPINE MANUFACTURING ENTREPRENEURS

Origins	Grand-father (1)	Father (2)	E's First Job (3)	Before Entrepre-neurship (4)	Philippine Male Labor Force (5)	Ratio of Columns (4) ÷ (5) (6)
Agriculture............63%	28%	8%	6%	68.3%	.01
Commerce.............20	27	38	43	4.9	8.8
Manufacturing.........12	19	26	31	6.0	5.2
Professional........... 0	7	18	4	2.2	1.8
Other................. 5	19	10	16	18.6	..
Total	100	100	100	100	100	

Source: John J. Carroll, *The Filipino Manufacturing Entrepreneur* (Ithaca, N.Y.: Cornell University Press, 1965). Column (6) not in original source.
    Definition of industrialist: entrepreneur in manufacturing employing at least 100 workers. Some peripheral activities (e.g. saw-milling) were excluded.
    Sampling basis: All industrialists (92) fitting the above definition.
    Approximate date of survey: 1962.

continuity, again as in the case of Greece, has been found among merchants' sons who tended to stay in trade until they became industrialists. Intergeneration comparisons also show large-scale movements out of agriculture into almost all other activities, but primarily into commerce and craftsmanlike small-scale ("preindustrial") manufacturing enterprises. The net result of these movements are included in the changing percentages shown horizontally in Table 2. "Getting off the land" thus appears to have been an important first step toward industrial entrepreneurship, a step taken by the grandfathers or fathers of the industrialists. In most cases this was a movement out of subsistence farming. Those who were in agriculture until just prior to their entry into industry were in all cases large commercial farmers. Finally, there is evidence that industrialists from commerce, agriculture, and "other industries" have constituted an increasing proportion of all industrialists in the more recent time periods, while those from "manufacturing" (i.e. craftsmen) have been decreasing proportionally.

Pakistan[4]

Merchants have also made a great contribution to the supply of industrialists in Pakistan. Table 3 summarizes the backgrounds of industrialists in that country. Persons whose primary occupation before 1947 (or before entering industry, if this was later) was trade furnished about 45 percent of the entrepreneurs for Pakistan's industry. These merchants were engaged both in domestic trade and in import-export. About 18

Table 3

INDUSTRIALISTS' OCCUPATIONS PRIOR TO 1947 OR TO ENTERING INDUSTRY (IF LATER) IN PAKISTAN

	Previous Primary Occupation		Father's Occupation
	Proportion of Industrialists	Present Investment	Proportion of Industrialists
1. Large and medium industry.................17%	16%	8%
2. Small industry, handicrafts.................18	6	17
3. Traders—import, export....................17	40	12
4. Traders—internal..........................28	29	34
5. Employees, professional, other.............16	6	16
6. Agriculture............................... 3	3	12
Total	100	100	100

Source: Gustave Papanek, "The Development of Entrepreneurship." *American Economic Review,* May, 1962, pp. 46–58.
Definition of industrialist: entrepreneur in manufacturing employing 20 or more workers.
Sampling basis: approximately 10 percent of industrialists.
Approximate date of survey: 1960.

percent of the industrialists were essentially recruited from the ranks of craftsmen (engaged in small industry and handicrafts and employing less than 20 persons). Relatively very few former farmers were found among the Pakistani industrialists. Merchants also set up the larger or more rapidly growing firms, controlling 69 percent of the private industrial capital. Former craftsmen on the other hand controlled only 6 percent of the capital. A large proportion, 46 percent, of all industrialists had fathers who were in trade. While this study does not offer a measure of each group's productivity in industrialists in terms of its relative size in the total population, it is more than likely that the merchants' productivity in industrialists must have again been the highest. Nearly half of the Pakistani industrialists had formerly been merchants, while the proportion of merchants in the total population is probably very small, as was the case in Greece and the Philippines.

---

[4] Gustav Papanek, "The Development of Entrepreneurship," *American Economic Review,* May, 1962, pp. 46–58.

The particular circumstances in Pakistan's economic environment which strongly influenced the decisions of merchants to become industrialists are worth pointing out because of similar developments in other countries.

The growth of industrial entrepreneurship in Pakistan became very rapid after the late 1940's, responding particularly to the very high rate of return on industrial investment which followed the export boom of the Korean War. A sharp drop in foreign exchange earnings necessitated a drastic import restriction. Domestic production was inadequate, while the importation of machinery was in effect subsidized by an undervalued rate of exchange. Under these conditions almost any investor in industry was guaranteed a profit. In some industries annual returns of 100 percent on investment were possible. At the same time opportunities for importers and exporters were substantially reduced. Importers and exporters as well as domestic traders readily responded to the new economic incentives. Profits accumulated in trade were crucial for starting industry, while the growth of industrial enterprises was supported by reinvestment of earnings.

Turkey[5]

The growth of industrial entrepreneurship in Turkey has some important similarities to industrial entrepreneurial development in Pakistan. In both countries industrial entrepreneurship has grown very rapidly since the late 1940's, merchants have made an exceptionally large contribution to the supply of industrial entrepreneurs, and changing conditions in the foreign trade sector have provided a major stimulus for merchants to become industrialists.

Table 4 summarizes the pattern of recruitment of industrialists in the Aegean Region of Turkey. There are reasons for believing that these findings approximately reflect the pattern of origins of industrialists in the country as a whole, although the proportion of merchants is probably a little higher than that found in the Aegean Region alone.

Traders are again the most important single group from which industrialists were recruited, accounting for the backgrounds of about 43 percent of industrialists. Former traders also tended to own the larger industrial enterprises, ranking only below second-generation industrialists in this respect. Farmers, along with craftsmen and skilled workers, contributed smaller proportions to the supply of industrialists, each of these two groups being roughly of equal importance. All those who had formerly been in farming had been owners of intermediate or large agricultural holdings.

---

[5] Alec P. Alexander, "Industrial Entrepreneurship in Turkey: Origins and Growth," *Economic Development and Cultural Change*, July, 1960, pp. 349–65.

Industrial entrepreneurship in Turkey grew very rapidly after the late 1940's. Conditions of excess demand had been created by import restrictions designed to meet the inflation-induced foreign exchange shortage, by an ambitious government investment program, and by high price supports for agricultural goods. As in the case of Pakistan, imports of industrial machinery were subsidized by the maintenance of an over-valued rate of exchange. The unprecedented expansion of domestic

Table 4

ORIGINS OF TURKISH INDUSTRIALISTS AND PRESENT SIZE OF INDUSTRIAL ENTERPRISE

		Present Size of Enterprise		
Economic–Occupational Activity	Industrialist's Former Activity	10–49 Workers	50 Workers and Up	Total
Farmer...................................	19%	82%	18%	100%
Craftsman.................................	17	100	00.0	100
Trader.....................................	43	70	30	100
Industrialist (father's activity)...............	8	66	34	100
Other......................................	13	96	4	100
Total...............................	100	80	20	100

Source: Alec P. Alexander, Industrial Entrepreneurship in Turkey: Origins and Growth,'' *Economic Development and Cultural Change*, July, 1960, pp. 349–65.
Definition of industrialist: entrepreneur in manufacturing employing more than 10 workers.
Sampling basis: approximately 20 percent of a total of 380 industrialists in the Aegean Region of Turkey.
Approximate date of survey: 1956.

markets, cheap imports of machinery (for those who could secure import permits) and curtailment of consumer goods imports were the immediate factors which triggered the sharp increase in industrial entrepreneurship. Under these conditions importers and domestic merchants readily switched to industry.

The prominence of former traders among the Turkish industrialists underscores the significance of a preindustrial, commercial phase in the evolution of Turkish entrepreneurship. It is noteworthy that the period of commercial incubation of industrial entrepreneurship had been relatively very short. A merchant class as a significant social force (other than the foreign minorities) only came into existence in Turkey after the establishment of the Republic in 1923. Traditionally, the Ottoman Turks were contemptuous of business, leaving it to the foreign minorities, while their elite was composed of government administrators, military officers, large landowners, and church officials. Kemal Atatürk's radical secularizing and westernizing reforms under the Republic led to the decline of openings in the traditional careers, while at the same time opportunities in business and the professions began to attract talent and resources. The spirit of economic enterprise began to permeate the Turkish society. A merchant class, under favorable ecconomic conditions (which included the period of World War II neutrality), grew sufficiently in size and wealth to become the major source of recruitment of industrialists. The venture of entrepreneurs into industry had thus been preceded by a new social experience which had strengthened secularism and the desire for material profit and by an economic experience which had contributed to the accumulation of capital in private hands. The development of a commercial class had been a key feature of these experiences.

MERCHANT AND OTHER GROUPS AS SOURCES OF INDUSTRIALISTS

The evidence is conclusive that more industrialists have been re-cruited from the ranks of merchants than from any other group. Between 25 and 45 percent of the industrialists in the countries surveyed had formerly been merchants, in particular large merchants and to a smaller degree importers. The importance of trade and of mercantile capital for industrialization today is thus not unlike that suggested by Mantoux, Pirenne, and others for the early period of industrialization in Western Europe.

The data from two countries (Greece and Philippines) also show that a high proportion of merchants who later became industrialists had fathers who had also been merchants. This differs substantially from the experience of industrialists of other backgrounds more of whom tended to "move out" of their fathers' activities and into something else before becoming industrialists. It thus seems that not only merchants but also second-generation merchants are more likely to possess whatever is needed in entrepreneurial motivation or capital or in other qualifications to effect the switch from trade to industry. The contribution of mer-chants, whether first or second generation, emphasizes the importance for industrialization of the earlier development of trade and of a commercial class. The Turkish experience offers a striking example of the importance of a period of commercial incubation of industrial entrepreneurship.

Several distinct reasons account for the merchants' high productivity of industrial entrepreneur: (1) Unlike other potential industrialists, mer-chants are already entrepreneurs. The market economy is already their milieu; they are accustomed to responding to market incentives and to exposing themselves to business risks. (2) Merchants also possess busi-ness skills, albeit of a particular kind. Merchants are skilled in buying, selling, employing others, and in making contracts. (3) Merchants are also likely to possess capital which may be substantial if past conditions have favored the accumulation of mercantile profits. The possession of financial resources confers a special advantage on potential industrialists, especially in countries in which the financial system is undeveloped and the possibilities of drawing on other people's resources are limited. (4) Merchants are also more likely to be able to cope with uncertainty as a major obstacle to entry. This is not only because of their particular skills but also because they probably already have their own networks of wholesale and retail outlets, they are more sensitive to particular product specifications, and they are generally closer to the market on the demand side of their contemplated industrial projects. These conditions also help explain why merchants often go into the production of goods which they were formerly trading. For all these and probably other reasons, merchants more readily respond to opportunities in industry. It can be assumed that the greater these opportunities are, the greater will be the disparity noted between the merchants' productivity in industrialists and that of other groups of potential industrialists.

Ranking behind merchants, craftsmen have also contributed substantially to the supply of industrialists. Excluding the Philippines, where the definition of this group was less precise, approximately one fifth of all industrialists surveyed had formerly been craftsmen. Our data also suggest that the craftsmen's productivity in industrialists is considerably smaller than that of merchants.

A craftsman becomes an industrialist (the precise demarcation line between the two is arbitrary) usually by expanding the scale of his operations in the same type of activity. This places the craftsman in an advantageous position for "entry" into industry. Yet, the craftsmen's relatively moderate or small productivity in industrialists suggests that this group also faces serious obstacles to entry. The vast majority of craftsmen typically have very small establishment, so that a manifold increase in size may be needed before their operations can be classified as industrial. (Thus in Greece, for example, 90 percent of all craftsmen employ fewer than five workers and the bulk of them employ only two workers). The generation and reinvestment of substantial profits are necessary conditions for growth. But these are not easy to bring about. Profits may be limited because of competition from other craftsmen, from mass production industries, or from imports, or because of inability to respond to changes in tastes. The typical traditional craft shops in underdeveloped countries operate on shoestrings. The difficulties for craftsmen are aggravated when growth beyond a certain level requires discrete jumps in size as well as radical changes in technology and organization. Perhaps most important, in contrast to merchants, craftsmen are not necessarily "entrepreneurs," and therefore they may not be responsive to favorable external conditions even if these conditions exist. Many craftsmen, however, are entrepreneurially inclined, and it is from among these that industrialists are more likely to be recruited.

In at least some countries it was craftsmen rather than merchants who contributed more heavily to the supply of industrialists during the very early stages of industrialization. The data are too limited to permit any generalization, but it is not too difficult to see why it may be easier for craftsmen to become industrialists in the early rather than in more advanced stages of industrialization. Smaller industrial establishments using simple technology and producing traditional types of goods are more likely to be profitable in the beginnings of industrialization, thus making it easier for craftsmen to expand their operations to the level of industry. But as larger and more complex initial operations become necessary, craftsmen lose these advantages to other groups. One can expect that as industrialization proceeds, the contribution of craftsmen to the supply of industrialists will decline, both because there will tend to be relatively fewer craftsmen in the working population and because their productivity in industrialists will also diminish.

The contribution of professional men, business executives, and of men from other services to the supply of industrialists in the now developing economies has so far been small. However, the limited empirical evidence available suggests that the professional men's productivity in industrialists is high. This is particularly true of such professional groups as engineers, chemists, and businessmen. Possession of technical and managerial skills offers some comparative advantages to potential industrialists. These advantages are greater, the more sophisticated industrial technology, products, and business operations become. In the Greek study it was found that several men from these fields moved into industries in which they had previously been employed and had thus acquired a particularly good understanding of specific industrial and business processes. A major disadvantage facing professional men and business executives who aspire to become industrialists may still be the insufficiency of their personal resources. But as industrialization proceeds, the financial system also develops, so that the possibilities of floating stock or of borrowing from credit institutions increase. Under these conditions potential industrialists can draw on other people's resources. It may be hypothesized that as an economy develops and the proportion of professional men and of business executives increases, the proportion of industrialists recruited from the ranks of these groups will also tend to increase. This increase will come about at the expense of other groups, probably including the merchants.

Our data show that the direct contribution of farmers to the supply of industrialists has generally been small and in some cases insignificant. Those industrialistts who came from agriculture had almost exclusively been recruited from the ranks of the larger landowners. It was also found that in Turkey farmers who became industrialists tended to concentrate on the processing of agricultural products. The greater financial capability of this group and their exposure to the industrial processing of products which they had themselves been supplying to other manufacturers must have facilitated their entry into industry. On the other hand, a significant proportion of all the industrialists' fathers had been farmers. Their sons' "getting off the land" and into something else, especially trade, before becoming industrialists, is thus an important feature of the intergeneration mobility which leads to the formation of the industrial entrepreneurial group.

The interpretations of industrial entrepreneurial recruitment offered so far can be incorporated in a more general framework. Recruitment has been viewed as the set of movements of people originating in various groups in society and converging on a single locus, namely, the industrial entrepreneurial group. A set of propositions may be presented which briefly summarize the effects of a variety of factors affecting these movements. Our immediate concern is the growth of industrial entrepreneurship, but some of the discussion applies to entrepreneurship in general.

The growth of industrial entrepreneurship is the result of effects emanating both from the demand and supply sides. The demand for entrepreneurship is the demand for goods and services which can be produced by entrepreneurs. Whatever determines the actual or potential demand for entrepreneurial output therefore, by derivation, also determines the demand or the opportunity structure for entrepreneurial inputs. The scope of these opportunities will be greater the faster income per capita is rising. When incomes are rising opportunities for positive-sum entrepreneurial activities are possible and profitable. On the other hand, in a stagnant economy entrepreneurial activities are of the zero-sum type where one entrepreneur's gain is another's loss. Not only the actual but also the anticipated rate of growth in income per capita affects entrepreneurial opportunities. When a high rate of growth in income per capita is anticipated, an entrepreneur will respond without making allowance for the fact that other entrepreneurs will also respond. The actual rate of growth in income per capita will thus tend to be greater than anticipated, and within this environment entrepreneurial activities of the positive-sum are more likely to thrive.

At least three sets of factors affect the supply of industrial entrepreneurship. These are: factors which are complementary to entrepreneurship, the economic-occupational structure of a society, and the overall social values and psychological motivations.

A given stock of potential entrepreneurship becomes actual the more easily it can be complemented with certain other factors. These include capital, managerial inputs, technological skills, and the flow of information affecting decision making. The need for these complementary factors tends to be greater the more industrialized an economy is. Thus, in the beginning of industrialization, small enterprises needing little capital and using simple technology and organization may be viable, while in a more advanced industrial economy larger enterprises using more complex technology and systems of management and more heavily relying on information about a large number of variables become necessary. On the other hand, not only the need for, but also the availability of, these factors increases as an economy advances. In the early stages of development an entrepreneur must also be the capitalist, whereas later he can rely more on other people's money on which he can draw through the more developed financial system. The same is true of the other factors. In a more advanced economy the entrepreneur can rely on the greater availability of technically trained men and managers and on the greater flow of information provided by private and public services. In sum, the more advanced an economy is, the easier it will be for an entrepreneur to rely upon his economic environment for the provision of the needed complementary factors.

The relevance of the economic-occupational structure of a society to the supply of industrialists is threefold. First, regardless of the level of entrepreneurial proclivities of the population as a whole, some economic-occupational groups may be more entrepreneurially inclined than others. Thus we have assumed that among the different groups from which industrialists are recruited, merchants are the most entrepreneurially inclined.

Second, economic-occupational groups tend to have a differential ability to command the complementary factors cited as the need for and availability of these factors increase in the course of development. Thus, in the early phases of development when small and simple enterprises are more viable, craftsmen may have an advantage as potential industrialists. They can expand the scale of their operations to the level of a small industrial firm without great changes in technology and management methods and without having to rely on a great deal more information about their market environment. Later on, however, as industrial enterprises increase in size and complexity and the need for the complementary factors is greater, the differential advantage for entry may shift to the merchants. Apart from the fact that merchants are already entrepreneurs, they have the advantages of possessing at least some capital and some special management skills and of having access to certain types of market information. At still more advanced levels of development the need for understanding and appreciating sophisticated technology and managerial methods confers some advantages to the now more numerous technically trained professional men and business executives or to those who can mobilize these talents. The need for capital and the flow of information are, of course, also greater, but these are more easily forthcoming from the more developed economic environment.

Third, the relative size of the various economic-occupational groups in the total working population is also relevant. It is this size along with each group's productivity in industrialists which determine the total supply of industrialists.

The importance of psychological motivations and of social values for entrepreneurial growth have been stressed by several theories in the social sciences. These have been identified with such concepts as the protestant ethic and more recently with the need for achievement and the withdrawal of status respect.[6] It will be difficult to assess the relevance of these and other noneconomic theories of entrepreneurial growth to particular times and places, and no such attempt can be made within the context of the present study. It can be argued, however, that these cannot be accepted as single-cause explanations. Any level of entrepreneurial inclinations in a given society, no matter how it is explained, must be combined with, and be conditioned by, the several "objective" factors surveyed in this study before entrepreneurship becomes effective.[7]

The role of merchants as suppliers of industrialists may be briefly reviewed in the context of this scheme. Given a certain opportunity structure in the economy and a certain level of motivations in the population as a whole, the merchants' productivity in industrialists will probably always be relatively very high. Further, the larger the relative size of the group of merchants in the population, the greater will their relative contribution to the supply of industrialists be. On the other hand, the merchants' differential advantages for entry into industry, while always strong, will probably tend to change as an economy develops. Thus we have explained that in the initial, as compared to later, stages of industrialization, craftsmen find it much easier to become industrialists, and correspondingly the merchants' relative advantages for entry into industry may not be as pronounced. In at least some countries, we have seen, craftsmen are indeed the largest suppliers of industrialists in the initial stages of industrialization. Merchants, on the other hand, probably enjoy their maximum advantage as potential industrialists at perhaps more intermediate levels of development. The greater requirements for entry into industry in terms of capital, flow of information, and managerial and other skill can more easily be met by the internal economies generated by the merchants' existing firms. At the stage of the "take-off," therefore, the merchants' contribution to industrialization can be decisive. In all of the countries we have surveyed, merchants were indeed the biggest contributors to the supply of industrialists. At still more advanced levels of industrialization, however, requirements for entry into industry

---

[6] David McClelland, *The Achieving Society* (Princeton, N.J.: D. Van Nostrand, Inc., 1961); Everett E. Hagen, *On the Theory of Social Change* (Homewood, Ill.: Dorsey Press, 1962).

[7] An assessment of some of these noneconomic models is included in Alec P. Alexander, "The Supply of Industrial Entrepreneurship," *Explorations in Entrepreneurial History*, Vol. IV, No. 2 (Winter, 1967), pp. 136–49.

are even more exacting, but also the environment becomes sufficiently richer in external economies (in terms of the availability of factors complementary to entrepreneurship), so that the mercantile firms' differential advantages for entry diminish. It may be hypothesized that under these conditions the mercantile origins of industrial entrepreneurship may relatively decline. Such other sources of recruitment of industrialists as professional men (especially those trained in advanced technologies) and business executives may increase in relative importance. This is not only because the changing environment provides greater accessibility to the factors that must complement industrial entrepreneurship but also because members of these groups may themselves possess some of the more exacting technological and managerial skills which are now necessary for entry. Further, in the more developed and therefore occupationally more pluralistic economies, the relative size of these other groups in the working population is likely to be greater, thus also increasing their importance as potential sources of recruitment of industrial entrepreneurs.

MERCHANT ORIGIN AND INDUSTRIAL BEHAVIOR

There is still another way in which the economic-occupational structure of a society may affect industrial entrepreneurship. Relations may exist between the quality of performance of industrialists and their economic-occupational origins. Indeed, some interesting although limited information is available on some links between the origins and behavior of industrialists in the four countries surveyed.

These relations have been more clearly discerned in the case of industrialists who have been recruited from the ranks of craftsmen. Former craftsmen generally tend to be more conservative as industrialists. They own firms which are usually the smallest and also technologically and organizationally the least advanced. No former craftsmen in the sample of Turkish industrialists owned firms which employed more than 50 workers (Table 4). Pakistani industrialists who had backgrounds in small industry and handicrafts remained small industrialists. The approximately 18 percent of Pakistani industrialists falling in this category controlled only 6 percent of industrial capital (Table 3). Greek industrialists who had been recruited from the ranks of craftsmen own the relatively smallest firms, practically none of which is of the corporate type (Table 5). Former craftsmen in Greece also tend to have the lowest level of formal education, probably contributing to their observed rigidity and conservatism as managers and entrepreneurs. In Greece as well as in the Philippines former craftsmen were found to be the least progressive as industrialists by almost any criterion used.

This type of entrepreneurial performance by former craftsmen is re-

Table 5

CHARACTERISTICS OF GREEK INDUSTRIALISTS BY ECONOMIC-OCCUPATIONAL ORIGIN

Former Activity	Average No. of Workers Employed in Industrial Enterprise (1)	Legal Form of Industrial Enterprise (Percentages)			Education of Industrialists (Percentages)			
		Proprietor-ships/ Partnerships (2)	Corporation (3)	Total (4)	Less than Six Years (5)	Six Years through High School (6)	University (7)	Total (8)
Craftsman.................	95	99	1	100	16	75	9	100
Big merchant.............	210	41	59	100	3	72	25	100
Small merchant...........	118	87	13	100	7	73	20	100
None: father industrialist..	200	50	50	100	..	53	47	100
Professional man..........	255	19	81	100	..	..	100	100
Business executive........	192	29	71	100	..	25	75	100
All Industrialists..........	171	58	42	100	4	61	35	100

Note: See notes to Table 1.

lated to the way in which they "enter" industry. Because of the necessarily arbitrary distinction between craftsmen and industrialists, the transition from one status to the other can be accomplished by a change in the scale of operations but not necessarily in organization, technology, or outlook. Whereas entry into industry of entrepreneurs recruited from other sources involves a radical change in the nature of their activities and constitutes an entrepreneurial act of the highest order that tests their abilities and ambitions, there is no similar screening involved in the entry into industry of former craftsmen. The test for them often comes later, when, after a certain point, continued growth of their "industrial" enterprises increasingly requires changes in the methods of production. It is then that many former craftsmen prove unwilling or unable to undertake these changes. Their firms, therefore, remain small and organizationally and technologically at an elementary level.

The pattern of industrial entrepreneurial performance of former merchants tends to be more diverse and consequently more difficult to describe. Judged in terms of size and overall progressiveness, the industrial operations of former merchants in all of the countries surveyed are generally far more advanced than those of former craftsmen. On the other hand, some of the most striking examples of progressive industrial entrepreneurship have been observed in the activities of industrialists of other backgrounds. In Pakistan, we have seen, merchants set up the largest and most rapidly growing firms. But in Greece former merchants (especially if big and small merchants are combined in one group) lagged behind industrialists of some other backgrounds in terms of the size of their enterprises and the extent to which these enterprises were of the corporate form (Table 5). Among the small number of truly progressive industrialists in Greece, there was a heavy concentration of former professional men and of business executives. In the Philippines it was found that in terms of their progressiveness as industrialists, former merchants were ranked somewhere between former craftsmen and other industrialists coming from a variety of backgrounds.[8]

It is difficult to generalize from these observations about the quality of performance of former merchants. The available data are obviously very limited. Allowance must also be made for the possibility, noted earlier, that as an economy grows, there are shifts in the groups which are best situated to respond to changing entrepreneurial opportunities. Consequently, the relative progressiveness of former merchants as industrialists at a given time and place may have been influenced by the level of industrialization. By the same token, the relative "backwardness" of former craftsmen may only be recent, reflecting the inability of craftsmen

---

[8] Carroll, *op. cit.*, p. 175.

to respond to the increasingly more demanding requirements of progressive industrial entrepreneurship.

One particular aspect of industrial entrepreneurial performance deserves comment. A tendency has been observed among industrialists in at least some developing countries, including Greece and Turkey, to concern themselves more with the marketing aspects of their activities and less with problems of production, management, efficiency, and long-term planning. Profit maximization emphasizing high prices rather than low unit costs and greater production may be said to be a reflection of this attitude. One explanation of this phenomenon may be traced to the large proportion of former merchants among industrialists who, one may argue, are carrying over into industry their ingrained habits and ways of thinking. This may be especially true in those frequently observed cases where merchants retain their trading activities even after they become industrialists. In these cases it may be difficult for the merchant-industrialist, especially if he is the owner and manager, to use compartmentalized approaches to profits.

This explanation, however, valid as it may be, does not tell the whole story. The study of Greek industrialists, for example, has shown that there are conditions in the economic environment which contribute to a "commercial" orientation of industrial entrepreneurs even among those whose background is not trade. These environmental conditions are not unique to Greece. In varying degrees and forms they exist in other countries whose economy is still relatively underdeveloped. Because of their wider relevance the explanations for the "commercial" attitudes of Greek industrialists will be repeated here.

First, increases in prices, percentage-wise much larger than decreases in cost, were more easily accomplished in the past under the shelter provided by the Greek government's protectionist tariff policies. Even a moderate decrease in unit costs by means other than substantial changes in the size of the enterprise requires the serious application of special managerial abilities. The typical entrepreneur-manager did not possess these abilities, nor did he have the incentive, until recently at least, to acquire them or to hire other persons possessing them. On the other hand, tariffs in Greece have been high, long in existence and granted almost indiscriminately in response to lobbying on the part of interested entrepreneurs. Tariffs have thus not been used in a way which could be justified by the "infant industry" argument, but have instead encouraged inefficiency.

Complementing the effects of tariffs, other circumstances made it easier for industrialists to increase profits through higher prices rather than lower costs. Until very recently the state (Ministry of Industry) had the authority to declare an industry "satiated" and to refuse the granting of the license needed for establishing a new enterprise in this industry. Lobbying often influenced the government's decisions in these matters. Finally, varying degrees of monopolistic policies in different industries have had effects upon prices and costs similar to those of tariffs and government restrictions on entry.

Second, the instability of the Greek market has contributed to the relative indifference of industrialists to problems of efficiency. Past fluctuations in demand, often confined within particular industries rather than extending to the economy as a whole, were responsible for considerable fluctuations in profits and losses. Poor forecasting methods also contributed to this effect. In the face of these fluctuations, there was a feeling on the part of at least some industrialists that improved efficiency would not add appreciably to their profits during good times and would not prevent losses during bad times. After the realization of profits during periods of strong demand, production, but not necessarily price, is cut back until the next boom. Pressures on profit margins lead to lower total costs through lower production but seldom to improved efficiency. In an environment of instability, what counts is to pick the right moment to buy or sell.

Third, the "mass markets at low unit profits" philosophy is only possible when a mass market exists. Given the size of the Greek population, the level and distribution of income cannot support mass production except, perhaps, of a few durables and consumer goods. Market conditions, from this point of view, have improved in recent years, but until recently at least, if not still today, a lowering of prices was not expected to lead to more than proportionate increases in sales. When demand tends to be price inelastic, the high-price-per-unit philosophy is consistent with rational profit maximization.

Finally, a high price per unit is desirable because it can accommodate an element of insurance against risks. Prices and costs in the postwar period in Greece have moved erratically, often affecting particular industries rather than the economy as a whole. A high profit per unit, if it is possible, includes a cushion against unforseeable changes.

Professor Miracle draws upon West African examples to show the ways in which control of marketing processes and control of capital may be related to each other and thus lead to profoundly anticompetitive results. While Professor Mintz stresses the competitive characteristics of small-scale trade, Miracle argues that even markets with large numbers of buyers and sellers may be subject to cartelization based upon the power inherent in the cartel leader's capital resources. The marketing process, in turn, is often the best available source for capital accumulation in developing countries. These considerations lead to a discussion of policies designed to promote freedom of market entry and increased access to capital accumulation opportunities.

MARVIN P. MIRACLE*

Market structure in commodity trade and capital accumulation in West Africa[1]

The literature on industrial organization has long focused on the effect of market structure on consumer sovereignty and the efficient use of resources at a given level of output. Relatively little attention has been given to ways in which market structure influences the rate and character of economic growth, and much of the literature on this topic has centered on two sets of arguments against competition—infant industry arguments and the Schumpeter argument concerning the possible benefits of having spots in the economy sheltered from the harsh winds of competition where innovations can be nurtured. Most of the arguments concerning beneficial effects of competition on economic development are found in an article by Willard F. Mueller and a monograph by Reed Moyer.[2]

This paper argued that in at least one large subset of the underdeveloped economies, the economies of West Africa—but probably in the rest

* University of Wisconsin.

[1] West Africa is herein defined as Cameroun and all of sub-Saharan Africa west of it. The author wishes to express his gratitude to Peter Helmberger for his helpful comments on an earlier version of this paper. Much of the research was done in West Africa in 1965 under a grant from the Social Science Research Council, but all opinions and conclusions are those of the author alone.

[2] Willard F. Mueller, "Some Market Structure Considerations in Economic Development," *Journal of Farm Economics*, Vol. XII, No. 2 (May, 1959), pp. 414–25; and Reed Moyer, *Marketing in Economic Development*, Michigan State University, International Business Occasional Paper No. 1, 1965, pp. 12–19.

of tropical Africa as well and perhaps in parts of other underdeveloped areas—adding effective policies that promote competition to the cluster of policies aimed at stimulating economic development will, in general, contribute to economic development in additional ways not covered by Mueller or others. This article extends Mueller's discussion of West Africa by arguing that in that group of underdeveloped economies, promotion of competition will not only increase the efficiency of the distributive sector but, because of the nature of the major obstacles to capital accumulation and the organization of agricultural production, will raise the rate of capital accumulation by peasants and may well help reduce the gap between the known potential and actual productivity in agricultural production.

THE ECONOMIES OF WEST AFRICA

The national economies of West Africa, like those of most countries at an early level of development, are predominantly agricultural and heavily dependent on one or two agricultural exports. In most of the countries of West Africa well over 90 percent of the population is still in rural areas, even though a number of urban centers are growing rapidly.[3] Most countries have begun some industrialization, but manufacturing is largely limited to a handful of factories. Economic growth in the past half century has been largely based on agricultural exports, except for recent development of a petroleum industry in Nigeria and of mining in Sierra Leone and Liberia.[4]

National income estimates in West Africa are too rough to have much meaning for many of the purposes for which they are usually used; nonetheless, they may be adequate for assessing the relative importance of sectors of the economy. According to estimates of the late 1950's, the agricultural sector accounted for from 48 to 63 percent of gross domestic product in Guinea, Ivory Coast, Ghana, and Nigeria, the most industrialized of West African countries for which estimates are available.[5]

Quantitative data are not available on the importance of trade, but it is clear that a large proportion, if not all, of the tribal economies found within the national economies of West Africa do not fit the stereotype of a subsistence economy that is commonly used in economic development

[3] An exception is Western Nigeria where there are at least six cities of over 100,000 within a 100-mile radius of Ibadan, itself a city of over a million.

[4] See B. F. Johnston, "Changes in Agricultural Productivity," in M. J. Herskovits and M. Harwitz (eds.), Economic Transition in Africa (Evanston, Ill., 1961), pp. 156–160.

[5] See United Nations, Economic Bulletin for Africa, Vol. XI, No. 2 (June, 1962), p. 12, and République de Côte d'Ivoire, Min. Finances, Affaires Économiques, et du Plan, Direction de la Statistique, Les Comptes Économiques de la Côte d'Ivoire 1958 et 1960, p. 23.

models. In the forest zone where cash crops such as cocoa, coffee, palm oil, bananas, and rubber can be grown, there is a heavy flow of migrant labor, and fairly heavy dependence on nonfamily labor is the rule. Such farmers tend to be fairly highly specialized, devoting available labor and land to cash crops and buying a large proportion of the foodstuffs needed to feed their families and laborers. In addition, there is substantial internal trade in foodstuffs between tribal economies because of geographical differences in starchy staples produced and quality differences in the same foodstuff.

This paper focuses on increasing the capital formation of farmers because they constitute such a large proportion of the population, and on the effect of market structure in the distributive sector on capital accumulation in agriculture because increasing capital formation in the agricultural sector by some means is clearly prerequisite to greater agricultural production and productivity.

Problems of market structure research in West Africa

Market structure research in West Africa is usually frustrating because of the lack of nearly all, if not all, of the data needed. Not only is there a total void of basic data needed for developing such things as concentration ratios, profit levels, prices, volumes of output and sales, price elasticities and cross-elasticities of demand, economies of scale, and technological changes over time, but defining the industry and relevant market, always a major problem anywhere, is made especially difficult because of lack of grades and standards and the predominance of commodities unknown in the temperature zone—e.g., manioc, yams, taro, plantain, palm oil, and kola nuts.

The researcher must generate all his own data, and even so, is denied use of some familiar tools because of the impossibility of getting reasonably trustworthy estimates of production, volumes of commodites moving in commerce, or the financial position of buyers or sellers. Getting information from businessmen on details of their operations is difficult in any country, but when a non-African or one of his assistants attempts to ask African sellers questions about prices, costs, income, or net returns, it is difficult to get any information at all, and there is little hope that anything obtained will be reasonably reliable. Apart from suspicion of strangers and fear of the consequences should either the government or rapacious relatives learn of the seller's true financial position, a large portion of transactions are not written down.

Until West African countries can provide the staff and funds needed to collect more and better statistics, meaningful market structure analysis must proceed largely by examining the kinds and causes of collusion and other departures from the competitive model with little possibility of satisfactorily quantifying the market structures found or showing more than the direction of associated conduct and performance.

THE STRUCTURE OF FACTOR MARKETS

Factor markets vary greatly in West Africa according to the factor and to the tribal economy. Probably most imperfect are the land and capital markets, with certain characteristics of systems of land tenure contributing to the thinness of capital markets and concentration of lenders, which, in turn, facilitates concentration in product markets. Labor markets are not discussed here because they are of little relevance to later discussion.

Land

Communal land tenure systems, under which land cannot be sold, still predominate, although considerable erosion of the traditional tenure systems can be seen everywhere. In a number of areas an embryonic market for land has developed.

Because of the land tenure systems, land usually cannot serve as collateral, and most farmers have little or no other collateral except growing crops which lending institutions do not accept. Private crop buyers do make loans against crops, and often are able not only to make a good return on the lending operation but an added return from their commodity trading if they lend enough to get some degree of control over crop supplies.

Capital

All evidence suggests that capital markets to which farmers have access are highly oligopolistic, although, like labor, capital markets have not yet been the focus of careful detailed studies.

Most rural West Africans make no use of banks or of other formal savings and lending institutions. Governmental credit agencies have very little credit to extend, and nongovernmental banks are generally not interested in making loans to Africans because they rarely have acceptable collateral, and are considered extremely high-risk borrowers.

The main sources of capital for Africans are moneylenders, which in some communities may be non-African as well as African, commodity buyers, and friends or relatives. Where non-African money lenders are encountered, they are typically Lebanese or Syrian merchants who, as a group, unlike Africans, can get loans from private banks. The risk of lending to Africans is much lower for Lebanese and Syrian traders than for banks because most of the traders live—or have lived—in rural areas, fraternizing with Africans and learning African languages and customs.

Lebanese and Syrian money lenders, in contrast to bankers, know, or can readily determine how honest most Africans with whom they might deal have been in the past; whether they have debts outstanding; who their associates are; and something of their ability to succeed in the planned venture. And, unlike bankers, moneylenders are not restricted in the interest they charge.

African moneylenders operate much as the Lebanese and Syrians, except that they usually must rely entirely on profits from moneylending itself, or revenues from some other enterprise, since they rarely have the option of lending again the money borrowed from private banks. They may have access to banks, however, through their loans from Lebanese and Syrian moneylenders. The Lebanese and Syrians will lend money to Africans who would appear to be their competitors because of the political power of African moneylenders who being better informed than others, may be able to make loans to some Africans with less risk than even the Lebanese and Syrians. Thus African moneylenders vis-à-vis the Lebanese and Syrians have the same role with respect to a portion of the African borrowers that the Lebanese and Syrians have vis-à-vis private banks for all African borrowers.

My informants widely report that the principal moneylenders are large commodity buyers who use their loans strategically to control supplies. Thus the amount of concentration in product markets often is directly related to concentration in the capital markets. Once concentration among commodity traders develops to the point that they can earn supernormal profits, such profits can be fairly easily perpetuated and increased by strategic use of credit to control supplies. The greater the supernormal profits in product markets, the greater the concentration of loanable funds in a few hands and the easier it is to make supernormal profits in moneylending, leading to still greater concentration of loanable funds and even tighter control of commodity supplies.

The only checks on the concentration of loanable funds are savings held by friends or relatives and injections of capital from national or world capital markets through Lebanese and Syrians. However, savings by friends or relatives appear not large or reliable enough to prevent control of the tribal capital markets by a few lenders.

Access to capital markets outside the tribal economies via non-Africans is also limited. First, Lebanese and Syrians are not found in numbers in all West African countries (Nigeria, for example, has very few relative to her population) and are unevenly distributed among the tribal economies in countries where they are relatively numerous. Secondly, Lebanese and Syrians are well aware of their guest status in West Africa and are careful not to antagonize politically powerful groups in the communities in which they operate. Wealth and political power appear as highly correlated in West Africa as anywhere; hence the Lebanese and Syrian traders are much more likely to use private banks to finance established commodity traders than to assist those who would like to challenge them if enough capital were available. Thus it would appear that once established individuals or groups get control of product markets they also get control of the capital market and have little threat to their position.

MARKET STRUCTURE IN PRODUCT MARKETS

Pure competition among farmers appears to be characteristic throughout West Africa. There are many producers of almost any commodity that can be produced; none is large enough to affect prices perceptibly. So far only a start has been made on study of market behavior in distribution, but enough has been done to show that the amount and kind of competition varies considerably by commodity and area. For all major products there seems clearly to be large departures from pure or atomistic competition.

The prevalance of oligopoly among importers from overseas markets has been well discussed by Bauer, Cox-George, Haik, Guillard, and Le Masson.[6] In most of Francaphonic West Africa, Lebanese and Syrians dominate internal trade in many available manufactured goods. Most African shopkeepers and peddlers depend on Lebanese or Syrian merchants for credit or for merchandise consigned to them, and are under obligation not to undercut prices prevailing in the Lebanese and Syrian shops. The small number of Lebanese and Syrian merchants in most towns and the clannishness of these cohesive immigrant groups strongly encourage oligopolistic behavior.

For any storable commodity whose production is seasonal, or any nonseasonal commodity not produced in quantity within a few miles of a given marketplace, one finds a considerable amount of collusion which frequently takes the form of well-organized cartels. This collusion stems from the enormous barrier to entry which capital requirements create and because of the social and economic ties between sellers which make maintenance of cartel discipline easier here than in most Western countries.

A number of the more conspicuous cartels are run by a single tribe or family. There are a number of examples of tribal dominance in trade. The cattle and kola cartels in Western Nigeria are controlled by the Hausa and the butcher rings by Yoruba. In the southern Ivory Coast,

---

[6] P. T. Bauer, "Concentration in Tropical Trade: Some Aspects and Implications of Oligopoly," *Economica* (November, 1953), pp. 302–21; N. A. Cox-George, *Report on African Participation in the Commerce of Sierra Leone* (Freetown, 1960); and G. Haik, R. Guillard, and C. Le Masson, *La Distribution en Côte d'Ivoire* (Paris, 1963), pp. 26–68.

tribes from north of the forest belt—the so called Dioulas—dominate the cattle, kola, and dried fish trade. In the same area Yorubas are said to dominate commerce in certain lines of manufactured goods; the Senegalese control the production and sale of "African types" of wheat bread; and the charcoal cartels are run by the Bambara from Mali.

African traders I have interviewed consistently stress their dependence on the goodwill of other sellers of the same commodity. That they should feel a greater mutual dependence than Western businessmen is not surprising, considering the greater social pressure for group-approved behavior in West Africa as reflected by the existence of strong loyalties to the extended family, clan, and tribe. Moreover, in West African societies collusion in selling and participation in cartels seem to be every seller's ambition and carry no stigma.

But mores and social structure aside, there are economic reasons to expect a higher degree of mutual dependence among rival sellers. As was the case with pioneer farmers on the American frontier, the goodwill of one's neighbors is about the only insurance against disaster from fire or theft and may be crucial in times of illness or financial emergency.

Awareness of mutual dependence is often heightened because of cultural isolation. A high proportion of the larger West African traders operate in tribal economies other than their own. There they form into tight, cohesive cultural groups in a strange, if not hostile, community. Like the Lebanese and Syrians who find themselves in exactly the same situation and respond to it in the same manner, their relationship to others of their cultural group makes collusion easy, if not mandatory. It also creates stability in what might otherwise be unstable collusive arrangements.

In the Ivory Coast, Ghana, and Nigeria, at least there exist well-organized cartels for most major commodities. Each is run by a powerful head who is usually a woman (called a "queen" in Ghana). Usually the queen has much more capital than other members of the cartel, and she uses it to maintain discipline in the cartel. Any seller wishing to sell in a given marketplace must obtain her permission and agree to follow policies of the cartel. He is then assigned a location in the marketplace.

The queen is usually elected by the other sellers. She must have enough capital to finance supplies of the commodity she deals in. She usually can buy any supplies arriving at the marketplace where she is established and may provide local storage for some surpluses. If more of the commodity arrives than she can finance, she can always refuse a place in the market to the potential entrant and enforce her decision with action by the rest of the cartel. Such collective pressure is apparently largely political and social in nature. None of my informants would admit that they ever resorted to violence but would mention it as a remote possibility.

Queens sell mainly at wholesale to the remainder of the cartel, whose members are usually retailers. Sales from the queen to members are usually on credit. Typically the queen alone sets the price to retailers and the price at which the commodity is to be retailed. Undercutting the queen's price may be punishable by a fine or expulsion from the cartel and, perhaps, economic exile. If the offense is sufficiently grave, the cartel may prevent the seller from joining any other cartel or from selling any of the minor, largely unorganized, commodities in the same market-place.

Queens also frequently control supplies at the farm level by giving advances on crops before they are harvested. By this use of credit and by dividing supply zones among themselves, they largely eliminate competition among buyers at the farm level and in small rural marketplaces.

One of the best known cartels is in the cattle trade. In the main consuming areas of the forest zone the cattle trade is controlled by cartels such as those in Ibadan, Nigeria, the largest city in West Africa, with over a million inhabitants and Abidjan, the capital of the Ivory Coast. In 1963 the cattle cartel in Ibadan had 12 members, two of which were much larger than the others; there were seven sellers in the cartel in Abidjan, one of which was greatly larger than any of the others.[7]

Members of such cartels buy animals from dealers who have purchased them in small markets in the supply zone, then drive or ship them by rail to the forest zone. Cattle drives take 20 to 45 days, depending on the point of origin, the destination, and the condition of grass along the route. Both shippers and drovers may sell some of their animals along the route, but only drovers sell in small towns and villages. A good proportion of the drovers' herds pass through the cartel then back to small towns and villages because butchers generally cannot buy animals unless they are given credit, and drovers do not know the credit rating of most butchers whereas cartel members do.

Cartel members offer a common price to suppliers and to butchers, but they may practice intense nonprice competition.[8] Cartel members try to firmly attach suppliers, and reportedly most drovers and shippers rarely

---

[7] The only measure of the relative size of members of the cattle cartels is the number of inns each maintains to house, feed, and entertain suppliers. In Ibadan in 1963 the largest cattle merchant had six inns; the second largest had four; two others had two inns; and the other eight sellers had only one each (A. Cohen, "The Social Organization of Credit in a West African Cattle Market," *Africa*, January, 1965, p. 10). The largest seller in the Abidjan cartel reportedly had 37 "houses" which may include rental property as well as inns, and my informants did not have information on the other six members of the cartel.

[8] Cohen states that cattle dealers in Ibadan receive only a fixed small commission, but from his discussion of their behavior it is clear that they control cattle supplies and prices and engage in vigorous nonprice competition. (Cohen "The Social Organization of Credit in a West African Cattle Market," *op. cit.*, p. 14). Thus if they are only brokers they must make gains beyond their fixed commission by collecting a higher price from the butcher than they report to the supplier.

switch from one member of the cartel to another. Frequently cartel members have a number of clients who have sold to them for years. The goodwill developed may be passed on from father to son along with tangible assets the son inherits. However, clients not firmly attached may be vigorously wooed. Emissaries may be sent to intercept drovers when they are still over a hundred miles away, to promise them good quarters, fine food, and lavish entertainment. A present is commonly given to suppliers when they have disposed of their animals and leave the forest zone to collect another herd.

The cartel derives its power from its capital through which it controls suppliers and, therefore, supplies. Local butchers have no alternatives. They lack the capital to buy their own animals in the supply zone or even to buy directly from shippers and drovers for cash. Shippers and drovers usually do not know butchers well enough to know their credit reputation, and time spent in the forest belt trying to collect bad debts has high opportunity cost in terms of returns they could make in the supply zone buying another herd.

Suppliers prefer to sell to members of the cartel because cartel members have enough capital to buy the whole herd at once. Even when the supplier must give the cartel two or three weeks of credit, as is frequently the case, the supplier need not fear default and the cartel sees that his wait is costless and pleasant. Moreover, should suppliers sell directly to butchers the cartel can then boycott the butcher involved as they do when a butcher is behind on his debts. The butcher gets a few animals, perhaps at a much lower price than the cartel charges, but he is cut off without any cattle for six weeks or two months until the supplier he dealt with returns with another herd.

The cartel blacklists any butcher who is badly behind on his debts. Where butchers are themselves organized, as they are in Ibadan and parts of the Ivory Coast, the cartel may boycott all members of the organization to which a delinquent butcher belongs.

Nonprice competition in dealing with butchers consists of differences in the amount and length of credit granted and the amount of advertising done by boys or other employees of the individual cartel members. These agents circulate among butchers pointing out the good features of their masters' animals and at the same time act as spies reporting to their master if a butcher is seen talking to an agent for a rival seller.

In addition to giving more or longer credit, cartel members in the Ivory Coast reportedly attempt to get butchers to somewhat overextend themselves so that they are perpetually slightly behind in payments.[9]

Butchers often are also organized and maintain common prices and a

---

[9] M. Lacrouts and J. Tyo, *Les Ressources Animales de la République de la Côte d'Ivoire* (Paris, April–May, 1961), p. 63.

debt relationship to slaughterers as they themselves have with the distributor's cartel, but with a much shorter time period. Butchers who buy cattle on one to four weeks credit have the animals slaughtered daily and give only 24 hours credit to the slaughterers.[10]

Well-organized cartels are also documented for the kola[11] trade, the fish trade, and the transportation industry.

In 1965, I found kola cartels in the Ivory Coast, Upper Volta, and Niger much like those in cattle, except that the geographical direction of trade is reversed—from the forest zone to the savanna. Cohen describes similar cartels in Nigeria.[12] Data on the fish cartels are provided by Bauer, Jancene, and Alix.[13] My own field work on the inland fish trade strongly suggests organization parallel to the cattle and kola cartels, although I was unable to find informants who would provide details on how discipline is maintained among sellers or on forms of nonprice competition other than credit relationships. Those reported are exactly as in the cattle and kola trade. For transportation, I have details only on the cartel in the Ivory Coast, but informants in Ghana state transportation is similarly organized there,[14] and it is likely that the same is true elsewhere in West Africa. In the Ivory Coast, transporters tightly regulate rates and allocate market shares by forcing each driver to wait his turn. Drivers who do not cooperate reportedly run the danger of having their tires slashed.

Marketing of minor commodities that can be grown locally, such as tomatoes or peppers, frequently is less organized and more competitive, but even for such commodities there is probably nothing close to pure competition in distribution anywhere in West Africa, although S. La Anyane suggests something nearer pure competition than monopolistic competition is characteristic of rural markets in Ghana.[15]

In areas I have visited in Ghana, Togo, Dahomey, Nigeria, Ivory

---

[10] Butchers organize the slaughter of animals; slaughterers are those who actually kill and dress animals and retail most of the meat. Butchers may do some retailing, and even if their retail sales are a small proportion of the total, they frequently have some control over the prices charged by other retailers because of their position in the credit chain.

[11] The kola nut, *cola nitida*, is a seed resembling a chestnut in size and texture that is munched as a stimulant and a thirst-quencher throughout West Africa, and consumed the world over as an ingredient of *Coca-Cola*.

[12] A. Cohen, "Politics of the Kola Trade," *Africa*, January, 1966.

[13] P. T. Bauer, *West African Trade* (Cambridge, 1954), p. 390, and Mesdames Jancene and Alix, Min. Finances, Affaires Économiques, et du Plan, Direction de la Statistique, *La Peche Industrielle en Côte d'Ivoire* (Abidjan, 1960), pp. 8–9.

[14] Polly Hill also suggests such cartels in Ghana (Polly Hill, "Some Characteristics of Indigenous West African Enterprise," in Nigerian Institute of Social and Economic Research, *Conference Proceedings March, 1962* [Ibadan, Nigeria], p. 120).

[15] (In Ghana) "Comparatively restrictive tendencies are ineffective. Crowds of buyers bargain freely with the large number of sellers of similar commodities. . . . "S. La Anyane, "Agriculture in the General Economy," in J. B. Wills (ed.), *Agriculture and Land Use in Ghana* (Oxford: Oxford University Press, 1962), pp. 194–95.

Coast, Senegal, Mali, Upper Volta, and Niger, rarely have I found anything more competitive than monopolistic competition—and oligopoly is common—even in large open-air marketplaces, many of which have over a thousand buyers and several hundred sellers. Apparently, pure competition is absent in all these marketplaces. To the casual observer the fairly large number of sellers of some commodities and the apparent homogeneity of items sold may suggest islands of pure competition, but this is illusory.

Commodities that look similar often have important quality differences that buyers can detect. For example, recently harvested oil palm fruit can be used either for cooking or as an ingredient in making soap, but as palm fruit ages, its free fatty acid content rises, making it progressively less suitable for cooking. African men often cannot identify palm fruit that is too old for cooking, but all African housewives in the palm oil belt can.

Moreover, people working in marketplaces are not necessarily sellers. Some sellers may have employees or dependents working for them, and even a fairly large group of sellers may act jointly. I have encountered cartels in Ivory Coast marketplaces with as many as 42 members.

Finally, a large majority of commodities are sold by heap rather than by weight. Commonly a "gift" of an extra unit, or part of an extra measure—like the extra loaf in the baker's dozen—is given at the end of the transaction. Therefore a seller trying to meet competitors' prices must do so by offering the same volume of the commodity, since the monetary unit per heap is the same for all sellers, and often is invariable from day to day and season to season. "Gifts" may be large relative to the purchase, and sometimes are even of equal size. They often come from stocks not on display, and frequently they are of a different quality from the portion purchased. Sellers often are too busy bargaining with their own customers to keep visible competitors under surveillance, hence they find it difficult to determine how frequently "gifts" are given, or their size and quality when offered. Through "gift" strategy, and through nonprice competition such as providing special services—like wrapping produce purchased, changing money for the customer in transactions he makes with sellers of other commodities, or in guarding purchases while the customer visits other parts of the marketplace—sellers ever strive to tie certain customers to them, and often manage to do so.

Other factors aside, the number of sellers of any one commodity, even in a large marketplace, is frequently small enough to encourage oligopolistic behavior, even if there are no collusive agreements among sellers.

CURRENT WEST AFRICAN POLICIES RELATED TO MARKET STRUCTURE

Antitrust legislation is not part of the heritage from the colonial powers, and the governments of West Africa have as yet no explicit policy concerning creation or preservation of competition. Nor has there been much, if any, conscious effort to promote competition indirectly by improving the money market or increasing the quality and quantity of market information. So far policy measures explicitly dealing with market structures are oriented in the opposite direction. They consist of statutory government monopolies or protected monopsonies or monopolies granted to private enterprises in the belief that such restrictions of competition will stimulate economic development.

Obstacles to capital formation by West African farmers

West African land tenure systems are complex and vary greatly, but they uniformly discourage capital accumulation by farmers by discouraging investment in agriculture and by limiting the mobility of farmers; the latter is especially important for reasons discussed presently.

In general, land is allocated by some tribal authority—a chief, a group of elders, or a lineage head—and may be cropped free. Land not in use, with some exceptions, may be given to farmers lacking land and sometimes even to farmers from other tribes.

Polygyny prevails, and in most instances land for foodstuff production is actually allocated to women, the size of the parcel often being determined by need or ability. A farmer usually is obligated to give some help to each of his wives in producing their crops, but the amount of his assistance varies enormously from one ethnic group to another. In most instances husbands at least participate in clearing land, providing they are not employed away from the farm as migrant laborers at clearing time. The husband shares in any surplus obtained from the harvest, but the size of his share varies from one society to another.

Thus an ambitious farmer can increase his income by investing outside of agriculture, by investing in increased production of livestock and crops, including trees, that he can grow or have sharecroppers or laborers grow, or by obtaining additional wives. To obtain another wife a specified collection of goods, or a sum of money, or both—erroneously called "bride price" by many popular writers—must be accumulated and given to the bride's kinsmen. (Usually a similar sum must be accumulated and repaid to the husband or his kinsmen in case of divorce.)

In some cases men do much of the work involved in producing certain crops, for example, tree crops like cocoa and coffee, and in some areas even some starchy staples and are obligated to share little or none of their net returns with their wives. In such cases men obtain land in much the same way as their wives do.

Trees having value can be and often are owned even though the land on which they grow cannot be bought or sold. All other material goods, including livestock, usually are owned, but grazing lands are not.

Women, as well as men, are permitted to save and invest, in the process of which they frequently sell commodities to, or buy commodities from, their husbands. Relatively wealthy women traders are so conspicuous in Nigeria and Ghana that they have been featured by the popular press.

No matter how, or by whom, savings are generated among farmers, they are always in danger of disappearing before they can be invested, because of the rapacity of kinsmen. Africans strongly feel an obligation to share their fortunes with any needy relative or friend, if asked to do so. Individuals who become prosperous rarely must wait long until a less fortunate kinsmen moves in, unless distance makes it costly for him to do so.

The strength of the concern over the rapacity of relatives is well-illustrated in consumption patterns. African housewives usually buy nondurables in extremely small quantities sufficient for only one day or one meal, for example, single cubes of sugar, half cups of cooking oil, sixth's of a loaf of bread, single or half cigarettes, single matches. Local African observers argue that there is demand for such small quantities because of a lack of purchasing power and storage facilities. However, Africans I have asked about this phenomenon repeatedly have emphasized the hazard of having visible stocks in the reach of friends or relatives.

Concern over demands by relatives is likewise reflected in the reluctance of Africans to use deposit accounts in banks. Informants from a number of West African countries, and from widely scattered areas, give as the first reason for not using banks fear that through bribery or gossip relatives may learn of the existence and size of savings. In the Ivory Coast even bank clerks who are given accounts and are paid through them rarely keep money on deposit for fear that someone may divulge the size of their balance to a prying relative.

Farmers have little escape from kinsmen, since by the current land tenure system both the land one has a right to use and one's kinsmen are found in the same geographical area. Farmers must be skillful in hiding savings or rapidly converting them into nonliquid forms in order to accumulate capital. Thus, although capital formation may be noteworthy among some African farmers, it is here argued that it amounts to less than it would if farmers were free to save without fear that their savings would be dissipated by kinsmen. Moreover, farmers' investments are reduced from the pressure quickly to convert gains into nonliquid forms.

Traders, unlike farmers, can, and frequently do, escape the depressing effect of the social structure on savings by operating at some distance from home so that the degree of their success is not well known in their home areas, or by permanently locating outside their ethnic group. In fact, the more successful African storekeepers seem nearly always to be found in areas a considerable distance from their own ethnic group, although to date we have no quantitative data on this phenomenon.

Marketing policy and capital accumulation

One can rule out as politically unfeasible attempts to change directly such fundamental aspects of social structure as attitudes toward kinsmen. Therefore, land tenure and marketing policy are the main avenues through which farmers can be freed from the rapacity of relatives.

Land tenure systems in West Africa are evolving toward ownership of land in many areas. Any change in policy to accelerate this trend will, of course, improve the possibility of capital accumulation among peasants by giving them opportunities to sell current rights to land and to purchase others some distance from kinsmen.

But whatever the trends in land tenure policy, the rate of capital accumulation by farmers will be greater if they also have the alternative of freely entering commerce. Most African farmers as yet have no other economic alternative that will isolate them from relatives. Not only are other opportunities few, but most African farmers lack the education or training needed for the openings that exist outside of farming and commerce.

The repercussions of a reduction of barriers to market entry in distribution can perhaps be traced most easily by assuming for simplicity that rural West African economies have only two sectors—production and marketing—and by starting with the limiting case of no competition among buyers and only one middleman between producers and consumers—either a single buyer or a group of buyers who by agreement act as a monopsonist.

The industry supply curve is the sum of farmers' marginal cost curves (because of pure competition among producers) and is also the monopsonist's average outlay curve. Also relevant is the monopsonist's marginal outlay curve (labeled MO in Figure 1). The rational monopsonist will equate marginal outlay and marginal revenue, buying OQ_1 of the commodity, paying OP_1 to the producer and charging consumers OP_2. Elimination of barriers to entry will, *ceteris paribus,* cause a shift of the supply curve to the left (assuming farmers enter trading either because they are attracted by the supernormal returns earned by the monopsonist or because of the desire to escape the rapacity of kinsmen, or both, and assuming that some of the farmers leaving agriculture have a positive marginal physical product, which seems likely since some of them will have savings to protect).[16]

---

[16] The other possibility, negative marginal physical product, is very probably not found in West African agriculture; there are certainly no prominent examples of it. Nor is it clear that zero marginal physical product is common. Charles H. C. Kao,

Suppose after entry is sufficient to eliminate supernormal returns by the monopsonist that the supply curve has shifted to S^*; the price charged consumers will be OP^* (a reduction of P_2P^*) and that received by the producer will be OP^*, less a normal return to the middleman (or middlemen), and sufficient to induce production of OQ^* of the commodity.

Figure 1

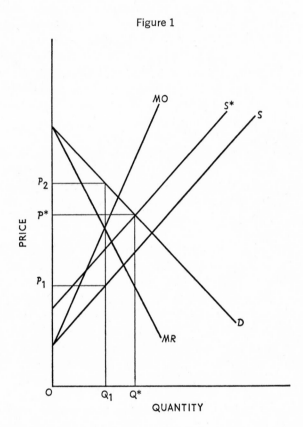

In the general case, where there is some restriction of competition among middlemen but less monopsony power than in the limiting case, and where marketing policies may not succeed in fully eliminating

Kurt R. Anschel, and Carl K. Eicher conclude, after a survey of the literature on disguised unemployment in the agricultural sector of underdeveloped countries, that there is little reliable empirical evidence to suggest zero marginal physical product for more than 5 percent of agricultural laborers in the underdeveloped countries; unfortunately, because of the paucity of empirical studies, little of the work they reviewed was on West Africa (Charles H. C. Kao, Kurt R. Anschel, and Carl K. Eicher, "Disguised Unemployment in Agriculture: A Survey," in Carl K. Eicher, and Lawrence W. Witt [eds.], *Agriculture in Economic Development* [New York, 1964], p. 141).

barriers to entry, the result is some upward pressure on producer prices and some reduction of prices charged consumers, with a decrease in the size of supernormal returns earned by middlemen.

The ultimate effect of the influx of farmers into trading on capital formation depends on what further assumptions are made. If one assumes that there is not enough change in the difference between the level of returns in agriculture and in trading, after the influx of farmers, to encourage movement of some traders or trading capital into agriculture, the net effect on capital formation is that farm savings that otherwise might have been dissipated by kinsmen flow into trading. The effect on agricultural production is indeterminate without knowing the price elasticity of supply and demand and the strength of the attraction of farmers to commerce.

If, on the other hand, one assumes—either because of elimination of monopsony power (which would be relevant for all traders but those with lowest costs); because of a rise in producer prices in agriculture (which might be relevant even for the lowest cost traders); or because of external diseconomies in trading[17]—that some traders find less than normal returns in commerce after the influx of farmers, there would be a flow of capital and entrepreneurial skills from the marketing sector to agricultural production.

As a rule, traders can invest in agriculture in West Africa even though ownership of land among Africans is not yet common. In most, if not all, West African countries there is already some opportunity to buy or lease land. Traders can easily invest in livestock and poultry production or in crop processing, which, under West African conditions, is particularly relevant to agricultural productivity because mechanized grinding of starchy staple foodstuffs and mechanized hulling of coffee enormously reduces the time women must spend grinding or pounding by hand. This frees them for additional work in the field at critical times when yields suffer because of labor bottlenecks.

Such a flow of capital from marketing to the production sector in agriculture might come either from established traders or from farmers who are new at trading. In either case it seems probably that traders

---

[17] For example, it is possible that there would be an increase in the proportion of times that any one trader would make a trip to a supplying area without finding the commodities sought, or would get a smaller quantity relative to needs than before the increase in the number of traders. West African traders now sometimes fail to find the amount of commodities expected in supply areas because of purchases made by other buyers during the interval between their receipt of market information and their arrival in the supply zone. However, there is as yet little basis for determining how frequently this happens.

An increase in the number of traders would tend to raise the probability of any one trader finding smaller supplies than expected, providing there is no increase in the efficiency of dissemination of information stemming from the expansion of the number of traders.

It is here assumed that if there are external diseconomies of this sort in trading that they are not the only source of existing monopsony power.

investing in agriculture are likely to be less tied to traditional agricultural enterprises and techniques than farmers. Also, they are in a better position to consider all of the alternatives in investment decisions, since they are not rushed to convert savings into nonliquid forms because of pressure by relatives. Therefore the entry of traders into agricultural production may well result in an increase in the rate of innovation, or an acceleration of the rate of adoption of innovations, in agriculture.

It is easy to think of situations in which traders would be better informed than farmers on the availability of productivity-increasing inputs, such as chemical fertilizers, hybrid seed, or pesticides. There is some evidence to support this view. P. T. Bauer reports that a Hausa trader contributed considerably to the development of the Nigerian peanut industry by encouraging farmers to try growing peanuts for the export market when the industry was in its infancy.[18] In the Ivory Coast the number of large-scale African egg producers who inoculate birds for disease, buy mixed feed for them, and otherwise use recommended "modern" production techniques, has grown from zero to about 100 since 1953. According to André Bey, the president of C.O.P.R.A.V.I., the producer cooperative at Abidjan which accounts for about 80 of the African producers, only about 10 percent of Africans investing in this new venture are farmers. A large proportion are traders. Sidney W. Mintz states that in Haiti, an economy much like those of West Africa in many respects, one of the characteristics of the trader (usually female) is that she "stimulates improvements in agriculture,"[19] but he does not give details.

If one adds to the assumptions already made appropriate lags in the response of farmers and traders, one can get an unstable situation, not unlike the cobweb type, in which there is too much influx of farmers in trading followed by an excess exodus of traders into agriculture; but whatever one assumes about the path which adjustments take in this hypothesized unstable case, it still provides a needed periodic escape of farmers from their relatives and a healthy entry into agriculture by entrepreneurs with relatively large amounts of capital and new ideas about development possibilities.

Other considerations

It might be argued that the cost of increasing competition among several hundred petty traders in each of many open-air marketplaces

---

[18] P. T. Bauer, *Economic Analysis and Policy in Underdeveloped Countries* (Durham, N.C., 1957), p. 76, cited in Willard F. Mueller, "Some Market Structure Considerations in Economic Development," *op. cit.*, p. 418.

[19] Sidney W. Mintz, "The Employment of Capital by Market Women in Haiti," in Raymond Firth and B. S. Yamey (eds.), *Capital, Saving and Credit in Peasant Societies* (Chicago, 1964), p. 285.

would be extremely costly and not obviously relevant to capital accumulation.

There is reason to think that this is not the case. Greater competition even among the smallest sellers is probably of considerable significance for capital accumulation. The smallest traders may operate on a small scale, but the cost of living is low. Even petty trade may well generate enough savings to foster development of entrepreneurial talent and adoption of some needed innovations. Thus obstacles to market entry at any level would appear to be relevant.

As to costs, considering that legislation to require selling by weight and to require posting prices would go a long way toward eliminating barriers to entry in small-scale selling, it is not clear that the cost of implementing and enforcing policies to promote competition at this level would be prohibitive. Local governments have long charged even the smallest traders a daily fee for use of the marketplace in most areas (now from 25 to 50 CFA francs or $0.10 to $0.20, depending on commodity, in some areas of the Ivory Coast). These proceeds are used for such purposes as building roofs over marketplaces, constructing stalls within them, and disposing of debris left by vendors. Local governments could also provide sellers with scales, probably at a relatively small increase in market fees. An 8 percent increase in the smallest market fee usually charged in Grand Bassam, Ivory Coast, would pay for the cheapest and most durable kind of scale[20] now used by the few vendors with scales, in only a little over a year.

Collectors of market fees could be used to help illiterate vendors post prices and translate price changes from variable weight per monetary unit to variable monetary unit per given weight until they learned to write numbers and gained some facility in the new way of expressing price changes. A companion measure needed would be increased minting of the smallest coin, or creation of smaller ones, a measure that would help reduce problems of indivisibility now solved by altering the size of heaps sold.

Although mandatory use of scales and posting of prices are here proposed because of their possible effects on capital accumulation, they would also yield obvious benefits by making it easier for consumers to allocate expenditures rationally.

Another argument to be considered relates to the loss of welfare resulting from individuals escaping the rapacity of their relatives. It might be argued that when the strength of obligations to kinsmen is as strong as in West Africa, individuals benefit from what might be called customary social security, and that one of the repercussions of policies designed to help undermine it is therefore some loss of welfare. The

---

[20] A simple balance suspended from a beam.

question is whether the gains in welfare through economic growth—induced by (1) greater capital accumulation of individuals who have escaped relatives and related adjustments such as those already discussed and by (2) the increased productivity of parasites who would be spurred to be more productive because of loss of opportunity to depend on kinsmen—are greater than the loss from reduction or elimination of customary social security. This question is unanswerable because of unsolved problems in measuring utility. However, the position of those who believe that the loss of utility through the reduction of customary social security is greater than that gained through economic growth is weakened by the fact that political considerations have caused most African countries to create some form of legislated social security. It is highly likely that for similar reasons coverage will be progressively extended.

A third argument to be considered is one concerning the benefits of certain kinds of coercion that could be exercised by those with monopsony power. Some believe that the prospects are so dismal for rapidly increasing the productivity of African farmers through conventional means, for example, improved and expanded extension services, improved credit facilities, and improved transportation, that use of coercion by governments, or private monopsonies they protect, is justified. The argument here usually is that the most rapid means of increasing agricultural productivity where there are small economies of scale in production is to allow farmers to sell only to a single buyer who provides them productivity-increasing inputs, and buys the crop only if recommended practices are followed, deducting from the price paid producers costs of inputs and services or supervision provided.[21]

Data are as yet insufficient to demonstrate adequately either the effectiveness of such arrangements in West Africa or of the more conventional programs for increasing agricultural productivity. Until there is conclusive evidence that there is no equally effective alternative to monopsonies, or other forms of restricted competition, as means of increasing the productivity of West African farmers, the possibility that an increase in competition in distribution will lead to greater capital accumulation by farmers is relevant, and there is perhaps reason to give marketing in West Africa more study than it would receive if the relationship between market structure and capital accumulation were ignored.

---

[21] Such monopsonies are now found in pineapples, cotton, and tobacco production in the Ivory Coast.

Summary

The issues raised in the introduction to this volume have been illuminated, but not resolved, by the papers presented here. The contributors to this volume are in total agreement on few of the major questions concerning marketing aspects of economic development. The authors' appraisals of existing marketing institutions and arrangements differ widely, as do their recommendations for future action. This lack of unanimity is deliberate, rather than accidental. The papers included in this book were not designed to present an artificial and misleading consensus concerning something as perplexing, as controversial, and as important as the process of economic development.

The discussions included here join around 10 points. These 10 points are not a decalogue of developmental injunctions, but rather they constitute a set of important issues explored or implied on the preceding pages.[1]

1. The authors, the coeditors (and probably most readers of this book) appear to have little disagreement about at least one point. Apparently all of us regard economic development as a good and desirable thing. This attitude is to be expected among people interested in a volume such as this, and the point is so elementary and so self-evident that there may seem to be little need for expressing it explicitly. Nevertheless, this fundamental evaluation should be made clear for two reasons.

First, we should be aware that it is not necessarily a universal attitude. We should recognize that some views and some philosophies, including at times those of some colonial administrators, have held that the less change the better. Concepts of "The Noble Savage," of "the peaceful pastoral existence," of "the idyllic Eden," suggest that economic growth is a curse rather than a blessing. The authors and the editors would be inclined to reply to those concepts in the words of David McCord Wright:

If therefore, we wish to solve the economic problem along the lines of passivity and "satisfaction," removal of desire will be the first requisite; but there are economic requisites as well. These economic foundations are best seen in discussing that most drastic of solutions now advocated for current problems, the "abandonment" of the machines and "return to the farm.". . .

---

[1] N.B. This summary chapter has not been submitted to the authors for their approval. Hence the editors alone are responsible for any errors of interpretation in this chapter.

If we want to make a genuine appraisal of the virtues of rural life, in and of itself, we must not ask a weekend commuter to Connecticut, nor a tourist traveling through picturesque Mexico, nor a bondholder leading the "simple" life in Tahiti or Hawaii with a radio, icebox, screens and comfortable flow of dividends. We must ask instead the drudging farmer's wife on the primitive farm, bowed down and dulled with childbearing and heavy work; the cripple embittered by injury incurable to rural medicine; the anemic starving peasant children of India, and the famine-ridden Chinese farmer. These are the real judges.[2]

Thus the question of economic growth versus stagnation seems, at least to us, almost rhetorical. But the fact that such a question could even be considered points to a second and more important reason for making our values explicit. The question of economic development versus stability can arise in any serious context only because development is not an unmixed blessing. It is no curse, but it is not without its pains, its penalties, and its costs. As Mintz notes, the process of Western industrialization involved much misery and suffering. Similarly, some of the steps toward economic growth outlined in this volume will conflict, most uncomfortably, with traditional values and ways of life. Berg particularly outlines many of the costs of growth, and both Berg and Currie note how the rationalization of trading institutions can easily lead to the displacement of many of the people now employed in those institutions. Miracle demonstrates the way in which the concept of the extended family (which even by our standards is in many respects a highly admirable institution and which must be even more highly regarded by most of the participants), is to some extent incompatible with marketing progress.[3] Consequently, those who advocate marketing development must be prepared to recognize the costs, and they must be prepared to offer programs for mitigating the pains of their recommendations.

2. The editors and most, probably all, of the authors would also naturally agree in decrying the traditional academic and administrative indifference to marketing in the developing economies. As noted in the introductory chapter, this attitude is now being replaced by one of growing interest on the part of scholars and development officials in the economically advanced nations. But as Abbott so thoroughly documents, planning officials in most parts of the Third World are still inclined to neglect or to completely overlook the marketing sectors of their economies.

The contributors to this volume have undertaken diverse assignments.

---

[2] *Democracy and Progress* (New York: Macmillan Co., 1948), pp. 13–14.

[3] Alice Dewey suggests, on the other hand, that the concepts of extended family and clan can be helpful to marketing, at least among people above a subsistence level, by providing a means for the enforcement of trading obligations. See her discussion of credit relations among the Chinese traders of Indonesia, in *Peasant Marketing in Java* (New York: Free Press of Glencoe, 1962), pp. 44–50.

Some were asked to analyze environmental influences on the marketing system, while others were invited to trace the ways in which marketing influences the environment. Regardless of their assignments, they undoubtedly differ in the extent to which they consider marketing as a leading sector and as a prime mover in development. But in spite of these inevitable differences in view, the papers included here demonstrate many of the ways in which marketing can be a help or a hindrance in economic growth. Many of the writers have pointed out how marketing activities can be a source of capital for growth, a school for entrepreneurship, and a device for distributing scale and other economies; they and other contributors have also shown how retrogressive institutions can be a tax and a burden upon society. All of the authors would unite, we think, in urging increased attention to marketing problems.

3. The papers presented here also demonstrate both the existence and the importance of another sort of refocusing. Just as the fashions in the study of economic theory have tended to oscillate between political economy and the theory and strategy of the firm, so too the central locus of marketing interest has fluctuated between societal and technical poles. Managerial problems have dominated marketing thought and literature throughout the postwar period. Now something of a reaction and synthesis of interests seems to be emerging. This change has been sparked, in part, by the apparent rise of "consumerism," i.e., conscious and avowed attention to consumer problems, in the developed countries. But in part this reaction has come from concern, as illustrated here, with the marketing aspects of development. Explicitly or implicitly, practically all of the chapters in this volume display the reciprocal nature of the relationship between marketing systems and public policy.

For example, several writers (Glade and Udell, Miracle, and Henley) note the deleterious effects that flow from the absence of viable antitrust legislation in the developing world. But the effects of law and public policy cited herein reach far beyond the conventional boundaries of antitrust. Bauer explores the harmful impacts of restrictive and ethnocentric regulation upon trade and society. Berg shows the marketing effects of general economic and political philosophy. Miracle demonstrates how something as fundamental as the land tenure system can influence the capital supply for marketing. And since the rate of enforcement may be as significant as the letter of the law, it is worthwhile to note the arbitrage and other effects of smuggling, as discussed by Berg and Henley.

4. The papers are also united in explicit and implicit indication of the problems that arise from the severe undersupply of ancillary marketing institutions and services in the developing countries. The efficiency and performance of developed country manufacturers, wholesalers, and retailers rests in good part upon the external economies provided by a host

of governmental and private agencies. The developed country firm can draw upon a wide variety of credit and financial institutions; it can delegate its physical distribution tasks to many different types of consolidators, carriers, and warehousemen; it can advertise in a wide selection of media; it can look to specialized agencies for the preparation of its advertising (and those agencies, in turn, can draw upon specialized graphic, photographic, art, and production services); it can buy its market research and analysis from specialized contractors and subcontractors; it can seek advice from many different kinds of consultants; and it can obtain information ranging from dealer credit ratings to mailing lists of automobile owners from an almost inexhaustible bank of data sources. Weights and measures are standardized; censuses achieve impressive levels of accuracy; and most important of all, the developed societies produce large numbers of skilled and semiskilled people ranging from typists, statisticians, and programmers to management and marketing specialists. Marketing becomes substantially more difficult when such services and people are not readily available. The characteristic tendency of businessmen in the less developed nations toward underestimation of market opportunities, discussed in several papers and especially in Glade and Udell's, is at least partially due to the dearth of ready information about those opportunities.

Unfortunately, however, the problem of creating and providing ancillary services resembles the classic chicken and egg question: which comes first, the demand or the service? Neither the staff nor the other types of support that the ancillary agencies require are likely to appear until marketing develops to a point that insures their relatively full utilization. This is especially true in view of the scarcities of both funds and trained specialists in the developing countries. Yet the absence of these services tends to keep marketing from growing to the point at which the services will be automatically supported. Perhaps the best programmatic advice is to rely where possible upon demand creating its own supply. Henley, for example, shows how specialized transport and smuggling services emerged in response to felt opportunities. But some services, such as censuses and marketing education, are not likely to appear as automatic responses to the market mechanism. Consequently, development officials must be especially sensitive to needs for those services and anticipate their requirements.

5. As indicated above, one of the developing country needs is for better macroscopic data, such as population, employment and business censuses, national income and product reports, and input-output analyses. It is interesting to consider the extent to which the divergences of opinion in this volume and in other discussions of marketing development rest upon diverse impressions that could be resolved through better data. For example, the debate over the relationship between marketing

employment and developmental level, which Preston seems to have resolved, is essentially a question of fact and thus susceptible to solution through information. Some of the questions concerning performance, discussed below, are also partially questions of fact arising out of the inadequacy of information about marketing inputs and costs. (We should quickly note, however, that the available information on these topics is inadequate everywhere, and not only in the so-called under-developed countries.) But in good part the debate over performance is a matter of definition and, more fundamentally, of philosophy. What is the output or function of marketing institutions? Is it to maximize consumer supply of existing products, is it to encourage innovation, is it to mini-mize the costs of allocating a given supply, is it to maximize producer revenue, is it to increase opportunities for local employment, or is to perform some other task?[4] And finally, even when there is agreement on objectives, debate can arise over method. Is competition (defined in one of many possible ways) a better device than monopoly or oligopoly for achieving some given marketing goal? Again, the answer is partially a matter of information: What has worked in the past or elsewhere? But since the situations are never exactly the same, differences in judgment and analysis are inevitable.

6. Not surprisingly, questions concerning the value and nature of competition form one of the issues on which the contributors tend to disagree. Much of the discussion here echoes similar discussions of the role of competition in the more prosperous nations, but there are some important differences. To summarize briefly and somewhat unfairly, most writers on the subject tend to favor competition, regardless of the eco-nomic level involved, but differ over its definition. This statement is probably applicable to the present discussion, subject to some significant reservations. Both Alexander and Miracle indicate that trading profits are needed or are useful to finance industrial expansion in the developing countries, an argument that would not apply to countries with more advanced economies. Presumably, of course, at least some trading profits could arise under any sort of "reasonable" or "workable" competition, and neither author urges monopoly per se. Nevertheless, their position does suggest that some degree of monopoly surplus in trade might not be as horrendous as neoclassical economics would have it. Moreover, in the absence of a satisfactory number of properly equipped actual and poten-tial competitors, at least some of the authors probably would urge a somewhat higher degree of government intervention in the marketing

---

[4] In a witty and sadly neglected *reductio ad absurdum*, Richard Lundy shows how efficiency judgments about a marketing system are completely dependent upon definition of function. See his "How Many Gasoline Stations Are Too Many?" in Wroe Alderson and Reavis Cox (eds.), *Theory in Marketing* (Homewood, Ill.: Richard D. Irwin, Inc., 1950), pp. 321–33.

process than they might recommend for more developed economies. But actually most of the papers here that deal specifically with government intervention are critical of official tendencies toward protected monopolies. Adams, Bauer, and Berg clearly oppose restrictions on entry, and Henley's argument for common markets centers around the competitive stimulus of increased rivalry. Abbott does urge more intervention through the planning process, although he too has some severe words for the protected monopoly.

The authors divide somewhat more sharply on the question of structural versus performance definitions of competition. Both Abbott and Miracle point out that large numbers are no guarantee of competitive behavior. Preston joins them in this position. Currie and Preston both note that the presence of large numbers of traders in the marketing system may involve technologically excessive and wasteful labor inputs. Currie, however, feels that the impact of this technical redundancy is offset by the limited alternatives available to the workers involved, so that the opportunity cost is low. Bauer agrees, or goes even further, and argues that the market labor would not be sustained as such if it were not economically viable. Mintz also seems to feel that, at least in the developing country context, crowded marketplaces and large numbers of sellers are beneficial.

These differences of opinion as to the optimum number of marketers tend to reflect diverse views on the performance of existing marketing institutions. A belief in the benefits of numbers, at least in the absence of cartelization, is likely to accompany a conclusion that highly fragmented, minutely divided native marketing systems are an efficient and flexible response to the needs of the developing economies. Considerable evidence, including the competitive difficulties that cooperatives and expatriates have faced, does suggest that indigenous retailing and agricultural assembly are often efficient, low-margin activities. However, not all authorities would agree that the evidence is conclusive. Those who feel that scale economies and rationalization result from large-scale enterprise are more likely to favor systems that entrust the marketing task to fewer and bigger institutions.

7. Debate concerning the performance of indigenous marketing systems also shows up in evaluations of the expatriate and alien trading firms that are so frequently found in the developing nations. Abbott, Bauer, and Berg conclude that, on balance, these firms have been helpful to the economies in which they operate. Adams finds that the alien traders can be of great assistance up to a certain developmental level, but that they can then become a severely inhibitive factor. Glade and Udell suggest a somewhat similar position, although their strictures seem to apply almost equally to native and alien firms. Mintz, and quite possibly, Miracle, also seem to have very mixed opinions of the foreign merchants.

Discussions of this sort often founder on a definitional problem: What is an alien or expatriate firm? The term is often applied, quite properly, to the great British and European firms engaged in substantial export-import operations in Africa and other developing areas. It is also frequently applied, often with less justification, to establishments operated by members of minority ethnic groups, even though these peoples may have lived in and have been citizens of the country of operation for decades or generations. The two types of businesses may have very different operating styles, very different degrees of interest in importing, exporting, wholesaling, and retailing, very different cost structures, very different price policies, very different attitudes toward majority group participation in the enterprise, and very different impacts upon the economy. Consequently, discussions that unceremoniously lump the two categories together and that also ignore differences between individual enterprises within each category usually tend to muddy, rather than clarify, the issues. Fortunately, that has not happened here. The authors in each instance are quite clear as to the types of merchants they are discussing.

Thus the debate rests upon more fundamental questions. Evaluations of expatriate merchants are likely, but not necessarily, to be reciprocals of the authors' impressions of the truly (somehow defined) indigenous traders, a source of differences already noted here. Another cause of disagreement in the evaluation of alien traders may be, as Adams suggests, variations in the environments in which those traders are operating, as well as variations in the degree of competition to which they are exposed. This suggests an issue to which we must ultimately turn: the extent to which the developing nations can be treated as a homogeneous unit or continuum for analytical purposes. But the most fundamental debate, both on these pages and elsewhere, centers around the choice of patterns for development. Should developmental programs encourage specialization, and thus exploit comparative advantage, or should they try to foster self-supporting, import-substituting economies? What are the appropriate sources and uses for capital? What sectors of the population should be encouraged to change, and in what ways?

8. There are many dimensions to the debate concerning how well indigenous and expatriate retailing perform their tasks. As indicated above, much of the discussion focuses on costs, margins, and prices. However, a special question also persists, as a sort of minor theme in developmental strategy, and is reflected in this volume. The problem concerns the extent to which available merchandise offerings are attractive enough to induce wage employment and market production. Put in its baldest form, this incentive goods argument holds that at least one cause of low output in the poorer countries is the fact that labor has little incentive to seek employment and that farmers have little cause to

produce for the market, since cash returns cannot be converted into desirable consumer inventories. One well-known investigation, conducted in East Africa in the early 1950's, concluded that this belief was erroneous and that both farmers and potential wage earners could find many attractive outlets for their incomes reasonably close at hand.[5] Among the present authors, Currie explicitly agrees with this finding, and concludes that lack of suitable expenditure outlets seldom inhibits production. Both in his paper here, and in the larger study from which that paper is drawn, Adams takes a somewhat intermediate position. He sees the reservation trader as rationing supplies in his isolated market so as to evoke labor up to a level compatible with apparent existing nondisruptive earning possibilities, but as throttling consumer acquisitions, particularly of transport equipment, that would increase labor and consumer mobility. Both Glade and Udell, and Abbott, on the other hand, are inclined to support the incentive goods argument and would urge increased supplies for their impact upon production.

9. Expressed in this way, the incentive statement refers mainly to countries at the lowest per capita income levels. However, a somewhat similar concept is sometimes advanced for countries at an intermediate growth level. In their case, the argument holds that developed country distributive institutions should be imported to provide the types of items that will foster a "middle-class ethos." This seems to mean a desire for orderly individualistic economic and material progress and is reflected in consumer investment in durable goods. Thus, one study of Sears' influence in Mexico comments:

. . . the broad effect of the Sears operation is to hasten the establishment of this middle class by giving a large proportion of the people a much wider choice of goods than they formerly had. . . .
It is not just money that makes a middle class, but rather goods, especially durables, and a wide choice among them. More value for your money is more effective in bringing about a social change than just more money. More money is only too often spent for additional food, drink and personal luxuries. But more value for your money can mean the purchase of furniture and appliances and all the wares that go to build up a home.[6]

In general, the present authors do not deal directly with this particular formulation of the issue, although Mintz points out in some detail that we often suffer from erroneous impressions of both the nature and the location of "middle-class" values. If middle class is defined as entrepre-

---

[5] Fergus Chalmers Wright, *African Consumers* (Colonial Office Research Studies No. 17 [London: H.M.S.O., 1955]).

[6] Richardson Wood and Virginia Keyser, *United States Business Performance Abroad . . . The Case Study of Sears Roebuck de Mexico, S.A.* (Washington, D.C.: National Planning Association, 1953), p. 50.

neurial, he suggests that we ought to look to the petty traders, to the people who appear to American eyes as a commercial proletariat, rather than to the bureaucratic bourgeoisie. However, the book does include a diversity of opinions on the general question of the transferability of developed country institutions to the developing areas. Henley reports beneficial effects from the entry of developed country firms at the manufacturing level. Currie proposes certain types of intermediate and modified distributive agencies, adapted to local conditions, that might be useful. Abbott thinks that the creation of Western-type capital-intensive agencies is wasteful and inefficient, particularly if appropriate training and supportive arrangements are not available. Both Bauer and Berg report disappointments in the establishment of various types of cooperatives patterned on British and Scandinavian models.

10. Finally, perhaps the most interesting question this volume raises is whether the concept "developing country" (or any more or less euphemistic synonym) is a worthwhile construct for marketing study. In other words, can we offer useful generalizations concerning marketing-environmental relationships across the entire category, "developing area?" Can we make meaningful marketing statements that will equally apply to Dahomey, Pakistan, Mexico, Tibet, Greenland, and American Samoa? Or would it be better to group countries under entirely different rubrics, completely without regard to per capita income and other standard development measures. Conceivably, better analyses might result from classifying countries according to location, perhaps in terms of Huntington's climatic zones, so that we would try to make statements about tropic versus temperate areas, rather than about developing and developed ones. The number of taxonomic possibilities is limited only by the classifier's imagination. Political system, past or present status as an independent or colonial area, religious and ethical orientations, familial system, etc., are all conceivable bases for categorization.[7] Or, conceivably, each country's marketing system may be so different from all others, so much *sui generis*, that there is no point in attempting any sort of international, cross-cultural, or comparative analysis.

Certainly the developing country marketing systems do exhibit diversities that cannot be explained by available knowledge of either the developmental process or of other environmental factors affecting marketing. Some of this apparent diversity may be an illusion due to errors or gaps in the available data concerning the systems under question, some may rest upon inadequacies in our current analytical approaches. For

---

[7] Robert Bartels offers a well-developed classificatory outline in the appendix to his *Comparative Marketing: Wholesaling in Fifteen Countries* (Homewood, Ill.: Richard D. Irwin, Inc., 1963). Another, more recent, attempt to classify markets is found in the Marketing Science Institute's volume, *Comparative Analysis for International Marketing* (Boston: Allyn & Bacon, Inc., 1967).

example, we are uncertain as to the pattern of specialization among distributive agencies in the poorer countries, to say nothing of being able to explain whatever pattern may exist. The comment that one of the editors of this volume made three years ago is equally valid today: "At this point about all that can be said is that both specialized and unspecialized trade exists in underdeveloped economies—not a very satisfactory conclusion."[8]

The relative prevalence of cash and credit trading is equally obscure. David Carson perhaps sums up the situation best when he says, "There is, however, no uniformly positive relationship between the use of consumer credit and the standard of living."[9] The available reports seem conflicting and inconsistent. It may be that a rural-urban dichotomy must be imposed on the analysis before the place of consumer credit in the developing countries becomes clear. Several of the case studies included in a recent symposium indicate that at least retail consumer credit is much more likely to be prevalent in the rural than in the urban sectors of the poorer countries.[10] Nevertheless, many other variables will have to be introduced into the analysis before the role and nature of credit is fully explained.

But even though such diversities are still unexplained, the authors and editors of this volume are hardly ready to reject comparative analysis. Rather, since the diversities are not likely to be purely random phenomena, they would call for more, not less, comparative study. Moreover, as the mere act of engaging in the preparation of this volume suggests, they do seem to have faith in the usefulness of the developing-developed categories for marketing study. This does not imply any naïve belief that the marketing situations are the same in all developing countries, or that a hard and fast line separates the developed and the underdeveloped nations. Rather, it suggests a belief in the existence of relationships, discovered or as yet undiscovered, between marketing and the degree of development.

Some of these regularities are noted in the cross-cultural papers included in this collection. Preston's study, for example, reports a basic correlation between developmental level on one hand and trade/nontrade employment ratios on the other. Alexander finds similarities in the marketing origins of industrialists in Greece, Turkey, Pakistan, and the Philippines. Mintz notes similarities among peasant markets in many

---

[8] Reed Moyer, *Marketing in Economic Development* (International Business Occasional Paper No. 1 [East Lansing: Bureau of Business and Economic Research, Michigan State University, 1965]), p. 21.

[9] David Carson, *International Marketing: A Comparative Systems Approach* (New York: John Wiley & Sons, Inc., 1967), p. 370.

[10] Raymond Firth and B. S. Yamey (eds.), *Capital, Saving and Credit in Peasant Societies* (London: George Allen & Unwin, Ltd., 1964).

parts of the world, although he also reports many variations in pattern.[11]

Moreover, similarities also exist among the situations described in the one-country papers included here. As already noted, many of the authors describe the extent to which distributive trade is in the hands of ethnic minorities within the developing countries. As Glade has suggested else-where[12] this phenomenon seems to have held true of peasant societies across time, for example, in Medieval Europe, as well as across space. Another illustration of uniformities (unfortunately not entirely confined to the developing countries although there do seem to be differences of degree) is the characteristic tendency of developing country business-men toward underestimation of their market opportunities.

Uniformities of this last-mentioned type probably provide the strong-est argument for the study of developing country marketing. Regardless of whether marketing is a leading sector or not, regardless of the particu-lar patterns of marketing activity found in the developing countries, and regardless of the diverse recommendations for improvement of that activ-ity, agreement can be had on one point. This point is banal and should be apparent to all, but as Abbott indicates, it has frequently been ignored in practice. It is that marketing improvements (whatever their nature may ultimately turn out to be) can, at the very minimum, provide outlets for increased production, encourage business activity, facilitate profitable exportation, and increase consumer supplies within countries that very urgently need such help.

The present authors have indicated the avenues that must be explored in the search for those improvements. Their work, and the work of those who join them in that search, should bear fruit in greater comfort and well-being for a substantial portion of all mankind.

---

[11] For further cross-cultural discussion of developing country marketing similari-ties, see Morton R. Solomon, "The Structure of the Market in Underdeveloped Economies," *Quarterly Journal of Economics,* August, 1948, pp. 519–37, and Stanley Shapiro, "Comparative Marketing and Economic Development," in George Schwartz (ed.), *Science in Marketing* (New York, John Wiley & Sons, Inc., 1965), pp. 398–429. Shapiro considers the interesting question of whether countries can be assigned to stages of marketing development at pp. 410–12.

[12] William P. Glade, "Approaches to a Theory of Entrepreneurial Formation," *Explorations in Entrepreneurial History,* 2nd Series, Spring/Summer, 1967, pp. 245–59. Also see Lloyd A. Fallers, "Comments on 'The Lebanese in West Africa,'" *Comparative Studies in Society and History,* April, 1962, pp. 334–36. Both Glade and Fallers draw upon such classic studies as Park's, Simmel's, Veblen's, Sombart's, Pirenne's, and Mantoux'.

Selected Annotated Bibliography

Abbott, John C. "Marketing and Area Development Studies," in Stephen A. Greyser (ed.), *Toward Scientific Marketing,* pp. 424–38. Proceedings of the 1963 Winter Conference of the American Marketing Association, Chicago: American Marketing Association, 1963.

Market studies and organizational improvements are a critical success determinant for area development and settlement projects. This paper analyzes what is involved in making such studies and programs on the basis of experience in Europe, Latin America, and the Near East. Greatly improved marketing organization may be essential to take full advantage of favorable production opportunities. Often in the past, development projects have been undertaken which, while technically feasible, failed because of an inadequate market structure or marketing organization. These failures could be prevented through the use of adequate research and planning techniques.

————. "The Role of Marketing in the Development of Backward Agricultural Economies," *Journal of Farm Economics,* Vol. XLIV (May, 1962), pp. 349–62.

The author discusses the inefficiencies of existing food marketing systems in underdeveloped countries. He presents alternative approaches for the improvement of these systems. He suggests that an important characteristic of food marketing problems in developing countries is that problems arise simultaneously in many areas, i.e., production, assembly, processing, distribution, etc. Improvement is needed both in the coordination of production and marketing programs and in the training of marketing personnel.

Alpert, Paul. *Economic Development: Objectives and Methods.* New York: Free Press of Glencoe, 1963.

A description and analysis of all major aspects of development. The author stresses the importance of a transportation network for the establishment of a nationwide domestic market. The problems of development are analyzed principally from an economic viewpoint, although some interesting implications for marketing can be derived from the study.

Baker, Raymond W. "Marketing in Nigeria," *Journal of Marketing,* Vol. XXIX (July, 1965), pp. 40–48.

Mainly a description of the prevailing marketing system. Trends apparent (at least before the 1967 Civil War) included increasing Nigerian participation in all phases of marketing, enlargement of trading units, shortened channels of distribution, increasing use of mass media for promotional purposes, changes in the product mix, and expansion of both industrial and consumer markets. However, continuance of these trends is here based upon an assumption of political stability.

Baldwin, K. D. S. *The Marketing of Cocoa in Western Nigeria with Special Reference to the Position of Middlemen.* London: Oxford University Press, 1954.

A detailed study of marketing channels. Concludes that while cocoa-buying middlemen do receive good incomes, the middleman system is more flexible and more advantageous to the farmers than any cumbersome, government-operated system would be. The impacts of various government price policies are examined.

Banerjee, Tarasankar. *Internal Market of India: 1824–1900.* Calcutta: Academic Publishers, 1966.

An historical study, showing the way in which the elimination of internal trade barriers, improvements in communication and transport, and standardization of weights and measures contributed toward the development of an integrated, national market.

Bartels, Robert (ed.). *Comparative Marketing: Wholesaling in Fifteen Countries.* Homewood, Ill.: Richard D. Irwin, Inc., 1963.

Studies of the wholesaling systems of 15 countries are presented. Editorial chapters discuss (1) the instrumental use of wholesaling in order to achieve some social and economic ends; (2) social influences upon wholesaling; (3) the expectations of this marketing institution; and (4) the relationship between patterns of wholesaling structure and social-political objectives. Several of the individual country studies are concerned with developing nations.

Bauer, P. T. "Concentration in Tropical Trade: Some Aspects and Implications of Oligopoly," *Economica,* Vol. XX (November, 1953), pp. 302–21.

Primarily a statistical analysis of the relative market shares held by large firms dealing in the import and export of agricultural products in Ghana and Nigeria. The author concludes that there appears to be, "a degree of concentration in trade which is rather exceptional and noteworthy." He feels that this concentration has not stifled competition or prevented the entry of new firms, but that legislation has been passed in both countries in recent years designed to protect larger firms.

————. *West African Trade: a Study of Competition, Oligopoly, and Monopoly in a Changing Economy.* Cambridge, England: Cambridge University Press, 1954.

A definitive study of the structure of West African internal and external trade. Major subjects covered include: the number and diversity of local traders; the rationale for their large numbers; the growth of restrictive practices in trading shares of import trade handled by various racial groups; the effect of concentration in import-export trade on competition; the existence of barriers to entry in import trading; effect of immigration policies on competition in trading; the operation of statutory marketing boards—their scope, price policies, and assessment of their economic impact; and a discussion of various proposals for marketing reform, including reducing the number of intermediaries, setting up producer-controlled zonal monopolies for buying agricultural output, and eliminating abuses in marketing.

————, and Yamey, B. S. "Competition and Prices: A Study of Groundnut Buying in Nigeria," *Economica*, Vol. XIX (February, 1952), pp. 31–43.

The degree of competition found among buyers of groundnuts in nine different market areas of Nigeria is felt to be indicated by the amount by which payments to growers exceeded the legal minimum price, i.e., the higher the price, the greater the degree of competition. The authors conclude that the differences observed between the nine market areas examined are best explained on the basis of increased competition associated with increases in the social heterogeneity and numbers of buyers.

————. "The Economics of Marketing Reform," *Journal of Political Economy*, Vol. LXII (June, 1954), pp. 210–35.

Most of the market-restrictive administrative proposals for agricultural market reform in the developing countries are likely to have deleterious, rather than beneficial, effects.

Belshaw, Cyril. *Traditional Exchange and Modern Markets*. Englewood Cliffs, N.J.:Prentice-Hall, Inc., 1965.

An anthropological review of gift exchange and reciprocity systems and of monetized peasant marketing, leading to a description of salient aspects of modern marketing systems (e.g., appropriate value orientations, presence of entrepreneurs, complex information flows, feedback and adaptive mechanisms). The modernization process seems to require expansion motivations, insatiable wants (the consumption spur), financial and technological investment, and a healthy (but not excessive) amount of change-induced tension.

Bennett, Peter D. "The Role of Government in the Promotion of Efficiency in the Retail Marketing of Food Products in Greater Santiago, Chile," in Peter D. Bennett (ed.), *Marketing and Economic Development*, pp. 105–9. Proceedings of the 1965 Fall Conference of the American Marketing Association. Chicago: American Marketing Association, 1965.

Years of inflation in Chile have centered attention on food prices since food expenditures comprise such a large portion of consumers' budgets.

To improve food marketing efficiency, the government has adopted several measures, including price controls, regulation of market entry, the use of sales taxes, the provision of infrastructure and market information, and the assumption of the role of entrepreneur. Attention in the article focuses principally on the regulative and entrepreneurial activities of the government in food retailing. The author briefly assesses the relative merits of the government measures and is attracted to the second of these as an effective way to improve marketing efficiency. See also, Peter D. Bennett, "Retailing Evolution or Revolution in Chile?" *Journal of Marketing*, Vol. XXX (July, 1966), pp. 38–41.

Blair, T. L. V. *Africa: A Market Profile*. London: Business Publications, Ltd., 1965.

A very brief and general discussion of African economies followed by an optimistic forecast of rising living standards, suggestions for market research designs for consumer studies, and a somewhat more detailed review of media, methods, and problems in communicating with African consumers.

Bohannan, Paul, and Dalton, George (eds.). *Markets in Africa.* Evanston, Ill.: Northwestern University Press, 1962.

A collection of 28 detailed descriptions of indigenous economic systems in various parts of sub-Saharan Africa. An introductory essay notes that these societies divide into three groups: (1) Those in which the market principle (i.e., conventional Western exchange and price mechanisms) plays a minor role and in which there are few or no formal marketplaces. (2) Peripheral market societies in which "the institution of the market place is present, but the market principle does not determine acquisition of subsistence or the allocation of land and labor." (3) A relatively few societies dominated by the market principle and the price mechanism. Paradoxically, formal marketplaces play a minor role in the third group. Western contacts are inducing expansion of market-oriented economic activities throughout Africa, but some obstacles to change (for example, different values) are also noted.

Bonnen, J. T.; Eicher, C. K.; and Schmid, A. A. "Marketing in Economic Development" in V. L. Sorenson (ed.), *Agricultural Market Analysis,* pp. 35–38. East Lansing: Bureau of Business and Economic Research, Michigan State University, 1964.

The role of marketing in economic development may be analyzed in terms of "(1) static distribution costs and efficiency, (2) distribution, production and consumption interrelationships, (3) market structure." The authors draw upon examples from U.S. history to indicate the importance of attention to the linkages between physical transformation processes and related social systems. The law of contract, property, corporations, and credit, for example, played an important role in shaping the developmental impacts of the American marketing system.

Bose, Kumar Sailesh. "Problems of Mobilization of the Marketable Surplus in Agriculture in India," *Indian Journal of Agricultural Economics,* Vol. XVI (January–March, 1961), pp. 37–46.

An analysis of the role of agricultural surpluses in the growth of developing nations with special emphasis on the Indian case. After reviewing several different methods of mobilization, such as price manipulation, revision of land revenue charges, cooperative marketing and warehousing, etc., the author concludes that "creation rather than mobilization of surpluses is the prime need of the situation," and that "structural changes in agrarian, credit, or marketing organization or improvements in transport and storage facilities are but aids to greater mobility of stocks through space and time, but these by themselves cannot remedy a situation."

Boulding, Kenneth E., and Singh, Pritam. "The Role of the Price Structure in Economic Development," *American Economic Review,* Vol. LII (May, 1962), pp. 28–38.

The price structure is viewed as a powerful instrument for the redistribution of society along the lines of structural development. "In any given state of a society we can postulate an optimum price structure from the point of view of a stated goal of economic development." The possibilities of "manipulating the aggregate demand structure and the distribution of income by restricting consumption in certain areas and encouraging it in other" are also considered.

Boyd, Harper W.; El Sherbini, Abdel Aziz; and Sherif, Ahmed Fouad. "Channels of Distribution for Consumer Goods in Egypt," *Journal of Marketing*, Vol. XXV (October, 1961), pp. 26–33.
The article describes and evaluates the channels of distribution for consumer goods in Egypt. The authors feel that retailers and wholesalers are relatively more important in developing economies, because they, and not the manufacturers, typically perform most marketing activities.

————. "Egypt's Need for Marketing Management," *Business Horizons*, Vol. IV (Summer, 1961).
Although Egyptian businessmen often feel little need for modern marketing orientations and practices, because of tariff and entry restrictions on competition, there actually is a greater need for the marketing concept in a country such as Egypt which is industrializing, than in the more advanced nations.

Broehl, Wayne G., Jr. *United States Business Performance Abroad, The Case Study of The International Basic Economy Corporation.* Washington: National Planning Association, 1968, 314pp.
A detailed study of IBEC's food, housing, mutual fund, and manufacturing operations in Latin America, the Middle and Far East, and Europe. Its well known supermarket development programs for Venezuela, Puerto Rico, Peru, Italy and Argentina are described at length. The author notes that although manufacturing activities have contributed to IBEC's budget, the organization's real strength and contributions come from marketing know-how. ". . . IBEC has become a specialist in organizing markets and distribution channels, from producer to consumer, from saver to investor. Within this basic concept lie most of IBEC's innovations."

Burnet, I. D. "Stimulating Development Through Consumption-Oriented Policies," *International Development Review*, Vol. VI (September, 1964), pp. 21–23.
This study is basically a consumer-oriented approach to the process of economic and social development. The author argues that an appreciation of the consumption patterns of a developing area coupled with the optimization of the incentive system in existence, which in turn makes the most of existing productive capacity, are often more important in the promotion of economic development than a mere extension of productive capacity.

Campbell, W. K. H. *Practical Co-operation in Asia and Africa.* Cambridge, England: W. Heffer & Sons, Ltd., 1951.
Detailed discussion of the operating problems of cooperative societies in

developing economies. Although marketing is seen as a difficult and risky process, producers' marketing societies appear to be useful and appropriate devices for overcoming distribution problems. Even though the author is an advocate of cooperative activity, he notes that consumer cooperative stores are difficult to establish in the underdeveloped countries and are subject to a disproportionately high failure rate.

Carson, David. *International Marketing: A Comparative Systems Approach.* New York: John Wiley & Sons, Inc., 1967.

A comparative systems approach to international marketing, stressing the socioeconomic variations between regions and nations, and their influence on the development and structure of marketing organizations and practices. The book focuses on the marketing function as an entity (systems approach) rather than individual segments. "Comparative marketing is . . . an area inextricably involved with the behavioral sciences, geography, politics, and other social disciplines." The text emphasizes applications to real situations and everyday decisions. Many of the illustrations are drawn from sub-Saharan Africa and other development situations.

Chaturvedi, J. N. *Theory of Marketing in Underdeveloped Countries.* Allahabad, India: Kitab Mahal, 1959.

The author cites the need for different approaches to the marketing concept in developed and underdeveloped areas. Also, the concept of "forced" surplus as originating the process of marketing is explained. Marketing and its role in the developmental process are examined from several perspectives, and topics such as imperfect competition, the industrialization of underdeveloped areas, the role of agriculture, and the role of the urban-industrial sector are analyzed. Finally, the author attempts to develop a theory of marketing for underdeveloped countries, in which he holds that middlemen are an undesirable luxury, instead of forming a socially useful institution as in the developed economies.

Collins, N. R., and Holton, R. H. "Programming Changes in Marketing in Planned Economic Development," *Kyklos,* Vol. XVI (1963), pp. 123–35.

This study presents the argument that marketing is the "Cinderella" of economic planning. Few economic models recognize explicitly that society can benefit fully from increases in growth only if there is a developed marketing system that effectively bridges the gap between producers and consumers. Some obstacles are analyzed and strategies are suggested for designing facilitating mechanisms to help bring about the necessary structural changes.

Cook, Hugh L. "Observations on Market Structure and National Economic Development in the Philippines," *Journal of Farm Economics,* Vol. XLI (August, 1959), pp. 500–518.

A survey and analysis of Philippine employment (1955) found much small-scale economic activity. Two thirds of all workers surveyed were not employed in regular business establishments but operated household enterprises, market stalls, or engaged in street trading. The most highly developed industries exhibited the highest concentration ratios. The conclusion is that the less developed nations must accept a considerable measure of monopoly, in spite of its political unattractiveness, if they wish to achieve self-sufficiency.

Cundiff, Edward W. "Concepts in Comparative Retailing," *Journal of Marketing,* Vol. XXIX (January, 1965), pp. 59–63.

The author develops four hypotheses to account for the comparative evolution and adaptation of retailing practices. They are: (1) innovation occurs only in the highly developed systems; (2) a system's ability to adopt innovations successfully is directly related to its level of economic development; (3) adaptation may be helped or hindered, in countries where economic conditions are favorable to development, by local demographic, geographic, competitive, and social conditions or by government action; (4) aggressive firms can accelerate the adaptation process.

Four developments in retailing are used to test the hypotheses. These are: (1) the adoption of self-service; (2) use of low markups and emphasis on high stockturn; (3) development of groups of suburban retail outlets, and (4) development of automated retailing.

The evidence provides at least partial support for the hypotheses.

Dacca University Socio-Economic Research Board. *The Marketing of Jute in East Pakistan.* Dacca: Oxford University Press, Pakistan Branch, 1961.

An extremely detailed study, attributing the level of marketing costs (approximately 27% of the price at point of export) to the small size of the typical producing unit and the consequent loss of economies of scale in assembly. Improvement in transportation, grading and weighing, and market information systems would help. Traders believe that government price control and licensing of middlemen have hampered market operations, and neither the development of cooperatives nor increases in the degree of market regulation would be beneficial.

Dean, Edwin R. "Social Determinants of Price in Several African Markets," *Economic Development and Cultural Change,* Vol. XI (April, 1963), pp. 239–56.

Analysis of transactions in African markets revealed little intertribal price discrimination on the part of African sellers.

Demas, William G. *The Economics of Development in Small Countries with Special Reference to the Caribbean.* Montreal: McGill University Press, 1965.

After examining Rostow's "self-sustained growth" theory and applying some of its ideas to small underdeveloped countries, the author reviews the problems of economic development and economic planning in the Caribbean. The author concludes that the economics of integration between underdeveloped countries require: (1) development of adequate, efficient, and cheap transportation links within the region in order to widen the market for new industries; (2) devising of measures to safeguard existing industries; (3) application of measures for dealing with the problem of "polarization"; and (4) mutual agreement between territories to specialize in activities for which they are specially suited.

Dewey, Alice G. *Peasant Marketing in Java.* New York: Free Press of Glencoe, 1962.

The Javanese market system is considered as a whole, in its wider context, "showing the functional interrelationship between patterns of trade and the social and economic patterns of the peasant society." For example, an extended family system and great internal cohesiveness provide the resident Chinese trading community with the informal sanctions needed to enforce credit and contractual obligations. The Javanese peasant society, with its nuclear family concepts, does not provide these sanctions and consequently must operate on a cash basis. Nevertheless, the peasant marketing system demonstrates great flexibility in adjusting to the needs and limitations of the larger economy.

Drucker, Peter. "Marketing and Economic Development," *Journal of Marketing*, Vol. XXII (January, 1958), pp. 252–59.

"Marketing occupies a critical role in respect to the development of . . . growth areas. Indeed, marketing is the most important 'multiplier' of such development." Professor Drucker stresses the significance of marketing in economic development from several perspectives, and notes the absence of marketing in totalitarian forms of planned economic development.

Emlen, Woodruff J. "Let's Export Marketing Know-How," *Harvard Business Review*, Vol. XXXVI (November–December, 1958), pp. 70–76.

U.S. aid to underdeveloped nations usually takes the form of financial and technological assistance. The author feels that we are neglecting what is potentially our most productive exportable commodity—American marketing knowledge. "The adaptation of new marketing and distribution methods, so vital as productive capacity increases, will not only yield higher standards of living in these countries, but also help to create an important source of investable capital to support industrialization."

Erickson, Leo G. "Analyzing Brazilian Consumer Markets," *Business Topics*, Vol. XI (Summer, 1963), pp. 7–26.

A description of the difficulties of conducting market research in an area suffering from communications difficulties and a shortage of trained research personnel. The author does manage to construct geographical sales potential indices on the basis of available population, income, and commercial activity statistics and estimates.

Firth, Raymond. *Malay Fishermen: Their Peasant Economy.* 2d. ed. Hamden, Conn.: Archon Books, 1966.

A detailed description of the marketing institutions, credit system, income distribution system, and many recent developments within the Malay fishing communities.

The role of the middlemen in extending the social contact of the village to the external society is stressed. Other aspects of marketing are emphasized, including: a description of the middlemen's functions; colorful accounts of the bargaining process in fish markets; the price-making mechanism in fish marketing; the influence of credit on market transactions; an analysis of the relationships among wholesalers (who form loose coalitions) and between them and retailers; and problems encountered in the recent development of cooperatives in the fishing industry.

————, and Yamey, B. S. (eds.). *Capital, Saving and Credit in Peasant Societies.* London: George Allen & Unwin, Ltd., 1964.

As the title indicates, the 15 country studies of non-African peasant societies, prepared mainly by anthropologists, and the two chapters prepared by the editors, deal mainly with personal and agricultural capital formation problems rather than with marketing per se. However, many of the essays describe consumer and mercantile credit practices which seem to vary considerably between societies. Quite possibly, credit selling tends to prevail in supplying farmers whose cash income is highly seasonal, and tends to be more restricted in supplying anonymous urban consumers at low levels of economic development.

Fisher, Allan. "Marketing Structure and Economic Development: Comment," *Quarterly Journal of Economics,* Vol. LXVIII (February, 1954) pp. 151–54.

Even in the most primitive communities some fraction of work is devoted to tertiary production, and in more advanced economies its importance as a field of employment tends to grow more rapidly than the average rate of economic growth. As a corollary, it can be shown that there are important possibilities for increasing real per capita income simply by improving the distribution system.

Fletcher, L. B. "Commodity Markets and Marketing," in *Economic Development of Agriculture.* Iowa State University, Center for Agricultural and Economic Development. Ames: Iowa State University Press, 1965.

The author holds that marketing can serve as a "leading sector" in development. He looks for ways that the marketing sector can stimulate the transition from a traditional agricultural system to a "market-oriented" one in which input costs and farm prices influence output decisions and where production functions change over time.

He emphasizes the role of prices as a stimulant to production, and notes the typically ineffective use of price incentives in underdeveloped countries. He also cites the possibility of conflict between producers and consumers over agricultural price policies.

Other benefits from improved marketing include stimulation of farm production through the creation of rural retail outlets, a shift of output to profitable cash crops, and encouragement of the use of new techniques and equipment (facilitated by the extension of credit).

Frederick, William C. "The Market as a Factor in Economic Growth," *Southwestern Social Science Quarterly,* Vol. XLI (June, 1960), pp. 63–71.

A plea for a more behaviorally oriented theory of markets and economics in developing areas. ". . . market institutions cannot be relied upon to guide economic growth because they contain and interact with elements (taboos, mores, and ceremonial elements generally) that are inherently disequilibrating in a downward direction. . . . if one is to assess the role of the market in economic growth it must be done through a reconstructed economic theory. Market models must be built upon current understanding of culture process, not just upon inherited theoretical predilections."

Fritsch, W. R. *Progress and Profits: The Sears Roebuck Story in Peru.* Washington, D.C.: Action Committee for International Development, Inc., 1962.
    Case study of a successful transfer of U.S. retail technology to a developing country.

Galbraith, J. K., and Holton, Richard H. *Marketing Efficiency in Puerto Rico.* Cambridge, Mass.: Harvard University Press, 1955.
    This study deals with retailing and wholesaling in Puerto Rico. Suggestions as to how efficiency can be improved are offered in the following areas: chain store operations, consumer cooperatives, central warehouse and dock facilities, and promotion of price advertising. Major emphasis is placed upon improving efficiency in food wholesaling and retailing. Excessive atomization and redundancy of distributive institutions is found to be an undesirable disguise for underemployment, and forms a highly regressive levy on the Puerto Rican consumer.

Gallagher, John F. "Markets as a Basis of Industrial Development," in *Science, Technology and Development,* pp. 62–70. United States Papers Prepared for the United Nations Conference on the Application of Science and Technology for the Benefit of the Less Developed Areas. Washington, D.C.: U.S. Government Printing Office, 1962.
    A description of Sears, Roebuck del Peru, S.A.'s industrial development work in sponsoring, helping, and training indigenous sources of supply.

Geertz, Clifford. *Peddlers and Princes.* Chicago: University of Chicago Press, 1963.
    A comparison of entrepreneurial groups in two Indonesian towns, one a typical small commercial city, the other characterized by an entrepreneurial class of displaced aristocrats trying to work within the present social structure. Detailed description of the *pasar* (local market), including the functioning of the price system and the credit system, an explanation of the tendency of traders to think small (hence to reap small profits), and a discussion of the *pasar* as a social and cultural institution. Also describes retail stores outside of the traditional market system.
    Central theme is the contrast of a commercial, nonagricultural town whose work force is predominately petty traders and a rural, agricultural town strongly influenced by a local nobility.

Ghosh, Arabinda. *Market Structure of Indian Agriculture—An Analysis.* Department of Economics Monograph No. 4. Calcutta, India: University of Calcutta, 1963. Summary in *Indian Journal of Agricultural Economics* (October–December, 1963).
    This article attempts to analyze the structure of the market for agricultural products in India. Structural trends in Indian agriculture are also discussed. The author concludes that the, "effect of various (governmental) marketing orders on market structures are mostly not at all conducive to healthy market development and contrary to the desired objectives."

Halper, Donald G. "The Environment for Marketing in Peru," *Journal of Marketing*, Vol. XXX (July, 1966), pp. 42–46.

Emphasis is placed on personal income and distribution, household expenditure patterns, consumption behavior, demographic and geographical diversity, and cultural attitudes and traits. Resistance to change by various social groups, and Peruvian attitudes toward the value and utility of goods and services are considered.

Hamid, Hakima. "Marketing and Business Practices in Afghanistan," *Middle East Journal*, Vol. XIV (Winter, 1960), pp. 87–93.

Afghanistanian marketing practices tend to be highly inefficient. Supportive business services are grossly inadequate, the scale of operations is low, and sellers seek high margins rather than volume. Relatively modern department stores were introduced in Kabul in about 1925, with many advantages over more traditional outlets. However, in part because of their own inadequacies, the department stores have not displaced the smaller retailers.

Haring, Robert C. "Marketing in the Economic Growth of Alaska," in Peter D. Bennett (ed.), *Marketing and Economic Development*, pp. 38–43. Proceedings of the 1965 Fall Conference of the American Marketing Association. Chicago: American Marketing Association, 1965.

The rapid development of Alaska has placed relatively efficient marketing systems in large communities, while rural areas retain primitive barter economies. This is primarily due to a lack of mobility and education. This raises two development problems: Alaska's experience indicates a region can shift from barter to modern merchandising in a decade, but the transition brings economic problems; hence, Alaska's growth depends on its export sector to put natural resources into foreign markets.

Hawkins, E. K. "The Growth of a Money Economic in Nigeria and Ghana," *Oxford Economic Papers*, Vol. X (October, 1958), pp. 339–54.

After a careful careful statistical analysis of Ghana's and Nigeria's monetary system the author concludes that, "internal economic development—the spread of the market economy and of the use of money, together with associated internal investment—may be helped or hindered by a country's monetary arrangements. Changes in such arrangements will not in and of themselves initiate corresponding changes in economic development. On the other hand, such changes may remove obstacles which prevent such development from getting under way." The evidence suggests that since 1946, the internal trade sectors of the Nigerian and Ghanian economies, often overlooked in macroeconomic discussions, have grown faster than the export sectors.

Hirsch, Leon V. "The Contribution of Marketing to Economic Development —A Generally Neglected Area," in W. D. Stevens (ed.), *The Social Responsibility of Marketing*, pp. 413–18. Proceedings of the 1961 Winter Conference of the American Marketing Association. Chicago: American Marketing Association, 1961.

Improvement in the method or scope of distribution in any economic system can aid in development, both by leading to a more efficient use of presently existing productive resources and by encouraging their future generation. It can result in an expansion of market size which can lead to economies of scale and eventually to mass production. Another advantage of efficient distribution is the reduction of a community's need to keep working capital tied up in storing goods for future consumption, i.e., a reduction in the nonmonetized sector of the economy.

————. *Marketing in an Underdeveloped Economy: The North Indian Sugar Industry.* Englewood Cliffs, N.J.: Prentice-Hall, Inc., 1961.

A detailed study of the industry at all levels, from cane procurement to final sale to consumers and industrial users. Although the marketing activities are conducted within, and shaped by, the environmental context, including labor abundance and capital shortages as well as dietary and caste restrictions, the participants exhibit high degrees of rationality and economic motivation.

Holton, Richard H. "Economic Development and the Growth of the Trade Sector in Italy," *Banca Nazionale del Lavoro,* Vol. XV (September, 1962), pp. 240–58.

The author concludes that the rapid multiplication of retail stores in Italy may provide a partial explanation for the rising cost of distribution of consumer goods, i.e., retailers may be raising margins in order to compensate for shrinkage in sales volume. However, he feels that it is impossible to demonstrate conclusively that excess capacity exists in the retailing sector in Italy. To lower costs of distribution in the economy as a whole the author recommends a policy of free entry for large-scale retailers.

————. "Marketing Structure and Economic Development," *Quarterly Journal of Economics,* Vol. LXVII (August, 1953), pp. 344–61.

Distribution is considerably more important in the economic development of backward areas than is generally recognized. Real per capita incomes may be increased simply by improving the distribution system and thereby increasing payrolls and lowering the cost of living. The reasons for the neglect of this alternative are indicated.

Jefferys, James B. *Retail Trading in Britain: 1850–1950.* Cambridge, England: Cambridge University Press, 1954.

A detailed discussion of the history of the principal branches of the British distributive trades. Several overview chapters point out the ways in which rising productivity, industrialization, urbanization, and reliance upon imported foods contributed to the growth of mass marketing retail institutions.

Johnson, E. A. J. *Market Towns and Spatial Development in India.* New Delhi: National Council of Applied Economic Research, 1965.

Argues that the development of a network of 14,000 market towns (intermediate to the present village-city dichotomy) would foster India's economic development by encouraging market-oriented agriculture, facilitating sale of agricultural equipment and supplies on reasonable credit terms, and providing an appropriate setting for small industry and various public and private services.

Kahlon, A. A., and Reed, Charles E. "Problems of Marketable Surplus in Indian Agriculture," *Indian Journal of Agricultural Economics,* Vol. XVI (January–March, 1961), pp. 46–50.

The study concludes that, "expansion of marketing outlets is, to a great extent, a necessary accompaniment of the process of economic planning." "Production, processing, and all levels of selling should become highly co-ordinated units of a single marketing system." The development of this system will tend to expand the effective demand for farm products. The accessibility of farmers to the national market will also increase. The final result will be that farmers will tend to shift from subsistence to cash crop agriculture thereby increasing the amount of "marketable surplus" in the economy as a whole.

Katzin, Margaret. "The Jamaican Country Higgler," and "The Business of Higgling in Jamaica," *Social and Economic Studies* (University College of the West Indies), Vols. VIII and IX (December, 1959, and September, 1960), pp. 421–40 and 297–332.

The first of these two companion articles describes a week in the life of a "country higgler," a rural woman who buys produce from nearby growers for sale in Kingston, with emphasis upon the amount of hard work involved and upon the importance of personal relations in the channel. The second article describes other types of higglers, including town residents and large-scale operators, with considerable attention to the price-making mechanism. The higglering system is seen as relatively efficient in view of Jamaica's labor surplus position.

————. "The Role of the Small Trader," in M. J. Herskovits and M. Horwitz (eds.), *Economic Transition in Africa,* pp. 179–98. Evanston, Ill.: Northwestern University Press, 1964.

Examination of trading and commercial activities in the former British colonies shows no shortage of African entrepreneurial spirit or of African entrepreneurs. However, few large-scale African firms have developed. Capital shortages, due to the traders' family obligations and prevailing poverty levels, are often considered to be the major barrier to firm growth, but some traders have amassed substantial sums. Lack of opportunity to gain large-scale administrative experience and lack of appropriate governmental support are more serious obstacles.

Kindleberger, Charles P. *Economic Development.* New York: McGraw-Hill Book Company, Inc., 1958.

Chapter 6, "Scale," discusses the importance of widening markets, in part through improved transport and communications. Wider markets lead to scale increases in efficiency at the primary producing levels, introduce external economies within the marketing process through encouragement of specialist and facilitating institutions, and increase the elasticity of both demand and supply.

Lamont, Douglas F. "A Theory of Marketing Development: Mexico," in Peter D. Bennett (ed.), *Marketing and Economic Development*, pp. 44–45. Proceedings of the 1965 Fall Conference of the American Marketing Association. Chicago: American Marketing Association, 1965.

The traditional production-oriented approach to the study of economic development did not identify the contribution of marketing to economic development. To examine marketing development quantitatively, an equation is formulated to measure the participation of people over time in a monetary transaction market economy. The marketing methodology and the traditional production-oriented approach are then applied to the Mexican economy. The author concludes that the marketing effort during the development of an economy is in fact an independent variable operating in conjunction with, but not dependent upon, the production effort. Also, by determining the propensity to participate, specific marketing developmental programs now can be designed to raise the level of marketing development within an economy.

Liander, Bertil; Terpstra, Vern; Yoshino, M. Y.; and Sherbini, Abdel Aziz. *Comparative Analysis for International Marketing*. Boston: Allyn & Bacon, Inc., for the Marketing Science Institute, 1967.

Primarily a discussion of problems of classifying countries to determine receptivity to similar marketing techniques and managerial policies. Recommends multidimensional scales in which economic development and internal homogeneity play important parts, instead of simple geographical classification (for example, South America, Far East, Western Europe).

Marcus, Edward, and Marcus, Mildred Rendl. *Investment and Development Possibilities in Tropical Africa*. New York: Bookman Associates, 1960.

An enthusiastic report on the economic potential of Tropical Africa. The role of foreign investment in developing natural resources and an industrial complex is discussed. Obstacles such as illiteracy, lack of technical knowhow, shortage of trained labor, poor work habits, lack of local entrepreneurial enterprise, and political and social ferment are all considered.

A chapter on trade is devoted to a description of the retail and wholesale distribution structure; to the problems involved in entering markets; to suggested ways of anticipating consumer needs; and to delivery problems. See also, Edward Marcus, "Selling the Tropical African Market," *Journal of Marketing*, Vol. XXV (July, 1961), pp. 25–31.

Martin, Lee R. "Some Marketing Problems in Pakistan and India," *Journal of Farm Economics*, Vol. XLI (December, 1959), pp. 1323–26.

The problems of improving marketing channels in Pakistan and India are largely problems of investment in human capital (education, research, and public health), and in tangible public infrastructure, including transportation, communication, urban, water and sanitary services, and research facilities.

McCarthy, E. Jerome. "Effective Marketing Institutions for Economic Development," in Stephen A. Greyser (ed.), *Toward Scientific Marketing*, pp. 393–

408. Proceedings of the 1963 Winter Conference of the American Marketing Association. Chicago: American Marketing Association, 1963.

"One reason that economic development plans have not always lived up to expectations is that marketing institutions are taken for granted. In this article, various stages of economic development of producers are studied. Effective marketing institutions are necessary and sufficient conditions for economic development. They are necessary because if they are not present development will be inhibited. But they are also sufficient, because if they are present then they will aid development, providing it is economically feasible."

Mehren, George L. "Market Structure and Procedures in Economic Development," *Malayan Economic Review,* Vol. IV (April, 1959), pp. 94–100.

"Few development programs seem really to conform to the basic requirements for economic policy. Market structure in all countries is in a sort of balance with all other segments of the food industries. Thus, changes in any segment—marketing or others—induced by governments are unlikely to be successful unless consistent changes are made in all segments. And changes in any one segment will almost always lead ultimately to changes in other functional levels. This is a major reason that faulty or inadequate economic research can lead to abject failure of economic policy."

————. "Market Organization and Economic Development," *Journal of Farm Economics,* Vol. XLI (December, 1959), pp. 1307–15.

A review of available hypotheses concerning market structures, commercial organization, and economic development leads to the discomforting conclusion: "The fundamental difficulty still unresolved is to find some means in each country, and perhaps differently in each country, to introduce modern commercial activities at some functional level in such a way that enterprises in other functional levels are induced to adjust themselves to the same kind of commercial, profit-motivated activity."

Miller, Clarence J. (ed.). *Marketing and Economic Development.* Lincoln, Nebr.: University of Nebraska Press, 1967.

The articles included here mainly deal with market structure, price-making mechanisms, and market research in the developed countries, especially the United States, and thus are best described by the volume's subtitle: "Readings in Agribusiness Research." Four items, including J. C. Abbott's "The Role of Marketing in the Development of Backward Agricultural Economies," annotated above, discuss underdeveloped situations. Shyam Nandan Sinha describes the importance of agricultural exports in India's economic affairs, but notes that concentration of a few products and destinations, increasing competition, and stagnant demand are producing adverse terms of trade. William O. Jones and Christian Merat suggest that per capita consumption of exotic, i.e., imported, consumer goods might prove superior to some conventional indices for gauging economic progress in tropical Africa. William E. Folz calls for more marketing research to determine areas of comparative advantage, to measure consumer preferences, and to set up standards of pricing and market efficiency. Some elegance of research models may have to be sacrificed for immediacy and specificity in action recommendations. The volume contains several valuable short bibliographies.

Minkes, A. A. "Statistical Evidence and the Concept of Tertiary Industrialization," *Economic Development and Cultural Change,* Vol. III (July, 1955), pp. 366–73.

An attempt to apply the Clark-Fisher hypothesis concerning tertiary employment to detailed employment censuses conducted in the early 1930's in eight southern and eastern European countries reveals a number of anomalies and deviations from the hypothesized patterns.

Mintz, Sidney W. "Internal Market Systems as Mechanisms of Social Articulation," in *Intermediate Societies, Social Mobility and Communication,* pp. 20–30. Proceedings of the 1959 Annual Spring Meeting of the American Ethnological Society. Seattle, Wash., American Ethnological Society, 1959.

The peasant markets of the Caribbean approach pure competition in their freedom from both internal and governmentally imposed price fixing. However, while noneconomic factors should not be overemphasized, custom tends to determine the range of products admitted to market trading (instead of being reserved to shops), and personal relations influence the matching of buyers and sellers. The markets provide an articulation mechanism between various social groups, and those who participate in the markets acquire at least some measure of flexibility and predisposition toward change.

————"The Jamaican Internal Marketing Pattern: Some Notes and Hypotheses," *Social and Economic Studies,* Vol. IV (March, 1955), pp. 95–103.

The small-scale farmer in Jamaica reduces risk in production through crop diversification, and generally sells infrequently and in small quantities. The market woman who buys from the small-scale farmer reduces her risk by carrying a selection of items. The consumer sector consists mainly of individuals with irregular incomes who, because of this, manifest irregular demand for goods. The author concludes that small-scale agricultural production is functionally related to the prevalent marketing arrangements, and that, in turn, both are related to the demand situation.

————"The Role of the Middleman in the Internal Distribution System of a Caribbean Peasant Economy," *Human Organization,* Vol. XV (Summer, 1956), pp. 18–24.

An interesting description of the women "higglers" engaged in the distribution of agricultural products in Jamaica and a review of proposals for "marketing reform." The author raises the questions: "What will be the source of capital for an increase in the scale of operations and will the peasant farmers benefit from it?"

Moyer, Reed. *Marketing in Economic Development.* International Business Occasional Paper No. 1. East Lansing, Michigan: Bureau of Business and Economic Research, Michigan State University, 1965.

This study regards marketing as more than the sum total of the intermediaries making up the distributive sector. The dynamics that account for the linking of local into regional and national markets are indicated. The role of marketing in economic development is spelled out, and considerable attention is focused upon the available methods for distribution in primitive and developing economies. The linkages between marketing institutions required to form a marketing system are analyzed. Areas for future research on the topic are suggested. See also, by the same author, "Structure of Markets in Developing Economies," *Business Topics,* Vol. XII (Autumn, 1964), pp. 43–60.

————"Trade and Progress: An International Comparison," *Journal of Business,* Vol. XL (July, 1967), pp. 270–79.

Both historical analysis of the percentage of the labor force engaged in wholesale and retail trade (for those countries for which time series are available) and cross-sectional analysis of current employment in a much greater number of countries provide little support for the Clark-Fisher-type hypotheses. Long-run Clark-Fisher effects are noted in such advanced countries as the United States and the United Kingdom, but even in those countries, short-run changes such as those induced by the great depression and wars may run counter to the hypothesis.

Mueller, Willard F. "Some Market Structure Considerations in Economic Development," *Journal of Farm Economics,* Vol. XLI (May, 1959), pp. 414–25.

In general, developing-country market structures seem to be more monopolistic and less competitive than those of the United States. Although economists differ in their evaluations of this condition, it probably is a serious obstacle to economic growth.

Mulvihill, Donald F. *Domestic Marketing Systems Abroad.* 2d ed. Kent, Ohio: Kent State University Press, 1967.

A substantial portion of the entries in this annotated bibliography, which is organized on a country-by-country basis, are concerned with descriptions of domestic marketing systems in developing societies.

Myers, Kenneth H., Jr., and Smalley, Orange A. "Marketing History and Economic Development: A Report and Commentary on Two Recent Conferences Concerning the Need for a History of Marketing in the United States," *Business History Review,* Vol. XXXIII (Autumn, 1959), pp. 387–401.

The correlation between individual liberty in the political sense, consumer sovereignty in the economic sense, and the acceleration in material well-being that has occurred in the United States, suggests that the marketing system developed here has been a fundamental stimulus of productive efficiency and of the attainment of a lofty scale of material well-being. They suggest that there is latent productive capacity in the underdeveloped economies which is not being utilized due to the lack of adequate incentives. Perhaps a marketing system similar to the one in the United States could provide the necessary incentives.

Nash, Manning. *Primitive and Peasant Economic Systems.* San Francisco: Chandler Publishing Co., 1966.

Considerable attention is given to market considerations. The author points out that the development of a monetized market system is not a sufficient condition for economiic growth, so long as the participants are households or other groups that have substantial noneconomic goals. "What is lacking is . . . an entity like the firm, an autonomous, corporate group dedicated to and organized for economic activity." He feels that innovative leadership, if it develops, is likely to come from a fairly well-defined social group possessed of external contacts, undergoing change in its relationship to the wider society, and filled with a sense of urgency and mission. Its tasks are largely organizational, and concerned with fitting customary means (for example, the old skills of the bazaar) to new ends (the operation of rationalized systems). A compact bibliography provides a handy guide to the major writings of such economic anthropologists as Belshaw, Firth, Herskovits, Malinowski, Mintz, and Tax.

Nicholls, W. H. "Domestic Trade in an Underdeveloped Country: Turkey," *Journal of Political Economy,* Vol. LIX (December, 1951), pp. 463–80.

The Turkish marketing system, here reviewed as of 1950, seems comparable to U.S. marketing circa 1820. Both are characterized by a proliferation of small-scale middlemen, operating on high margins, low turnover, and with little opportunity to exploit merchandising know-how. The Turkish system suffers from inadequate supportive public services in such areas as transport, standardization and grading, and market information. Increased industrial productivity is seen as a prerequisite to market development, since marketing is essentially a dependent variable in the growth pattern. However, importation of large-scale distributive enterprises, such as Sears, and improvements in advertising practices would provide healthy stimuli.

Ofer, Gur. *The Service Industries in a Developing Economy, Israel as a Case Study.* New York: Frederick A. Praeger, Inc., 1967.

The service sectors have occupied a disproportionately large share of the Israeli economy throughout the period 1931–61 when compared with other countries at similar per capita income levels. Up until the mid-1950's much of the "excess" service employment was in trade and other private enterprise, and could be explained in part by the occupational structure of the immigrants and in part by "bulging," the inability of agricultural and manufacturing sectors to absorb available labor. Since then the excess has been in government, education, health, and transport services, due largely to demand structure considerations.

Pfaff, Martin. "The Marketing Function and Economic Development: An Approach to a Systematic Decision Model," in Peter D. Bennett (ed.), *Marketing and Economic Development,* pp. 46–47. Proceedings of the 1965 Fall Conference of the American Marketing Association. Chicago: American Marketing Association, 1965.

This is a summary of the author's doctoral dissertation. The dissertation constructs a decision model for the long-run allocation of resources by the marketing executive and the development planner. It statistically relates marketing development to economic development for 60 countries from 1830 to 1960. Furthermore, a search for a "cause-effect" relationship is undertaken. Finally, the specific case of India is analyzed in some detail.

Polanyi, Karl; Arensberg, C.M.; and Pearson, H.W. (eds.). *Trade and Market in the Early Empires.* Glencoe, Ill.: Free Press, 1957.

A well-known collection of essays, drawing upon both ancient and contemporary developing societies for illustrations of market and nonmarket distributive systems. Much emphasis on the extent to which exchange and the allocation of output may rest upon reciprocity, obligation, and other grounds outside the neoclassical price-market mechanism.

Preston, Lee. "Marketing Organization in Arab Socialism," *Journal of Marketing,* Vol. XXXI (October, 1967), pp. 1–7.

Marketing is beginning to receive increased attention in the U.A.R. development plans. However, this attention is likely to be expressed through increased centralization, bureaucratic control, and loss of adaptability within the marketing system.

Rostow, Walt Whitman. *The View from the Seventh Floor.* New York: Harper & Row, Publishers, 1964.

Drawn principally from some of the author's speeches while in the State Department, only one chapter deals with a matter directly involving marketing. There Rostow concludes that the central problem of development is not the gap between the rich nations and the poor nations, but the gap between the rich and poor parts of the developing nations themselves. The need is to develop self-reinforcing industrial and agricultural expansion and to create national markets. To bring this about he prescribes: "a build-up of agricultural productivity; a revolution in the marketing of agricultural products in the cities; a shift of industry to the production of simple agricultural equipment and consumers' goods for the mass market; and a revolution in marketing methods for such cheap manufactured goods, especially in rural areas."

———. "The Concept of a National Market and Its Economic Growth Implications," in Peter D. Bennett (ed.), *Marketing and Economic Development,* pp. 11–20. Proceedings of the 1965 Fall Conference of the American Marketing Association. Chicago: American Marketing Association, 1965.

Marketing must play the role of diffusing industrial know-how and market incentives to the rural production areas of developing countries. Efficient distribution systems from farm to city and from city to farm also facilitate the exchange of expertise and incentives. This skill in "cross-fertilization of sectors" is the key to national, and later international, market penetration.

Rottenberg, Simon. "Note on Economic Progress," *Review of Economics and Statistics,* Vol. XXXV (May, 1953), pp. 168–70.

A criticism of the Clark-Fisher hypothesis. Holds that custom, trade-union activity, or government regulation will impose minimum wages in industrial production, forcing large numbers of surplus workers in the underdeveloped countries to enter unregulated self-employment in the distributive trades.

Rutman, Gilbert. "State Trading in Tanganyika," *South African Journal of Economics,* Vol. XXXIV (June, 1966), pp. 148–57.

The Tanganyikan government is fostering the development of agricultural cooperatives to replace private trading, which is erroneously believed to be entirely in Asian hands, but the cooperative program tends to hamper rather than encourage economic growth. It is true that few Africans are currently engaged in wholesale trade, but this is due to lack of commercial experience of capital and of "a competitive business outlook."

Samli, A. Coskun. "Wholesaling in an Economy of Scarcity," *Journal of Marketing,* XXVIII (July, 1964), pp. 55–58.

Although Turkish whosalers do not engage in advertising and other promotional activities or in advisory services to their customers, they do assume leadership over distribution channels. In this respect they resemble the American wholesalers of the late 19th century rather than their modern counterparts.

Schooler, R. "Marketing in the Central American Common Market," in Peter D. Bennett (ed.), *Marketing and Economic Development,* pp. 116–17. Proceedings of the 1965 Fall Conference of the American Marketing Association. Chicago: American Marketing Association, 1965.

This brief study considers the possible existence of intangible barriers to increased trade within the Central American Common Market. National origin of a product is correlated with consumer opinion of that product. It is determined that the consumer's attitude toward a given foreign country influences his preconceptions toward products originating in that foreign country. As a result it appears that area jealousies, suspicions, and fears still have a negative influence on regional economic integration within the Central American Common Market.

Shapiro, Stanley J. "Comparative Marketing and Economic Development," in George Schwartz (ed.), *Science in Marketing,* pp. 398–429. New York: John Wiley & Sons, Inc., 1965.

The author explores certain controversial topics on which much disagreement has been voiced. Specifically, the paper deals with: (1) a frame of reference for comparisons between systems, (2) the applicability of American marketing techniques in other countries, (3) the existence of marketing development stages, (4) "the role of market economy and of market structure in economic development," (5) the stimulation of consumer wants in developing countries, (6) "the wisdom of efforts to reform the marketing systems of underdeveloped countries," and (7) the contributions of marketing to economic development.

———, and Doody, Alton R. (eds.). *Readings in the History of American Marketing: Settlement to Civil War.* Homewood, Ill.: Richard D. Irwin, Inc., 1968.

Forty-six articles discussing significant aspects of pre–Civil War trade patterns, business practices, institutional growth, and environmental controls are included in this anthology, the first of a projected two-volume set. The collection demonstrates the interactions between marketing activities and other parts of the political, economic, and physical environment in the movement from colonial settlement to the development of a national market. Footnotes attached to the articles and an extensive bibliography provide an excellent guide to primary and secondary materials on U.S. marketing development.

Sherbini, Abdel Aziz. "Marketing in the Industrialization of Underdeveloped Countries," *Journal of Marketing*, Vol. XXIX (January, 1965), pp. 28–32.

Marketing difficulties have proven to be much greater problems than anticipated in many industrial development projects. One source of difficulty is that import-oriented marketing channels are often unsuitable or even hostile to local products.

Singer, H. W. "The Concept of Balanced Growth in Economic Development: Theory and Practice," *Malayan Economic Review*, Vol. III (October, 1958), pp. 1–13.

This study attempts to relate the structural change which is implicit in economic growth to the marketing problems which arise simultaneously. "Industry cannot expand because it needs expanded markets in agriculture. Agricultural marketing, in turn, is limited by the lack of employment opportunities in industry."

The balanced-growth concept is studied and discarded as inappropriate for underdeveloped countries. Balanced-growth advocates are correct in showing that marketing difficulties bring about a low-level equilibrium, but they fail to deal with the nub of the problem: the shortage of resources.

Several solutions to break the "marketing deadlock" (inadequate markets) are suggested, including the promotion of export trade and development of import-substitution industries under a protective tariff shield.

Skinner, G. William. "Marketing and Social Structure in Rural China," *Journal of Asian Studies*, Vol. XXIV (1964/65), pp. 3–44, 195–228, 263–99.

An anthropological and geographical study drawing heavily upon central place theory. The study focuses upon the concept of "standard marketing towns," i.e., the lowest level markets capable of supplying all of the peasantry's normal trade needs. Historically, these towns served as the national marketing system's entry points for peasant agricultural surplus and craft production. Collectivization schemes that did not take account of this traditional geographic structure encountered severe difficulties, and since 1961 Communist collectivization and marketing plans have increasingly and necessarily been geared to, and built upon, "the natural systems of earlier times."

Slater, Charles C. "The Role of Food Marketing in Latin American Economic Development," in Peter D. Bennett (ed.), *Marketing and Economic Development*, pp. 30–37. Proceedings of the 1965 Fall Conference of the American Marketing Association. Chicago: American Marketing Association, 1965.

A study of preliminary plans to explore the relationship of marketing to economic development. The hypotheses presented are: (1) that GNP for urban areas can grow through a reduction in food prices; (2) the velocity of capital will increase with a reduction of risk through communication and insurance; (3) to the extent that firms perceive demand as elastic, expansion will occur through lower prices (reduced margins); and (4) the pragmatic attitudes of new marketing organizations will push expectations upward.

Smith, J. H. "The Eastern Regional Market Board, Nigeria," *Journal of Agricultural Economics,* Vol. XIV (May, 1961), pp. 368–74.

This study presents an outline and an analysis of the price policy followed by the Eastern Regional Marketing Board of Nigeria. It concludes that "marketing boards have a necessary and an important role to play in the economic life of Nigeria and that criticism of them stems largely from the conflicting nature of the duties imposed upon them." Their main function should be to secure orderly and efficient marketing of produce. They should also ensure that available resources are used in the most profitable manner and in the best interests of the farmers.

Solomon, Morton R. "The Structure of the Market in Underdeveloped Economies," *Quarterly Journal of Economics,* Vol. LXII (August, 1948), pp. 519–37.

The discussion here is limited to densely populated underdeveloped economies, since the sparsely settled ones probably have entirely different market structures. Monopolistic controls, which in some cases flow from market imperfections, are strong in the agricultural staples and capital goods markets; they are more limited in the other sectors.

Stevens, Robert D. "The Influence of Urbanization on the Income Elasticity of Demand for Retail Foods in Low Income Countries," *Journal of Farm Economics,* Vol. XLV (December, 1963), pp. 1495–99.

A study of the demand function, leading to the conclusion that: "High income elasticities of demand for retail food (resulting from urbanization) point to the likelihood of considerable strain on the marketing system during development unless sufficient compensatory action is undertaken. Such action could either discourage workers from moving into urban areas through improved commuter transportation and the decentralization of industry, or provide for considerable expansion of the marketing system."

Stewart, Charles F. "The Changing Middle East Market," *Journal of Marketing,* XXV (January, 1961), pp. 47–51.

"The Middle East market is much narrower than the figures for oil revenues would suggest. Barring a broader distribution of this income through radical political change, hopes for a larger market must come from development programs . . . . The fact that the market is increasing only slowly probably accounts for the persistence of distributive methods developed for another age and for the continued concentration of many disparate lines in the hands of a single agent with the consequent lack of attention that each requires. . . . All of this adds up to a small market, but a small market is not necessarily a negligible one."

Tax, Sol. *Penny Capitalism: A Guatemalan Indian Economy.* Washington, D.C.: U.S. Government Printing Office, 1953. Chicago: University of Chicago Press, 1963.

A classic study of trade relations in the Guatemalan highlands with detailed descriptions of the amounts of goods and the traders moving through the marketplaces.

Taylor, Donald A. "Marketing in Brazil" in Peter D. Bennett (ed.). *Marketing and Economic Development,* pp. 110–15. Proceedings of the 1965 Fall Conference of the American Marketing Association. Chicago: American Marketing Association, 1965.

This paper examines the way economic and cultural differences in Brazil affect marketing practice. It reviews the developments in business administration education and the role of marketing as a field of study within the business education curriculum in Brazil. A major idea is that although there are environmental differences in Brazil, the thought processes used in developing marketing strategy should not differ greatly from those used in the United States. See also, by the same author, "Retailing in Brazil," Journal of Marketing, Vol. XXIV (July, 1959), pp. 54–58.

Thorne, Alfred. "Monopoly—Oligopoly—Economic Development," *Cartel,* Vol. X (April, 1960), pp. 58–66, 77.

This article attempts to draw attention to the dominance of monopolies and oligopolies in the economic structure of the underdeveloped nations of the Caribbean and Latin America and to indicate how this dominance affects the economic growth of these countries. The author also suggests avenues along which ameliorative measures might be found.

Triantis, S. C. "Economic Progress, Occupational Redistribution and International Terms of Trade," *Economic Journal,* Vol. LXIII (September, 1953), pp. 627–37.

Largely a defense of the Clark-Fisher hypothesis, based in part on both family and government budget studies in countries at various levels of development. Substitution of capital for labor is less likely at the tertiary rather than other levels, so tertiary employment is particularly susceptible to growth.

United Nations Advisory Committee on the Application of Science and Technology to Development. *Increasing the Production and Use of Edible Protein.* New York: United Nations, 1967.

Offers, among other things, a series of recommendations for improving food marketing techniques. Also urges intensive research into food consumption patterns and into techniques necessary to obtain acceptance for nutritionally superior diets.

United Nations, Food and Agriculture Organization. *Bibliography of Food and Agricultural Marketing.* Rome: Food and Agriculture Organization, 1965 (plus annual supplements).

An exceptionally comprehensive, annotated bibliography drawing upon sources in many languages.

Van Niewenhuijze, C. A. O. (ed.). *Markets and Marketing Factors of Development in the Mediterranean Basin*. The Hague: Mouton & Co., 1963.

A symposium dealing with the types of markets and marketing practices prevailing in the Mediterranean basin. Emphasis is placed upon developments that are already in process or that could readily be implemented. Obstacles impeding the development of markets and the adoption of new marketing practices are indicated. Alternative methods of overcoming these obstacles are presented. Considerable attention is devoted to the beneficial and adverse effects of land reform schemes, cooperative plans, and governmental controls. Research into improved marketing methods must pay careful attention to the human relations and social roles of all participants in the marketing process.

Van Roy, Edward. "The Introduction of Plantation Economy to North Thailand," *Explorations in Entrepreneurial History, 2nd Series,* Vol. V (Fall, 1967), pp. 36–57.

In spite of considerable government support and considerable political skill on the part of the entrepreneur involved, an attempt to develop a large-scale tea-growing and tea-processing organization in North Thailand has encountered considerable difficulties. These difficulties are largely attributable to peasant resistance to the substitution of impersonal raw material buying or wage employment arrangements for the traditional quasi-market or nonmarket reciprocal patron-client relations fostered by conventional wholesalers and assemblers.

Wadinambiaratchi, George. "Channels of Distribution in Developing Economies," *The Business Quarterly,* Vol. XXX (Winter, 1965), pp. 74–82.

Drawing upon eight reports of marketing in developing economies, the author concludes that peddlers, itinerant traders, open-garden fairs, small stores, and foreign import agents decline in importance with economic development; that number of levels of distribution, number of differentiated specialty stores, supermarkets, and department stores, average store size, and both wholesale and retail markups increase with development; and that wholesaling functions tend to be performed in North American fashion as the economy develops.

Ward, Barbara, "Cash or Credit Crops? An Examination of the Implication of Peasant Commercial Production with Special Reference to the Multiplicity of Traders and Middlemen," *Economic Development and Cultural Change,* Vol. VIII (January, 1960), pp. 148–63.

Both peasant commodity production and finished goods distribution and consumption in peasant economies often require credit financing. Traders and middlemen are prime sources of credit, but are not equipped for large-scale financial operations. Consequently, a large number of middlemen is not a social evil, but is rather an economic necessity to provide sufficient credit sources for the total requirements.

Westfall, Ralph, and Boyd, Jr., Harper W. "Marketing in India," *Journal of Marketing*, Vol. XXV (October, 1960), pp. 11–17.

This review of weaknesses and difficulties in the Indian marketing system concludes that American marketing methods are not easily transferable to a radically different environment, but that improved physical distribution techniques would be of immediate help. Increases in literacy are expected to improve communications and promotional techniques, which in turn, through increased brand differentiation, should lead to greater quality standardization.

Wigglesworth, Edwin F., and Brotan, Jiri. "Retailing Trends in Thailand," *Journal of Retailing*, Vol. XLII (Spring, 1966), pp. 41–51.

A discussion of retailing in Thailand, which points out the financial opportunities for progressive foreign retailers. There are brief descriptions of the Thai economy and of the structure of retailing in three major areas—general merchandise, food, and hard goods and vehicles. Also covered are the mode of operations in retailing, and a cursory view of sales promotion techniques used by retailers. A concluding section looks at the future for Thai retailing and finds it promising.

Wind, Yoram. "The Role of Marketing in Israel," *Journal of Marketing*, Vol. XXXI (April, 1967), pp. 53–57.

Marketing has not grown to a fully modern research-oriented basis in Israel, even though it is more appreciated there than in other developing countries. The lacks in marketing progress are at least partly due to dependence upon foreign assistance and governmental intervention, which in effect discourage private entrepreneurship and promote cooperative and similar institutions.

Winder, R. Bayly. "The Lebanese in West Africa," *Comparative Studies in Society and History*, April, 1962, pp. 296–333.

Studies the immigration of Lebanese into West Africa, and traces the origins of the movement, the numbers of immigrants, and the restrictions placed on them after their arrival.

The author analyzes the reasons for the movement of the Lebanese into trading, and presents sketchy data on the success of early Lebanese traders in outdistancing their European competitors. Recently though, the Lebanese traders' dominance of small retail trade has ended. Replaced by African traders, the Lebanese are moving into other fields: importing, manufacturing, real estate, entertainment, and smuggling.

Most of the article deals with the immigrants' economic life, their resistance to assimilation into the community, and their political activities.

The author concludes that the Lebanese businessmen have contributed substantially to economic development in the area.

Wood, Richardson, and Keyser, Virginia. *United States Business Performance Abroad: The Case Study of Sears, Roebuck de Mexico, S.A.*, Washington, D.C.: National Planning Association, 1953.

Emphasizes Sears' contributions to Mexican industrialization through the development of local sources of supply. Notes, however, that Sears' effectiveness followed abandonment of original plans to operate as a luxury-type outlet, and conversion to a more characteristic role of mass-marketer to the rising middle class.

Wright, Fergus Chalmers. *African Consumers in Nyasaland and Tanganyika.* Colonial Research Studies No. 17. London: Her Majesty's Stationery Office, 1955.

A study of the merchandise supplies available to native consumers in the indicated territories, with the conclusion that those supplies were fully adequate to serve as labor incentives.

Yoshino, M. Y. "International Opportunities for American Retailers," *Journal of Retailing*, Vol. XLII (Fall, 1966), pp. 1–10.

Opportunities for overseas branches of American retail firms, particularly in the developing countries, depend particularly upon the size and rate of increase of the middle class, upon receptivity to innovation, and upon the inability of local retailers to preclude foreign entries.